DEBUNKING PRETERISM

SECOND EDITION

DEBUNKING PRETERISM

HOW OVER-REALIZED ESCHATOLOGY MISSES THE "NOT YET" OF BIBLE PROPHECY

SECOND EDITION

DR. BROCK D. HOLLETT
B.S. ED., M.DIV., D.O.

Debunking Preterism

SECOND EDITION

Copyright 2023 Brock D. Hollett

ALL RIGHTS RESERVED. No part of this book may be reproduced, stored, or transmitted in any manner whatsoever without written permission from the author, except in the case of brief quotations embodied in critical articles or reviews.

Cover photo and design by Brock D. Hollett.

Illustrations by Travis Bennett and Tom Quinlan.

Unless otherwise indicated, most Scripture quotations are from the English Standard Version (ESV) of the Bible.

ISBN: 978-0-9889316-6-4

FOR INFORMATION CONTACT

Brock D. Hollett

brockhollett@yahoo.com

Printed in the United States of America by

Ingram Spark

ingramspark.com

(855) 997-7275

Dedicated to my friends at Colleen's garage

May they and all preterists joyfully receive the eschatology of the apostolic Church

CONTENTS

1. Defining Preterism 2
2. Time Indicators 8
3. The Meaning of "This Generation" 27
4. Two Questions at Olivet 41
5. The Beginning of Birth Pains 49
6. The Abomination of Desolation 58
7. Prophecy of the Seventy Weeks 77
8. The Day of Jesus Christ 84
9. Coming on the Clouds 99
10. The Olivet Discourse in 1 Thessalonians 4-5 123
11. Nero and the Mark 134
12. No Transition to the Distant Future at Matthew 24:36 156
13. The Already and Not Yet 170
14. The Millennium 190
15. The Cost of Consistency 204
16. The End According to Preterism 222

17	All Israel Will Be Saved	236
18	Restoring the Kingdom to Israel	243
19	Repenting of Preterism	260

Table One: The Abomination of Desolation in Daniel 8, 9, and 11-12 74

Table Two: Thrones of Judgment 105

Table Three: Matthew 24, 1 Thessalonians 4, and 1 Corinthians 15 122

Table Four: Parallels Between the Olivet Discourse and 1 Thessalonians 4-5 127

Table Five: Common Elements of the Man of Sin and the Beast 150

Table Six: Parallels Between Matthew 24 and Luke's Gospel 167

Table Seven: Parallel Passages of Daniel 11 177

Sources 264

Scripture Index 270

About the Author 282

1

DEFINING PRETERISM

PRETERISM IS A VIEW OF ESCHATOLOGY, or the study of last things, that claims that most of the prophecies of the New Testament were fulfilled by the end of the first century AD. The word preterism comes from a Latin word meaning "past." Most preterists place great significance on the events of the First Jewish-Roman War of AD 66-70, which they posit largely fulfilled the prophecies of Jesus Christ's Olivet Discourse and the book of Revelation. They believe that the Roman destruction of Jerusalem and its temple in AD 70 was the climactic event that finalized the replacement of the Mosaic covenant with the new covenant.[1]

Preterism argues for an alternate view of prophecy that is vastly different than traditional, futurist readings of Scripture. For example,

---

[1] Gary DeMar, *Last Days' Madness: Obsession of the Modern Church* (Atlanta: American Vision, 1999), vii; Kenneth L. Gentry, *The Olivet Discourse Made Easy: You Can Understand Jesus' Great Prophetic Discourse* (Draper, VA: ApologeticsGroup.com, 2010), Kindle 122-27; Kenneth L. Gentry, *The Book of Revelation Made Easy: You Can Understand Bible Prophecy* (Powder Springs, GA: American Vision Press, 2010), 21; Peter J. Leithart, *The Promise of His Appearing: An Exposition of Second Peter* (Moscow, ID: Canon Press, 2004), 1-2; N. T. Wright, *Jesus and the Victory of God* (Minneapolis: Fortresss Press, 1996), 323.

many preterists deny that the Olivet Discourse and the Apocalypse even address the topic of the Second Coming of Jesus. David Chilton, a preterist scholar, claimed, "The Book of Revelation is *not* about the Second Coming . . . In fact, the word *coming* as used in the Book of Revelation *never refers to the Second Coming.*"[2] As we will see, preterists reinterpret the biblical phrase "the coming of the Son of Man" to refer to an event that occurred in the first century. Much of this book will explore the differences between preterism and futurism, that is, the view that these prophecies will be fulfilled in our future.

Preterism exists in two primary forms, partial and full. Partial preterism agrees with the traditional Christian teaching that the return of Jesus, the resurrection of the dead, and judgment day will occur in our future. By contrast, full preterism, the so-called "consistent" preterism, sees these events as having been fulfilled in AD 70. Full preterists, unlike partial preterists, reinterpret the traditional Christian understanding of the nature of these events; for example, they deny the doctrine of the future, bodily resurrection of the dead. Many full preterists also deny that God will finally and completely eradicate human sin in the new heaven and new earth (cf. Rev. 21:1-4). Such positions contrast sharply with the apostolic Church's understanding of these biblical doctrines as articulated, nuanced, and clarified by the Church fathers, Ecumenical Councils, and Nicene Creed. It is no surprise, then, that Christianity rejects full preterism as heresy. This book primarily critiques partial preterism and the underpinnings of preterism as a hermeneutical system, although I interact directly with full preterism in a subsequent chapter.

Many Protestant prophecy pundits advocate partial preterism. Dr. Gary DeMar, a postmillennialist and the president of the Christian Reconstructionist organization, American Vision, published multiple preterist books and videos. Similarly, the Reformed postmillennialist Dr. Kenneth L. Gentry has advanced preterism among popular and

---

[2] David Chilton, *Paradise Restored: A Biblical Theology of Dominion* (Horn Lake, MS, 2007), 166.

academic audiences. Hank Hanegraaff, a former Protestant, talk show host of the *Bible Answer Man* radio broadcast, and president of the Christian Research Institute, formerly popularized preterism through his books and radio programs. Dr. R. C. Sproul was perhaps the most famous proponent of preterism. He founded Ligonier Ministries and hosted the *Renewing Your Mind* broadcast. A minority of other scholars and pastors have embraced preterism.

Preterists frequently attempt to normalize preterism. For instance, DeMar labels all Christians as preterists for believing that the prophecies about the first advent of Jesus Christ were fulfilled in the past, and he calls traditional Jews "anti-preterists" for denying that these prophecies have been fulfilled. He indicts modern Christians for not embracing preterism by arguing that they seek the future fulfillment of prophecies that have already been fulfilled, similar to the manner in which first-century Jews rejected Jesus as the Messiah.[3] DeMar also points out that many futurists have failed to correctly predict the timing of "the end" and that many reputable Bible scholars have endorsed preterism during the last several centuries:

> Today's speculative madness related to repeated failed attempts at predicting the end must be a gross misunderstanding of Bible prophecy. As I soon learned, I was not alone in coming to this conclusion. For centuries great Bible expositors had taught that many New Testament prophecies had already been fulfilled. They taught that many texts that are often futurized actually describe events in the first century. This literature made sense of the passages that millions of Christians struggle to understand.[4]

Many preterist authors are Protestants who adopted their preterist eschatology after becoming disgruntled with dispensational premillennialism. This perspective is the eschatological view that Jesus Christ will rapture Christians prior to a seven-year tribulation period that

---

[3] DeMar, *Last Days' Madness*, vii, 36-37.

[4] DeMar, *Last Days' Madness*, 15.

is followed by a thousand years of world peace. It maintains a strict distinction between Israel and the holy apostolic Church. DeMar is a former Roman Catholic who, prior to his conversion to Christianity, was introduced to the pretribulational school of dispensationalism while reading Hal Lindsey's *The Late Great Planet Earth* in 1973.[5] He laments,

> My dissatisfaction with the Lindsey system forced me to go digging for answers to solve the hermeneutical puzzle. . . . I soon learned that today's prophetic scenario, so popular with radio and television evangelists and multi-million-copy best sellers, has a short history. The system of prophetic interpretation that is familiar to most Christians had its beginning in 1830.[6]

Similarly, Kenneth Gentry discusses his years as a disgruntled dispensationalist who was finally delivered from this eschatological system by a professor who introduced him to preterism.

As well, these authors attempt to establish the veracity of preterism by contrasting it with the excesses and flaws of pretribulational dispensationalism, and they rarely interact with other eschatological positions in any meaningful way. For example, Hank Hanegraaff argues his preterist position by contrasting it with dispensationalism throughout the entirety of his book *The Apocalypse Code*. Consequently, preterist works typically highlight the fallacy of limited alternatives, where the only option besides dispensationalism is preterism. Their arguments frequently imply that futurism itself must be invalid because of the erroneous claims of pretribulational dispensationalism.

DeMar and his colleagues have lost faith in modern prophecy experts who claim that our contemporary generation will witness the fulfillment of end-time Bible prophecy. He correctly points out that some Christians in every generation have believed this of themselves. He is also appropriately critical of preachers who "cry wolf" by

---

[5] DeMar, *Last Days' Madness*, 13.

[6] DeMar, *Last Days' Madness*, 14, 15; cf. p. vii.

espousing false doomsday predictions. Yet he goes further by asserting that the failed speculations of prophecy pundits have resulted from their failure to embrace preterism:

> The events in Waco [Texas] serve as a tragic lesson for those who maintain that the judgment themes depicted in Matthew 24, Mark 13, and the Book of Revelation are still in our future. How many more such tragedies will it take before Christians realize that these prophetic events have been fulfilled?[7]

This critique of futurism represents the guilt by association fallacy. Furthermore, the cautious reader will not assume that the careless speculations and predictions of some futurists assumes a wholesale failure of traditional Christian eschatology. At any rate, the failure of many believers to correctly ascertain the timing of the fulfillment of Bible prophecies has contributed to preterism gaining adherents.

DeMar is essentially pessimistic about the practice of looking to current events as the fulfillment of Bible prophecies, and he employs pejorative terms such as "newspaper exegesis" to describe this method.[8] However, he fails to recognize that the continued search for fulfillment of prophetic events undermines preterism and evidences their non-fulfillment in history. Prophecy teachers may not have calculated the precise date of the eschaton, that is, the time of the end, but it is clear that these events have yet to be fulfilled as preterists suppose. I hope to demonstrate this throughout this book.

But in fact, preterists are guilty of the very "newspaper exegesis" that DeMar criticizes. They rely heavily on the works of the first-century Roman historian Josephus to validate their claims of prophetic fulfillment. James Stuart Russell, a nineteenth-century Scottish preterist, asserted, "The only indispensable *apparatus criticus* is Josephus and the

---

[7] DeMar, *Last Days' Madness*, 28.

[8] DeMar, *Last Days' Madness*, 15.

Greek grammar."[9] Kenneth Gentry praises this approach, saying, "I highly recommend reading the Book of Revelation, Chapters 6 through 19, then reading Josephus, *War*, books 4-7."[10]

Historical events found in secondary sources should be used to validate whether prophecies have been fulfilled. However, we will see that it is equally certain that preterists engage in the same overly-realized eschatology as their futurist counterparts who engage in prophetic speculation, using a first-century historiography instead of twenty-first century newspapers. As we will see, preterism cannot adequately account for the prophetic details required by the biblical prophecies, and they are responsible for the same kind of force fitting as the prophecy experts that they criticize.

DeMar audaciously claims that preterism is a continuation of the Protestant Reformation, and to achieve this goal, he asserts that a Christian "should never fear having his [eschatological] 'system' scrutinized by the plain teaching of the Bible.[11] The purpose of this book is to evaluate the exegetical claims of partial preterism in light of solid biblical hermeneutics. My prayer is that the reader will arrive at a more comprehensive understanding of biblical eschatology by recognizing that preterism is not an adequate solution.

---

[9] J. Stuart Russell, *The Parousia: the New Testament Doctrine of Christ's Second Coming*. Edited by Edward E. Stevens. (Bradford, PA: International Preterist Association, 2003), 535.

[10] Gentry, *The Olivet Discourse Made Easy*, 31.

[11] DeMar, *Last Days' Madness*, x.

2

TIME INDICATORS

THE TIME TEXTS OF THE NEW TESTAMENT are the primary weapon in the preterists' arsenal. The time texts, variously called time indicators or time statements, are passages of Scripture that preterists utilize to demonstrate that eschatological events must have been fulfilled in the first century. None of the vast majority of the hundred or so passages specify a time or date of fulfillment, but most of these texts convey the meaning of nearness or imminence.

Many preterists describe the time statements as the "key" to understanding preterism. J. Stuart Russell asserted,

> It may truly be said that the key has all the while hung by the door, plainly visible to every one who had eyes to see; yet men have tried to pick the lock, or force the door, or climb up some other way, rather than avail themselves of so simple and ready a way of admission as to use the key made and provided for them.[1]

Gary DeMar argues that these time texts play a "defining role" in a proper understanding of Bible prophecy:

---

[1] Russell, *The Parousia*, 367.

The additional study that went into this edition of *Last Days Madness* has continued to solidify my conviction that the time texts are key indicators of when certain prophetic events will take place. Most books of prophecy do not interpret time texts literally. In fact, some books ignore the time texts altogether. . . To the contrary, "the time element" plays a major role in prophecy. In fact, it plays the defining role. Without precision of meaning for the time texts prophetic pronouncements are meaningless.[2]

DeMar charges non-preterists of mishandling the time texts. He states that "failing to recognize the proximity of a prophetic event will distort its intended meaning" and then accuses futurists of abusing the biblical text, stating, "There is no getting around this language, that most of the verses that many believe are yet to be fulfilled already have been fulfilled. Forcing the following verses to describe a time nearly two thousand years in the future is the epitome of 'Scripture twisting.'"[3] He contends that "an honest analysis" of these texts "jeopardizes" all futurist eschatological positions and that some of these systems arbitrarily deal with Scripture since "the entire thesis of futurism rests on a non-literal reading of the time texts."[4] He goes further by accusing the Church fathers and their contemporaries of erroneously believing that they lived in the last days "because they misapplied the time texts"![5]

The entire system of preterism is built around the primacy of the time indicators; therefore, our evaluation of preterism must include a thorough appraisal of these biblical texts. We will begin by evaluating many of the time statements concerned with the nearness of Christ's return and the day of the Lord. The evidence presented in this chapter will demonstrate that preterism fails to consider the time statements in their proper biblical framework and historical understanding.

---

[2] DeMar, *Last Days' Madness*, viii, 379.

[3] DeMar, *Last Days' Madness*, 37, 38.

[4] DeMar, *Last Days' Madness*, ix.

[5] DeMar, *Last Days' Madness*, 427.

DEBUNKING PRETERISM

NEAR, SOON, AND AT HAND

The apostle John provided the reader with several primary time statements in the book of Revelation. These verses demonstrate the *nearness* of Christ's return:

> The revelation of Jesus Christ, which God gave him to show to his servants the things that must soon take place. . . Blessed is the one who reads aloud the words of this prophecy, and blessed are those who hear, and who keep what is written in it, for the time is near. (Rev. 1:1, 3)

> "I am coming soon. Hold fast what you have, so that no one may seize your crown." (Rev. 3:11)

> And the Lord, the God of the spirits of the prophets, has sent his angel to show his servants what must soon take place. "And behold, I am coming soon. Blessed is the one who keeps the words of the prophecy of this book." (Rev. 22:6-7)

> "Do not seal up the words of the prophecy of this book, for the time is near. . . Behold, I am coming soon, bringing my recompense with me, to repay each one for what he has done. (Rev. 22:10, 12)

> He who testifies to these things says, "Surely I am coming soon." Amen. Come, Lord Jesus! (Rev. 22:20)

Seven of these time statements appear in the introductory and closing sections of the Apocalypse. This type of literary device is an inclusio; it consists of theological "bookends" which inform the reader that the nearness of the Lord's coming is intrinsic to the book's main theme. Preterists correctly teach that the Greek word groups translated "soon" and "near" frequently convey the idea of temporal nearness and likely do in the particular context of the book of Revelation, yet preterists define these words in a particularly restrictive manner that differs from the historical understanding of these texts.[6]

Russell asserted that these time statements are "the key" that unlocks the prophetic events described in the book of Revelation so that John's original audience could recognize the book's "connection with the events of their own day." He stated that this true key has always been visible, but it has been "allowed to lie rusty and unused, while all kinds of false keys and picklocks have been tried, and tried in vain, until men have come to look upon the Apocalypse as an unintelligible enigma, only meant to puzzle and bewilder."[7] According to Russell, these statements, combined with the book's then-contemporary relevance, mean that modern readers are "absolutely shut up by the book itself to the contemporary history of the period, and that, too, within very narrow limits."[8] He chides, "How could an event be said to be near, if it was actually further off than the whole period of the Jewish economy from Moses to Christ?"[9] He continued this discussion by accusing futurists of defying the grammatical rules regarding the time statements:

> It seems unaccountable that scholarly and reverent students of divine revelation should either overlook or set aside the explicit declarations of the book itself with regard to its speedily approaching fulfillment . . . and that they should then, in defiance of all grammatical laws, proceed to invent a non-natural method of interpretation, according to which '*near*' becomes '*distant*,' and '*quickly*' means '*ages hence*,' and '*at hand*' signifies '*afar off*.' All this seems incredible, yet it is true. Language serves only to mislead, words have no meaning, and interpretation has no laws, if the express and repeated declara-

---

[6] DeMar, *Last Days' Madness*, 384; Gentry, *The Olivet Discourse Made Easy*, 19; Frederick W. Danker, Walter Bauer, and William F. Arndt. *A Greek-English Lexicon of the New Testament and Other Early Christian literature*. 3rd ed. (Chicago: University of Chicago Press, 2000), 992-93.

[7] Russell, *The Parousia*, 532-33.

[8] Russell, *The Parousia*, 374.

[9] Russell, *The Parousia*, 41.

tions of the Apocalypse does not plainly teach the speedy and all but immediate fulfillment of its predictions.[10]

Preterists unanimously agree that futurist interpretations violate the plain meaning of the time indicators by maintaining that John's prophecies would be fulfilled in *our* future. Gentry argues that any view that sees a fulfillment in "the distant future, thousands of years away, is expressly contradicting John's opening and closing statements."[11] Hanegraaff retorts, "Are we really to suppose that the angel was referencing a time more than two thousand years hence? Of course not!"[12] David Chilton conveyed their mutual concern:

> John's first-century readers had every reason to expect his book to have immediate significance. The words *shortly* and *near* simply cannot be made to mean anything but what they say. If I tell you, "I'll be there *shortly*," and I don't show up for 2000 years, wouldn't you say I was a little tardy?[13]

Gentry contends that a preterist interpretation of the Apocalypse is "demanded" by John's time statements. His reasoning is that a first-century fulfillment logically follows from the concept of near fulfillment.[14] He notes that John's "stated expectation regarding *when* his prophecies will transpire" is "absolutely essential" to a proper understanding of the book of Revelation.[15] He warns that the "most destructive" mistake a reader can make is "overlooking the apostle's clearly-stated

---

[10] Russell, *The Parousia*, 534.

[11] Gentry, *The Olivet Discourse Made Easy*, 139.

[12] Hank Hanegraaff, *The Apocalypse Code: Find Out What the Bible Really Says About the End Times and Why It Matters Today* (Nashville: Thomas Nelson, 2007), 92, 94; Similarly, R. C. Sproul, *The Last Days According to Jesus: When Did Jesus Say He Would Return?* (Grand Rapids: Baker, 2015), 109.

[13] Chilton, *Paradise Restored*, 166.

[14] Gentry, *The Olivet Discourse Made Easy*, 137, 57.

[15] Gentry, *The Olivet Discourse Made Easy*, 15.

temporal expectation."[16] Gentry means by this that readers should avoid the mistake of avoiding a preterist interpretation of the Revelation.

Hanegraaff states that the meaning of the word "soon" in the Apocalypse is "self-evident" and that any attempt to place the fulfillment of these prophecies into the distant future should trigger our "baloney detectors." He believes that the futurist understanding of the time statements violates the grammatical principle of hermeneutics, and he is amazed that prophecy experts "could possibly be mistaken about something so basic."[17] DeMar agrees with Hanegraaff and argues that non-preterists deny the literal and plain interpretation of the words "near," "shortly," and "quickly."[18] He accuses traditional interpreters of inconsistently rendering these statements; he claims that they interpret these words figuratively when they appear in the Apocalypse and literally when they appear elsewhere in the Scriptures:

> Supposedly, while "near," "quickly," and "shortly" are used in a literal sense in every other New Testament passage where they occur, in the Book of Revelation we are told that they should be interpreted figuratively, except, of course, when they need to be interpreted literally. This line of argumentation is surprising when it is put forth by those who insist on a literal interpretation of Scripture. Why don't the literalists want to interpret "near," "quickly," and "shortly" literally in the Book of Revelation when they interpret these same words literally elsewhere in the Bible?[19]

DeMar and his colleagues teach that the book of Revelation was fulfilled no later than Jerusalem's destruction in AD 70. This conclusion is based upon statements in the book that its prophetic fulfillment was near for John's original audience and on the fact that the apostle

---

[16] Gentry, *The Olivet Discourse Made Easy*, 33.

[17] Hanegraaff, *The Apocalypse Code*, 73; cf. p. 91.

[18] DeMar, *Last Days' Madness*, 206, 382; cf. Hanegraaff, *The Apocalypse Code*, 17, 90; Sproul, *The Last Days According to Jesus*, 148.

[19] DeMar, *Last Days' Madness*, 390.

wrote the book, as most preterists suppose, during Emperor Nero's reign between AD 64-68.[20] DeMar believes that futurists simply "ignore the time texts that speak of a *near* coming of Jesus in judgment upon an apostate Judaism that rejected its Messiah in the first century."[21] Gentry essentially agrees with this assessment. He argues that preterism alone adequately accounts for the *Sitz im Leben* ("setting in life"), that is, the cultural and historical context that allows John's message to serve a function for his original audience, the seven churches of Asia Minor. He thinks that a futurist interpretation of the Apocalypse is "a mockery of their historical circumstances," even a "'be thou warm and filled' comfort of little help to these churches."[22] He writes, "Surely, he is not telling these persecuted saints that the time is near, that they must heed that which he is writing, that God is concerned with their persecution—but He will avenge you thousands of years in the future!"[23]

THE PROPHETIC PERSPECTIVE

Despite the claims of preterists, the apostolic Church has affirmed for two thousand years that Jesus will return soon. Robert Mounce, a preeminent Greek and New Testament scholar, explains:

> The most satisfying solution is to take the expression "must soon take place" in a straightforward sense, remembering that in the prophetic outlook the end is always imminent. Time as chronological sequence is of secondary concern in prophecy. This perspective is common to the entire NT.[24]

---

[20] DeMar, *Last Days' Madness*, 21.

[21] DeMar, *Last Days' Madness*, 37.

[22] Gentry, *The Olivet Discourse Made Easy*, 139-40.

[23] Gentry, *The Book of Revelation Made Easy*, 35; cf. Russell, *The Parousia*, 384-85, 396.

[24] Robert H. Mounce, *The Book of Revelation. The New International Commentary of the New Testament*, (Grand Rapids, MI: W. B. Eerdmans, 1998), 41.

TIME INDICATORS

The idea is that the eschaton is always being pressed into the present and portrayed as a foreshortened time of the end.

Several other commentators have embraced this prophetic perspective.[25] George Eldon Ladd, a distinguished New Testament professor at Fuller Theological Seminary, described the tension between the immediate future and distant future in Bible prophecy:

> The future was always viewed as imminent. . . . There is in biblical prophecy a tension between the immediate and distant future; the distant is viewed through the transparency of the immediate. It is true that the early church lived in expectancy of the return of the Lord, and it is the nature of biblical prophecy to make it possible for every generation to live in expectancy of the end. To relax and say "where is the promise of his coming?" is to become a scoffer of divine truth. The "biblical" attitude is "take heed, for you do not know when the time will come."[26]

The New Testament reflects the eschatological view that the end of the age had arrived during the apostolic period. The apostles taught that they were already living in the last days and at "the end of the ages" because the Son of God and His eschatological Spirit had arrived (Acts 2:16-17; 1 Pet. 1:20; Heb. 1:2; 9:26; 1 Cor. 10:11). Prior to the heavenly outpouring of the Holy Spirit on the day of Pentecost, only Christ understood the new covenant mystery of His two advents. He came to die for sins and to ascend to the Father's right hand but would return in glory many centuries later (cf. Acts 2:23-39; 3:20-21). He had been resurrected as "the firstfruits," but those who have died in Him must wait to be raised on the last day (1 Cor. 15:20-23).

These prophetic events about Christ meant nothing less than an unexpected and mysterious "breaking in" of eschatological realities

---

[25] Philip Edgcumbe, *The Book of the Revelation: A Commentary* (Grand Rapids: Eerdmann, 1990), 16, 241; George Eldon Ladd. *A Commentary on the Revelation of John* (Grand Rapids: Eerdmans, 1972), 22; Grant R. Osborne. *Revelation*. Baker Exegetical Commentary on the New Testament (Grand Rapids: Baker Academic, 2002), 55, 59, 781.

[26] Ladd, *A Commentary on the Revelation of John*, 22.

before His return on the day of the Lord. Similarly, the apostle John saw that the then contemporary arrival of antichrists signaled that "the last hour" had arrived in some real sense (1 John 2:18; cf. Rom. 16:20). This reinforces the concept that the day of the Lord was "at hand" (Rom. 13:12; cf. Heb. 10:25), and also, that believers should heed the apostolic admonition to patiently wait because Christ's return was "at hand" (Phil. 4:5; Heb. 10:37; James 5:7-9). The apostle Peter taught that Christians should live in holiness because "the end of all things is at hand" (1 Pet. 4:7; cf. 1 Cor. 7:29, 31; cf. 2 Pet. 3).

This prophetic perspective portrays "the end" as pressing into the present age and is divinely intended to compel believers in Jesus Christ to live in continual readiness for His return. The passages conveying nearness function to remind believers of the Lord's admonition to "stay awake, for you do not know on what day your Lord is coming" (Matt. 24:42; cf. Matt. 24:36, 44; 25:13). DeMar even admits that "the near and soon coming of Jesus in judgment [is used] as a way of spurring the church on to greater works."[27] Such exhortations have enabled Christians in every era to constantly live in patient, eager expectation of His glorious return. The holy Church has always maintained this eschatological understanding of these biblical texts.

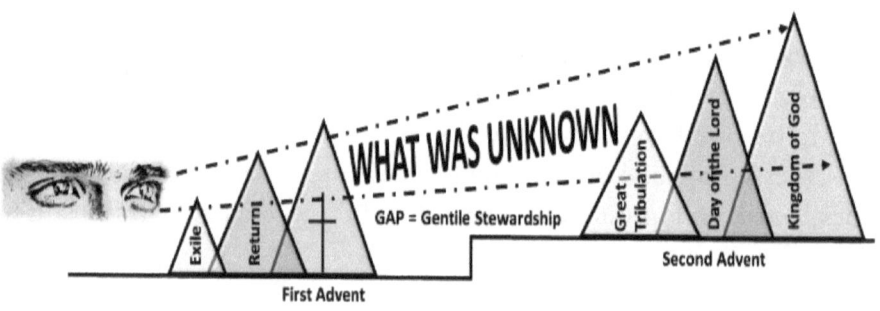

---

[27] DeMar, *Last Days' Madness*, 30.

TIME INDICATORS

The apostolic Church has maintained that the prophetic events in the book of Revelation were near and soon even in the first century, although the fulfillment of these events would not take place for two thousand years. This historic understanding of the time statements was crucial for John's contemporary audience and has remained relevant for every subsequent generation of Christians. The statements provide the theological reason why God's people can faithfully endure persecution, specifically, the persecution which will reveal its divinely-intended purpose when Jesus returns. The context of these statements consistently reveals the theme of patiently enduring tribulation that had resulted from faithfully adhering to the gospel (e.g., Rev. 1:9; 7:14; 22:12).

The book's theme is further developed in the letters to the churches in Revelation 2-3: The persecuted saints can "overcome" by "holding fast" to the gospel and remaining faithful in spite of false teachers and tribulation because the Judge is quickly coming to reward them and punish their persecutors (Rev. 2:2-3:21). The idea advanced by preterists, that is, that this coming refers merely to a first-century "judgment coming" of Jesus, threatens to rob post-AD 70 Christians of this theological basis for their faithful endurance.

Consistent with this theme of the encroaching return of Jesus Christ, the holy apostles contrasted the transient, temporary suffering—this "light momentary affliction" of Christians—with "an eternal weight of glory beyond all comparison" that will be ushered in at His return to vindicate and glorify His saints (e.g., 2 Cor. 4:16-18). Consequently, a few thousand years is only "a little longer" for those who partner together in "the patient endurance" of the persecuted saints (cf. Rev. 1:9; 3:10; 6:11; 14:12). As such, the glorious return of Jesus is always near when seen against the backdrop of the eternity that God has placed in our hearts (Eccles. 3:11). People living at every period of history sustain an impinging, existential proximity to this day of Christ, being either preserved for salvation or reserved for judgment. Christians should avoid deliberate sin and pursue love and obedience to Jesus, encouraging our

DEBUNKING PRETERISM

fellow Christians as we see the day of judgment drawing near (Heb. 10:24-27).

AS SOME COUNT SLOWNESS

The modern reader of the Apocalypse faces the challenge of reconciling the time statements with an apparent delay in Christ's coming. Some theologians call this dilemma "the problem of a delayed parousia."[28] R. C. Sproul claimed, "The crisis of 'parousia-delay' eschatology has been fostered in large measure by this problem. Perhaps no other problem has spurred the revival of different strands of preterism and realized eschatology more than has this one."[29] The apostle Peter addressed this issue when it first arose during his lifetime:

> This is now the second letter that I am writing to you, beloved. In both of them I am stirring up your sincere mind by way of reminder, that you should remember the predictions of the holy prophets and the commandment of the Lord and Savior through your apostles, knowing this first of all, that scoffers will come in the last days with scoffing, following their own sinful desires. They will say, "Where is the promise of his coming? For ever since the fathers fell asleep, all things are continuing as they were from the beginning of creation." For they deliberately overlook this fact, that the heavens existed long ago, and the earth was formed out of water and through water by the word of God, and that by means of these the world that then existed was deluged with water and perished. But by the same word the heavens and earth that now exist are stored up for fire, being kept until the day of judgment and destruction of the ungodly. But do not overlook this one fact, beloved, that with the Lord one day is as a thousand years, and a thousand years as one day. The Lord is not slow to fulfill his promise as some count slowness, but is patient toward you, not wishing that any should perish, but that all should reach repentance. But the day of the Lord will come like a thief, and

---

28   The Greek work transliterated "parousia" means presence.

29   Sproul, *The Last Days According to Jesus*, 57.

then the heavens will pass away with a roar, and the heavenly bodies will be burned up and dissolved, and the earth and the works that are done on it will be exposed. Since all these things are thus to be dissolved, what sort of people ought you to be in lives of holiness and godliness, waiting for and hastening the coming of the day of God, because of which the heavens will be set on fire and dissolved, and the heavenly bodies will melt as they burn! But according to his promise we are waiting for new heavens and a new earth in which righteousness dwells. (2 Pet. 3:1-13)

Peter reminded his readers that scoffers would cast aspersion on the prophetic certainty of the Lord's promise to return quickly. They will mock, "Where is the promise of his coming?" (2 Pet. 3:4). The apostle responded to this charge by explaining that the *apparent* failure of Jesus to faithfully keep His promises to return quickly is not an *actual* failure. Furthermore, the fact that He did not return *immediately* does not indicate a failure to return soon. The apostle affirmed that the Lord "is not slow as some count slowness" (2 Pet. 3:9).

The actual problem is a faulty *perception* of slowness, based on an erroneous reckoning of time by those who fail to appreciate the depth of God's patience towards His elect who have not yet repented (2 Pet. 3:9). Some of Peter's contemporaries accused Jesus of failing to return quickly but this is based entirely on their faulty human reasoning. The apostle alluded to Psalm 90:4 ("a thousand years in your [God's] sight are but as yesterday when it is past") to demonstrate that a divine reckoning of time is different than mere human reckoning; the idea is that his readers should recognize God's timetable and divine perspective instead of relying on their own fleshy understanding.

The apostle Peter explained that Christ's return will take the scoffers by surprise because He will "come like a thief" (2 Pet. 3:10; cf. Matt. 24:43-44; Rev. 3:3; 16:15). They follow "their own sinful desires" and "deliberately overlook" the fact that the same word of God that created the world, which was later destroyed by the flood, has also reserved the world for fiery destruction at the day of the Lord (2 Pet. 3:3-12). The motif of Jesus returning "like a thief" at night means that He will appear suddenly to those who are not expectantly waiting (1 Thess. 5:1-8). The Judge will appear sooner (read "soon" and "near") than many have estimated, and the wicked will be taken unaware and unprepared into eternal judgment (Matt. 24:39, 48-51; 25:11-13, 19, 30).

The apostle Peter's criticism of the scoffers in 2 Peter 3 echoes the sentiments of Jesus in the Olivet Discourse:

> But if that wicked servant says to himself, "My master is delayed," and begins to beat his fellow servants and eats and drinks with drunkards, the master of that servant will come on a day when he does not expect him and at an hour he does not know. (Matt. 24:48-50; cf. Luke 12:45-46)

Christ emphasized the idea, later echoed by Peter, that Christians should patiently obey and prepare for His return because it will occur at an unexpected hour that is soon, near, and at hand. Although Jesus predicted a delay of sorts (Matt. 25:5, 19), He rejected the idea of a long delay (Luke 18:7).

> But watch yourselves lest your hearts be weighed down with dissipation and drunkenness and cares of this life, and that day come upon you suddenly like a trap. For it will come upon all who dwell on the face of the whole earth. But stay awake at all times, praying that you may have strength to escape all these things that are going to take place, and to stand before the Son of Man. (Luke 21:34-36)

The preterist objections to the apostle's argument in 2 Peter 3 argument lack substance. Russell contended, "To have intimated that time was a variable quantity in the promise of God would have been to stultify his argument and neutralize his own teaching, which was, that 'the Lord is not slack concerning his promise.'"[30] However, Peter did not suggest that the timing of the promise was variable but only that it was soon and certain. Gentry acknowledges that the apostle's teaching is concerned with God's perception of time, yet he conjectures that the apostle was facing the "*slowness* of God's judgment" and that this

---

[30] Russell, *The Parousia*, 323.

contrasts with the directives of the Apocalypse to people in history.[31] Nevertheless, Gentry fails to notice that Peter also gave directives for his readers, specifically, that they reject the false teachings of the scoffers and prepare for the Lord's arrival. But more to the point, the apostle was certainly not "facing the slowness of God's judgment," despite Gentry's claim. To the contrary, the apostle specifically taught that "the Lord is not slow to fulfill his promise" (2 Pet. 3:9).

DeMar completely evades the evidence from 2 Peter 3 while objecting to the traditional interpretation of this prophecy:

> There is no indication in the Book of Revelation or the entire Bible that 'at hand' and 'near' are relative terms. There is no passage that points us to viewing time 'from the perspective of God' as if when God says 'near' He actually means an indefinite period of time. To make such a claim is practicing the fine art of *ei*segesis—reading an interpretation *into* a text so that it will say what you want it to say.[32]

Yet as we have seen, the apostle Peter contrasted God's reckoning of time ("with the Lord one day . . ." 2 Pet. 3:8) with the scoffer's reckoning of time ("as some count slowness" 2 Pet. 3:9) to provide the primary reason for rejecting the scoffer's claims that Christ had failed in His promise to return soon. Furthermore, the apostle John used the time indicators in the book of Revelation ("near," "soon," and "at hand") in the precise manner that the prophets had employed these time indicators in the Old Testament.

TIME INDICATORS IN THE PROPHETS

Despite DeMar's charge of eisegesis, the historical manner of interpreting the time statements finds its origins in the Prophets. The

---

[31] Gentry, *The Book of Revelation Made Easy*, 43, 44.
[32] DeMar, *Last Days' Madness*, 383.

prophets warned of an impending judgment upon the wicked at the day of the Lord:

> Wail, for the day of the LORD is near; as destruction from the Almighty it will come! (Isa. 13:6)

> Its time is close at hand and its days will not be prolonged. (Isa. 13:22)

> For the day is near, the day of the LORD is near. (Ezek. 30:3)

> Alas for the day! For the day of the LORD is near. (Joel 1:15)

> The day of the LORD is coming; it is near. (Joel 2:1; cf. Isa. 13:9; Mal. 4:1)

> For the day of the LORD is near in the valley of decision. (Joel 3:14)

> For the day of the LORD is near upon all the nations. As you have done, it shall be done to you. (Obad. 1:15)

> For the day of the LORD is near. (Zeph. 1:7)

> The great day of the LORD is near, near and hastening fast. (Zeph. 1:14)

> in a little while (Hag. 2:6)

Most of the Old Testament prophecies concerning the day of the Lord, in one sense, point to localized judgments which took place in antiquity. Based on this fact, preterist commentators generally assume that the Prophets convey *many* "days of the Lord" which occurred in history and that those days only foreshadowed the final day of the Lord. However, based on abundant biblical evidence, it is preferable to understand these historical judgments as revealing *aspects* of the day of the Lord, the solitary day which is penultimate and in our future.

The versatility of language employed by the Prophets for the day of the Lord does not give the interpreter license to imagine that these various expressions indicate multiple days of the Lord. To illustrate, the apostle Peter equated the day of the Lord with "the day of God" (2 Pet. 3:10-12; cf. Rev. 16:14). He also considered this to be judgment day ("the day of judgment and perdition of ungodly men" 2 Pet. 3:7) and the day when the Lord Jesus Christ will fulfill His promise to return in glory (2 Pet. 3:4-5). An exhaustive study of the linguistic variations for the day of the Lord serves to demonstrate that any attempt to divide this solitary day into multiple days or to extend it over a period of months or years is forced and contrived.

The primary reason for this is that the many prophecies about the day of the Lord form a single patchwork of overlapping events, wherein each prophecy provides details about the day, while leaving out other details. Consequently, the careful reader can observe the same recurring themes in these various passages; this collective weight of evidence strongly argues in favor of the interpretation that they all refer to the same day of the Lord. When comparing the Old Testament prophecies regarding the day of the Lord with the New Testament passages about the day of Jesus Christ, we can recognize that the apostles equated the two, which is the day upon which Jesus will return from heaven to save His people, judge His enemies, and consummate His kingdom.

At any rate, the Old Testament prophecies regarding the day of the Lord convey the theme of certain judgment for their audience, and this strongly suggests that the day was nearer than their stubborn, unrepentant hearts realized. The idea is that the wicked live as if they will live forever without being required to give an account of their deeds on judgment day (cf. Job 27:8, 17-22; Luke 12:19-20).

Keith Mathison, a preterist theologian, admits that the Old Testament prophets "regularly used terms implying 'nearness' to describe events that did not occur for centuries."[33] This concept of "nearness" illustrates our point and undermines preterism. Mathison provides an

---

[33] Keith A. Mathison, *When Shall These Things Be?: A Reformed Response to Hyper-Preterism* (Phillipsburg, NJ: P & R Publishing, 2004), 202.

overview of how the prophets utilized the time statements when referring to relatively distant historical events:

> Isaiah 13:22 and Habakkuk 2:3-4, for example, speak of the imminence of the judgment to come upon Babylon. It is interesting to note that Isaiah was writing between 740 and 701 B.C., while Habakkuk wrote sometime between 609 and 598. Yet both spoke of Babylon's judgment using short-term time texts. Isaiah says it is "near." Habakkuk tells the people that "it will not tarry." Babylon fell to the Persians in 539. . . . Isaiah 56:1 says that God's salvation is "about to come." Writing in the early sixth century B.C., Ezekiel says that "the fulfillment of every vision" is "at hand" (12:23). Writing after the Exile, in approximately 520, Haggai proclaims the following word from God: "Once more (it is a little while) I will shake heaven and earth, the sea and dry land . . . (2:6-7). . . Hebrews 12:26-28 seems to indicate . . . [that] "a little while" was more than 520 years.[34]

Preterists are faced with a critical dilemma. They insist that the time indicators "near," "soon," and "at hand" in the Book of Revelation must refer to first-century events and not to events that will immediately precede the Lord's return. Nevertheless, as Mathison explains, the apostle John borrowed these time statements from the day of the Lord passages of the Old Testament, passages that predicted events that did not take place for at least several centuries after they were penned. These same preterists condemn futurist interpretations of John's time indicators on the grounds that they require several centuries for fulfillment. In addition, a general consensus exists among biblical scholars that the "little while" of Hebrews 12:26-28 is an allusion to the "little while" prophecy of Haggai 2:6. Consequently, preterists must either admit that the writer of Hebrews referred to a different "little while" than Haggai intended or that such day of the Lord passages can have an eschatological fulfillment. This would mean either a dual fulfillment or "already and not yet" aspects of fulfillment regarding Haggai's original prophecy,

---

34 Mathison, *When Shall These Things Be?*, 165.

both of which are devastating to common preterist thinking about how prophecy is fulfilled.

DO NOT SEAL UP THE WORDS

Preterists often note the contrast between the angelic command for the prophet Daniel to seal the scroll of his prophecy "until the time of the end" (Dan. 12:4, 9; cf. Dan. 8:26) and the command for the apostle John not to seal up his prophetic scroll because "the time is near" (Rev. 22:10).[35] They argue that traditional eschatological positions inconsistently regard two thousand years beyond the apostle John to be in his near future while maintaining that around 2,500 years beyond Daniel to be in the prophet's distant future. Full preterist Don Preston summarizes the argument:

> This means it has now been *four times longer* from John to the present, than it was from Daniel to John. Yet, Daniel was told fulfillment was far off, and John was told it was near. . . Was 400 years a 'long time' to Daniel, yet John's vision, that was 'at hand,' has not been fulfilled 2000 years later? This contrast in temporal perspective is *prima facie* proof that the time statements of Revelation must not be 'elasticized' into meaninglessness.[36]

This argument fails to consider the different intended audiences and contrasting theological purposes between the book of Daniel and the book of Revelation. To illustrate, Daniel's prophecies contain mysteries that have been concealed from the larger nation of Israel. The prophet followed Isaiah's pattern of proclaiming a message of divine judgment that reinforced the nation's inability to see, hear, and understand his prophetic visions. Daniel, like Isaiah, described his message as an incom-

---

[35] Jay E. Adams and Milton C. Fisher. *The Time of the End* (Hackettstown, NJ: Timeless Texts, 2000), 111; Chilton, *Paradise Restored*, 167; DeMar, *Last Days' Madness*, 390; Gentry, *The Book of Revelation Made Easy*, 19.

[36] Don K. Preston, *Who is This Babylon?* (Ardmore, OK: JaDon Management Inc., 2011), 45, 192.

prehensible "sealed scroll" that would not be unsealed and understood by the nation until messianic times (Isa. 6:9-13; 8:16; 29:9-14; Dan. 8:26; 12:1, 4, 9-10; cf. Rom. 11:7-8). Consequently, the nation would not welcome the message of salvation until the time of the end as it was far removed and inaccessible to them due to their spiritually-hardened condition (Isa. 6:9-10; Dan. 12:10).

By contrast, Jesus Christ has given the secrets of His kingdom to the New Testament Church (Matt. 13:11; Luke 8:10), and the messianic secrets have been revealed as an "open scroll" to all whom God has given "eyes to see" and "ears to hear" (Matt. 11:15; 16:16-17; Mark 4:9, 23; Luke 8:8; 10:23; 14:35; 1 John 1:1). Unlike the recipients of Daniel's prophecies, John's receptive audience was comprised of Christians who had been given "the mind of Christ" and this open scroll of the gospel (Rev. 2:7, 11, 17, 29; 3:6, 13, 22).

The eschatological features of the day of Christ have been brought into the present age. Consistent with this theme, the New Testament presents Christians as the eschatological people, firstfruits of the new creation (2 Thess. 2:13; James 1:18; Rev. 14:4; cf. Rom. 8:23), and recipients of Christ who have been transferred by the Holy Spirit into His heavenly kingdom prior to the day of the Lord (Col. 1:13). Those who are in Christ participate in His resurrection (Rom. 6:4; Eph. 2:6; Col. 3:1). The former "times of ignorance," when God mercifully overlooked ignorant sin, have given way to the new covenant era when He "commands all people everywhere to repent because he has fixed a day on which he will judge the world in righteousness" (Acts 17:30-31). The eschaton, which was *chronologically* distant for Daniel's nation, has drawn near *existentially* by the apostolic revelation of the mysteries of the gospel which were hidden from previous generations.

3

THE MEANING OF "THIS GENERATION"

IN THE OLIVET DISCOURSE, Jesus Christ prophesied that the unprecedented tribulation (Matt. 24:15-28) will terminate with His glorious return on the day of the Lord (Matt. 24:29-33). Then He declared, "Truly, I say to you, this generation will not pass away until all these things take place" (Matt. 24:34; cf. Mark 13:30; Luke 21:32). Many preterists argue that the phrase "this generation" must refer to the period of Jesus' contemporaries because it always carries this meaning when it appears throughout the Synoptic Gospels. They contend that the term "generation" refers to all people living during a specific time frame, usually during a period of approximately forty years.

In addition, most preterists consider Christ's statement about "this generation" to be "the key" for properly interpreting the Olivet Prophecy.[1] Gentry considers it a "confident, clear, and compelling pronouncement regarding the time of the events" described in the verses preceding

---

1   Gentry, *The Olivet Discourse Made Easy*, loc. 1311; J. Marcellus Kik, *An Eschatology of Victory*. (Phillipsburg, NJ: Presbyterian and Reformed Publishing Company, 1971), 30, 59, 60.

it.² Chilton summarized the preterist interpretation of this verse: "This means that everything Jesus spoke of in this passage, at least up to verse 34, *took place before the generation then living passed away*. . . The question is, do you believe Him?"³ Preterists argue that "this generation" refers to the contemporary generation alive when Jesus delivered His discourse.⁴ Gentry considers this an "inescapable conclusion," and he confidently proclaims, "Thus, we may say (as strange as it may seem) that 'this generation means this generation.'"⁵ DeMar provides a glimpse into the rationale for understanding the verse in this manner:

> At first reading one gets the distinct impression that Jesus is saying that the people with whom He was speaking would live to see and experience the events described in Matthew 24. This seemed impossible! And yet, there it was. I looked up every other occurrence of the phrase "this generation," and each time I came up with the same answer: Jesus was referring to *His* generation, the generation of people alive when He uttered the words. Every Bible commentator danced around the text. "It means the generation alive when the events described in the previous verses begin to manifest themselves," one respected commentator wrote. If that's true, I thought, then this is the only place where "this generation" means a future generation. That's not sound Bible interpretation. . . My discontent grew. I was struck with the obvious, straightforward, literal, plain interpretation.⁶

DeMar and his colleagues reason that the expression "this generation" in the Olivet Discourse must refer to Jesus' contemporaries because

---

2 Gentry, *The Olivet Discourse Made Easy*, loc. 1072.

3 Chilton, *Paradise Restored*, 86; Similarly, Adams and Fisher, *The Time of the End*, 108; Sproul, *The Last Days According to Jesus*, 18, 72.

4 DeMar, *Last Days' Madness*, 159, 184; Gentry, *The Olivet Discourse Made Easy*, loc. 1150; Hanegraaff, *The Apocalypse Code*, 75; Kik, *An Eschatology of Victory*, 63; Mathison, *When Shall These Things Be?*, 179; Sproul, *The Last Days According to Jesus*, 18.

5 Gentry, *The Olivet Discourse Made Easy*, loc. 1204; cf. loc. 1150; Similarly, DeMar, *Last Days' Madness*, 26, 55.

6 DeMar, *Last Days' Madness*, 15.

it always carries this meaning when it appears throughout the Synoptic Gospels.[7] This chapter will demonstrate that this reasoning is incorrect and betrays an ignorance of the phrase's essential meaning and how Christ employed it throughout the Gospels.

Preterists also contend that it is "grammatically impossible" for Jesus to have meant anything other than His contemporary generation because "*this* generation" does not mean "*that* generation."[8] Hanegraaff posits that skeptics, such as Bertrand Russell and Albert Schweitzer, were correct in dismissing the supposed "grammatical gyrations" of futurists who argue that "this generation" refers to another generation.[9] However, R. C. Sproul correctly identified a fallacy with this critique of the traditional view:

> I think DeMar commits a basic error at this point. Futurists do not tend to argue that Jesus was not speaking to that generation of his contemporaries. Rather they argue that the term generation here refers not to a specific time-frame of forty years, but to a "kind" or "sort" of people. Some of these interpreters see "this generation" as a description of believers, while others see it as a description of the wicked.[10]

In other words, Sproul conceded that most futurists teach that the phrase "this generation" *includes* the contemporaries of Jesus but is not *restricted* to them, as preterists insist.

The Greek word translated "generation" refers to children or offspring, not to a group of individuals living during a specific time frame.[11] *The Theological Dictionary of the New Testament* notes that in

---

[7] The phrase "this generation" (ἡ γενεὰ αὕτη) in DeMar, *Last Days' Madness*, 56, 344; Gentry, *The Olivet Discourse Made Easy*, loc. 1111; Hanegraaff, *The Apocalypse Code*, 77; Kik, *An Eschatology of Victory*, 30, 31, 61.

[8] Hanegraaff, *The Apocalypse Code*, 79, 83, 94; Similarly, DeMar, *Last Days' Madness*, 58.

[9] Hanegraaff, *The Apocalypse Code*, 83.

[10] Sproul, *The Last Days According to Jesus*, 65.

[11] This is the Greek word translated *genea* (γενεὰ).

general usage this word means "birth or descent."[12] The word has a primary meaning of offspring which are sired, produced, brought forth, and generated.[13] English speakers sometimes use the word generation in this manner; for example, Christians believe in the eternal generation of the Son from the Father with reference to the Holy Trinity and the doctrine of regeneration, that is, a person receiving new life by the grace given by the Holy Spirit.

The New Testament word translated "generation" corresponds to the Hebrew word frequently translated "generation," which came over into the Greek-speaking synagogues through the Septuagint (LXX).[14] Throughout the Old Testament, this word often carries a qualitative meaning. In other words, this word describes a general quality or character of people, children, or offspring and is not primarily concerned with a specific time period. For example, the psalmist wrote about "the generation of the righteous" (Ps. 14:5), "the generation of his fathers" (Ps. 49:19), "the generation of Your [God's] children" (Ps. 73:15), and "the generation of the upright" (Ps. 112:2; cf. Ps. 12:7; 71:18).

Throughout the Synoptic Gospels, the expression "this generation" functions as a technical term (Matt. 11:16; 12:41-42; 23:36; 24:34; Mark 8:12; 13:30; Luke 7:31; 11:30-32, 50-51; 17:25; 21:32). I will demonstrate that Jesus used this expression as part of a larger thematic interweaving of Deuteronomic expressions (Deut. 1:35; 32:5, 20). In addition, Christ and His apostles developed this larger theme by adding adjectives to modify the word generation:

- faithless generation (Mark 9:19)

- faithless and perverse generation (Matt. 17:17; Luke 9:41)

---

[12] Gerhard Kittel, Gerhard Friedrich, and Geoffrey William Bromiley. *Theological Dictionary of the New Testament* (Dallas, TX: CDWord Library, 1989).

[13] The holy Church fathers regularly used the word "generation" (γενεά) in this manner.

[14] The Greek word *genea* was brought over from the Hebrew word *dor* (דור).

THE MEANING OF "THIS GENERATION"

- this wicked generation (Matt. 12:45)

- an evil and adulterous generation (Matt. 12:39; 16:4)

- an evil generation (Luke 11:29)

- this adulteress and sinful generation (Mark 8:38)

- this perverse generation (Acts 2:40)

- a crooked and perverse generation (Phil. 2:15)

We can discover how Christ and His apostles used these expressions once we properly understand what they meant in their original context within the book of Deuteronomy. The first expression, "this evil generation" (Deut. 1:35), refers to the Israelites who died because of their unbelief during the forty years of wandering in the desert (Deut. 1:34-39; cf. Heb. 3:7-19). As we will see, this expression in not primarily quantitative, limited to people who lived at the time of the exodus, but qualitative, referring to the offspring or children produced with an evil disposition.

The other two Deuteronomic expressions, located in the Song of Moses, categorically convey a qualitative meaning. In the preamble to the song, Moses rebuked the children of Israel for their evil inclination, which is bent toward rebellion and stubbornness (Deut. 31:21, 27). The song itself defines this wicked generation as the sired offspring of Israel, children brought forth with a sinful disposition: "They have dealt corruptly with him [God]; they are no longer his children because they are blemished; they are a crooked and twisted generation" (Deut. 32:5; cf. Hosea 2:2-5). Just verses later, God warned, "I will see what their end will be, for they are a perverse generation, children in whom is no faithfulness" (Deut. 32:20, cf. Deut. 31:17). The larger context characterizes the nation as a corporate offspring of "blemished" children who *perpetually* reject God and engage in idolatry. In point of fact, their corruption would continue long after Moses' death, reaching a crescendo in "the latter days" (Deut. 31:16-29; cf. Deut. 4:25-31). Therefore, the generation in question cannot be limited to a specific time period; it refers to offspring with a transhistorical inclination or disposition toward iniquity.

The prophet Isaiah borrowed from these themes in the Song of Moses for the introduction of his book: "Children have I reared and brought up but they have rebelled against me. . . Ah, sinful nation, a people laden with iniquity, offspring of evildoers, children who deal corruptly! They have forsaken the Lord, they have despised the Holy One of Israel" (Isa. 1:2-4). Once again, such passages emphasize that Israel's children are a corrupt, idolatrous "brood of evildoers," which has continued to rebel against God (cf. Num. 32:14; Isa. 1:2-4; 14:20; Matt. 3:7-9; 12:34; 23:33; Luke 3:7-8). We may conclude, then, that the New Testament motif of "this generation" is faithful to its Old Testament usage as a description of the largely unregenerate Israelite nation.

This evil generation does not refer to ethnic descendants of Jacob as such but to those with a degenerate disposition toward sin. This definition is further qualified by the appearance of the phrase in the apostle Paul's epistle to the Philippians:

> Do all things without complaining and disputing, that you may become blameless and harmless, *children* of God without fault in the midst of *a crooked and perverse generation*, among whom you shine as lights in the world, holding fast the word of life, so that I may rejoice in the day of Christ that I have not run in vain or labored in vain. (Phil. 2:14-16, emphasis added; cf. Deut. 32:5)

The unique feature here is that the Philippians "among whom" these Christians lived were predominantly Gentiles. Therefore, we see that "this generation" was not a uniquely Jewish identity; it includes all unregenerate mankind since the introduction of ancestral sin (Rom. 3:9; cf. Ps. 14:2-5), wicked people who will inhabit the Earth until the return

THE MEANING OF "THIS GENERATION"

of Jesus Christ. In addition, the text indicates that God's children are separate from this wicked generation.

In his seminal work, *Jesus and 'this Generation,'* Evald Lövestam painstakingly demonstrated that the concept of "this generation" should be understood qualitatively as referring to a character or type of people.[15] He demonstrates that the Synoptics include specific, repetitive themes to describe "this generation": First, the expression always has a negative tone and refers to people characterized by moral wickedness. In other words, "this generation" is decisively "evil" and "perverse." Consequently, Christ never included Himself in "this generation," and He generally excluded His disciples from this descriptor; furthermore, He frequently contrasted the people of the evil generation with the righteous. Second, God repeatedly sends preachers to them to proclaim a message of repentance. Third, while miraculous signs accompany this message, they react with doubt and disbelief. Fourth, they persecute and often murder God's righteous messengers. Fifth, they will be condemned on judgment day but the righteous messengers will be vindicated and receive rewards, having previously been rescued from "this crooked generation" (cf. Acts 2:40). Sixth, the New Testament links this pattern of rejecting "the sent ones" with similar narratives in the Old Testament. These consistent themes in Christ's teachings about "this generation" consistently highlight the Jewish nation's perpetual, consistent disposition of rejecting the message of salvation.

As Lövestam demonstrates, this salvific-historical pattern for "this generation" is evident in every pericope or section of material in which the expression appears. The repeated elements discussed above appear in the pericopes regarding the demand for a sign (Matt. 12:38-42; 16:1-4; Mark 8:11-13; Luke 11:16, 29-32), the parable of the playing children (Matt. 11:16-19; Luke 7:31-35), the epileptic boy (Matt. 17:14-20; Mark 9:14-29; Luke 9:37-43), the eschatological sayings about "this generation"

---

[15] Evald Lövestam, *Jesus and 'This Generation': A New Testament Study* (Stockholm: Almqvist & Wiksell International, 1995).

(Mark 8:38; Luke 17:22-37), the judgment on "this generation" (Matt. 23:34-36; Luke 11:49-51), the Olivet Discourse (Matt. 24; Mark 13; Luke 21), the apostle Peter's appeal on the day of Pentecost (Acts 2:40), and the epistolary references to "this generation" (Phil. 2:12-16; Heb. 3:7-4:11). This is conclusive evidence that the phrase "this generation" conveys a technical meaning referring to the transhistorical offspring of wickedness, as it does in the Song of Moses (Deut. 32:5, 20).

Clearly then, Christ's statements about "this generation" continue the theme established by Moses and the Prophets concerning this "perverse generation, sons in whom is no faithfulness" (Deut. 32:20; cf. Ps. 12:7). In addition, contrary to the preterist position as articulated by Gentry, the similar use of the expression in Matthew 23:36 and 24:34 does not prove that both expressions are quantitative and "must mean that [same] first century generation."[16] Seeing both passages as describing *only* the contemporaries of Jesus, DeMar states that both of these appearances of the phrase "form eschatological bookends for determining when the predicted events that occur between these two time markers are to be fulfilled."[17] The larger context of the first statement reads as follows:

> Woe to you, scribes and Pharisees, hypocrites! For you build the tombs of the prophets and decorate the monuments of the righteous, saying, "If we had lived in the days of our fathers, we would not have taken part with them in shedding the blood of the prophets." Thus you witness against yourselves that you are sons of those who murdered the prophets. Fill up, then, the measure of your fathers. You serpents, you brood of vipers, how are you to escape being sentenced to hell? Therefore I send you prophets and wise men and scribes, some of whom you will kill and crucify, and some you will flog in your synagogues and persecute from town to town, so that on you may come all the righteous blood shed on earth, from the blood of righteous Abel to the blood of Zechariah the son

---

[16] Gentry, *The Olivet Discourse Made Easy*, loc. 1111; cf. loc. 573, 695, 1161, 1210; Similarly, DeMar, *Last Days' Madness*, 52, 55-56; Kik, *An Eschatology of Victory*, 64.

[17] DeMar, *Last Days' Madness*, 55.

THE MEANING OF "THIS GENERATION"

of Barachiah, whom you murdered between the sanctuary and the altar. Truly, I say to you, *all these things will come upon this generation.* (Matt. 23:29-36, emphasis added; cf. Luke 11:47-51; 13:34-36)

Preterists and many futurists argue that the expression "this generation" must be understood quantitatively, referring only to Christ's first-century Jewish contemporaries. Certainly, the Lord's original audience, whom He identified as the scribes and Pharisees (Matt. 23:29), belonged to the evil generation in question. In addition, God's judgment upon "this generation" certainly included the destruction of the Jerusalem temple in AD 70 ("Your house is left to you desolate" Matt. 23:38). However, although "this generation" included Christ's contemporary audience, it was not restricted to them.

The scribes and Pharisees comprised only part of this larger generation—the transhistorical offspring of wicked children—as depicted in the Song of Moses and alluded to by the prophets. The text specifies that God held "this generation" responsible for the rejection of all the righteous "from the blood of righteous Abel to the blood of Zechariah" (Matt. 23:35; cf. Gen. 4:8-11). In other words, these evil children will be condemned for the heinous sins of the entirety of Old Testament history. Although the scribes and Pharisees did not personally commit the transgressions of their biblical past, Jesus explained that they maintained a corporate solidarity of guilt with their "fathers" who persecuted and rejected "all the prophets" of the Old Testament, a solidarity evidenced by their continued ancestral pattern of wickedness (Matt. 23:29-31; 34-35; cf. Matt. 5:12; 21:33-41). Under their leadership, the covenant nation soon murdered God's Son and persecuted His apostles (Luke 17:25; Acts 2:23; 5:30; 1 Thess. 2:14-15). For this reason, the apostle Peter also labeled them "this crooked generation" (Acts 2:40).

Christ taught that the scribes and Pharisees maintained culpability for their transgressions because they were children or offspring (read "the generation") of their fathers, who also committed these evil deeds (cf. Ps. 12:7; Jer. 2:30-31; Matt. 11:16-19; Luke 7:31-35). This is why He called them "children of hell," "sons of those who murdered the prophets," and "serpents . . . brood of vipers" (Matt. 23:15, 31, 33; cf. Deut. 32:33; Matt. 3:7; 12:34; John 8:44). Elsewhere, He scolded them: "You are of your father the devil, and your will is to do your father's desires" (John 8:44). In other words, Christ's contemporaries were the spiritual descendants of those who persecuted the prophets, and ultimately, of the devil himself! Thus, "this generation" refers to the qualitative, age-enduring offspring of the serpent (Gen. 3:15; cf. Deut. 32:33; Matt. 3:7; 12:34; John 8:44).

For this reason, these people deserve divine wrath including eternal damnation ("the condemnation of hell" Matt. 23:33). They soon filled up "the measure" of the guilt of their fathers by persecuting the apostles, as their ancestors had rejected and murdered the prophets (Matt. 23:29-36). The Judean Jews as a collective whole deserved divine retribution, as seen in the Pauline phrase *"as always* to fill up the measure of their sins" (1 Thess. 2:16, emphasis added; cf. Matt. 23:32). They perpetually deserved divine wrath ("as always" 1 Thess. 2:16; cf. Matt. 3:7) because they refused to repent for how they responded to the Lord's messengers.

Stephen, the first Christian martyr, spoke about their persistent, ancestral pattern of rejecting God's messengers: "You stiff-necked and uncircumcised in heart and ears! *You always* resist the Holy Spirit; *as your fathers did, so do you.* Which of the prophets did your fathers not persecute? And they killed those who foretold the coming of the Just One, of whom you now have become the betrayers and murderers" (Acts 7:51-52, emphasis added). Similarly, the people of Jerusalem continued this pattern of wickedness: "I [Peter] know that you acted in ignorance, as did also your rulers" (Acts 3:17).

Saint Luke recorded Jesus' contrast of the children of this world with the children of light: "For the sons of this world are more shrewd in dealing with their own generation than the sons of light" (Luke 16:8-9). Once again, Christ used the term "generation" as a synonym for sons or children who share common attributes; He contrasted the generations of the righteous and the wicked in apocalyptic dichotomy. And more to the point, He depicted them as existing simultaneously in the same

THE MEANING OF "THIS GENERATION"

contemporary setting! Neither of these trans-historical generations can be construed as being limited to a contemporary group of people living at the same time, as preterists argue.

Christ borrowed the phrase "all these things" (Matt. 24:33-34; cf. Matt. 23:36) from a series of Old Testament eschatological passages regarding the unprecedented tribulation and the subsequent salvation of the nation of Israel. The primary source for this phrase is found in the covenantal "blessings and curses" listed in the book of Deuteronomy. In these prophetic portions of Scripture, Moses warned that the covenantal curses would ravage the nation (Deut. 32:21-30), most particularly at its "latter end" (Deut. 32:29; cf. Deut. 31:17-18; 32:20) and "in the latter days" (Deut. 4:30; 31:29). The prophet connected this time period with Israel's tribulation and national repentance (Deut. 4:30-31; cf. Jer. 5:18-19). This new covenant promise is that the nation will return to God to mercifully receive a spiritual "circumcision," an event that will occur "when *all these things* come upon you [Israel], the blessing and the curse" (Deut. 30:1; emphasis added; cf. Deut. 30:1-10; Ezek. 37:21-28; Jer. 31:33-40; Dan. 12:7).

Consequently, the "all these things" will not be fulfilled until the glorious appearance of Jesus Christ, as He Himself predicted (Matt. 24:34; Mark 13:30; Luke 21:32). He remarked that this transhistorical generation—"this generation"—will remain until His glorious return. This is why His diatribe against the scribes and Pharisees ends with the statement, "See, your house is left to you desolate. For I tell you, you will not see me again until you say, 'Blessed is he who comes in the name of the Lord'" (Matt. 23:38-39). Then the persecutors of God's elect will come to a complete end.

Russell, a full preterist, argued that Christ employed the second person plural ("you") in this latter passage to show that He was promising to return to His contemporaries.[18] Partial preterists, however, do not eagerly adopt this interpretation. Gentry creatively, although uncon-

---

18 Russell, *The Parousia*, 52.

vincingly, argues that this passage does not refer to Israel's future hope but speaks of "a condition of indefinite possibility" (borrowing from R. T. France) that was fulfilled in their "constrained admission of Jesus' blessedness" which they made in their destruction in AD 70.[19]

However, the antecedent for the "you" addressed in this passage is Jerusalem (Matt. 23:37); this indicates that the name Jerusalem stands as a metonymy[20] for its *people* (cf. Matt. 23:1). As such, Jesus was prophesying that the people of Jerusalem will someday make a declaration of their Messianic redemption. This declaration is part of a psalm of thanksgiving that speaks of Yahweh returning to Jerusalem to deliver Israel from their distress (Ps. 118:26). The larger theme of the psalm is the national salvation of the Jews at Christ's return, but it is not consistent with the events of Jerusalem's demise in AD 70. J. Marcellus Kik, a preterist scholar, admits that this passage refers to the day when the Jews will be "included amongst the chosen."[21]

The preterist arguments regarding Christ's statement about "this generation" (Matt. 24:34; Mark 13:30) fall apart even if the phrase is understood quantitatively. A few examples will demonstrate the falsity of their contention that Jesus would have used "that" instead of "this" if He had wanted to speak of events in our future.[22] For example, the New Testament writers sometimes used the proximal demonstrative, commonly translated "this," to describe events occurring in a distant time from the speaker (e.g., Luke 23:7). Even in the Olivet Discourse, Jesus used the proximal demonstrative to speak of an event in the distant

---

19 Gentry, *The Olivet Discourse Made Easy*, loc. 826-842; cf. R. T. France, *The Gospel According to Matthew: An Introduction and Commentary*; Tyndale New Testament Commentaries (Leicester, UK: InterVarsityPress, 1985), 332.

20 A name of an attribute that is substituted for the object meant.

21 Kik, *An Eschatology of Victory*, 81.

22 The demonstrative ἐκεῖνος instead of οὗτος/ταύτη.

THE MEANING OF "THIS GENERATION"

future (Luke 17:34).[23] In addition, the writer of the book of Hebrews even used the proximal demonstrative in the phrase "this generation" to describe an event that occurred thousands of years prior: "Therefore I [God] was provoked with that [literally 'this'] generation" (Heb. 3:10). Finally, koine Greek has three distinct demonstratives (meaning "this [here]," "this," and "that"[24]) so one could use preterist "logic" to argue that Christ would have used the first of the three demonstratives ("this [here]") in the Olivet Discourse if He had wanted to only refer to His contemporaries or to a restricted time period.

To summarize, Jesus presented the Church with an enigma by using His phrase about "this generation" (Matt. 24:34; Mark 13:30). The interpreter who believes in the inspiration of Scripture is divinely hedged in by the biblical evidence to embrace the conclusion that the expression refers to the transhistorical offspring or children of iniquity. We can further identify them as "the sons of the wicked one" (Matt. 13:38), the spiritual offspring of Satan (Gen. 3:15), and the children belonging to the ruler and god of this world (John 12:31; 14:30; 16:11; 2 Cor. 4:4). As such, "this generation" includes anyone who has not escaped the corruption of "this present evil age" (Gal. 1:4) by trusting in our Lord Jesus Christ. These evildoers will continue to persecute the righteous until the end of the age at the day of Christ.

Christ's statement about "this generation" (Matt. 24:34; Mark 13:30) serves many purposes: For example, the transhistorical nature of this phrase helps preserve the unknowability of the timing of His return; it allowed for the possibility, at least in the minds of the first-century disciples, that they could have lived to see the day of His return. In addition, the statement allowed the destruction of Jerusalem and its temple in AD 70 to *partially* fulfill the Olivet Prophecy in a *typological* manner while demanding its exhaustive fulfillment await the end of the

---

[23] Although many modern translations render the phrase "that night" instead of "this night" in an attempt to provide clarity, the Greek text uses the proximal demonstrative.

[24] ὅδε, οὗτος, ἐκεῖνος

age. Furthermore, as chronicled by Eusebius of Caesarea, the Judean Christians illustrated the versatility of application inherent in Christ's warnings when they fled after seeing the Roman armies approaching Jerusalem (cf. Luke 21:20-21), enabling them to escape the onslaught of the Jews in AD 70. Nevertheless, this wicked generation, which persecutes Christ's disciples, will certainly not pass away until all the aforementioned eschatological events have occurred ("all these things" Matt. 24:34; cf. Matt. 24:4-33). Ultimately, the modern ambiguity regarding the meaning of Christ's statement about "this generation" stumbles academic presumption and demands that the reader humbly wrestle with the timing of the Lord's return and the age-enduring application of the prophecy.

4

TWO QUESTIONS AT OLIVET

A PROPER UNDERSTANDING of the Olivet Discourse is essential for any evaluation of preterism. The discourse is found in all three Synoptic Gospels, primarily Matthew 24, Mark 13, and Luke 17, 21, and each account parallels and augments the others. A preterist interpretation of this discourse and the Apocalypse formally sets one apart as a preterist. For preterism, as with most other eschatological systems, the Olivet Prophecy typically serves as the crux interpretum through which many other eschatological passages can be understood. According to preterism, this discourse was fulfilled in the Roman legions' destruction of Jerusalem and the Second Temple in AD 70. Most futurist interpretations see these first-century events as forming a prophetic backdrop upon which Christ spoke about distant events that will immediately precede His glorious return, including the destruction of a third temple in Jerusalem.

The Lord Jesus delivered the Olivet Discourse to His holy apostles while they sat on the Mount of Olives overlooking Jerusalem's temple from the east. This location was well known as the place where King David wept after leaving the city due to losing the widespread support of the Jewish nation and being threatened by the superior military force of his treasonous son, Absalom (2 Sam. 15:30-31). When Jesus delivered His discourse, He had also been rejected by the nation and was about to be crucified. As the ultimate Son of David, He wept prior to giving this final discourse, knowing that the consequence of the nation rejecting Him would be the destruction of the nation and temple. He approached the city and wept with the following words on His lips:

> Would that you, even you, had known on this day the things that make for peace! But now they are hidden from your eyes. For the days will come upon you, when your enemies will set up a barricade around you and surround you and hem you in on every side and tear you down to the ground, you and your children within you. And they will not leave one stone upon another in you, because you did not know the time of your visitation. (Luke 19:41-44)

The structure of the Olivet Discourse proper begins with Christ's statement that the temple would be destroyed and His lengthy response to the apostles' follow-up questions regarding this event.

> Jesus left the temple and was going away, when his disciples came to point out to him the buildings of the temple. But he answered them, "You see all these, do you not? Truly, I say to you, there will not be left here one stone upon another that will not be thrown down." As he sat on the Mount of Olives, the disciples came to him privately, saying, "Tell us, when will these things be, and what will be the sign of your coming and of the end of the age?" (Matt. 24:1-3)

Several important observations should be made about the questions posed by the disciples. First, their questions were in response to their initial observations about the existing temple complex and Jesus' statement that its stones would be completely dismantled, an event that occurred when the Romans destroyed Jerusalem in AD 70. Second, the content of the questions reveals that the apostles did not know the *timing* of these prophetic events. Third, the disciples thematically connected the destruction of the temple with the glorious coming of Jesus and the end of the age. This is seen by the fact that the disciples asked Him about these events, although He had not provided the timing for these events in the preceding context (cf. Matt. 23:38-39). Fourth, the grammatical form of the questions in Matthew's Gospel and the parallel accounts in the other Synoptics show that the topics of "the sign of your coming" and the end of the age comprise one question and not separate questions per se. This is evident because Mark and Luke combined these two questions into the solitary question "What will be the sign when all these things are about to be accomplished?" (Mark 13:4; cf. Luke 21:7). Most commentators, whether preterists or traditionalists, do not consider these observations to be controversial.

Preterists disagree over the meaning of Jesus' phrase "the end of the age." Those who see the entirety of the Olivet Discourse as having a first-century fulfillment believe that His references to "the end" mean, as DeMar defines it, "the *end* of the Old Covenant redemptive system and nothing else."[1] DeMar and several of his colleagues teach that "the end" signaled the termination of "the temple, the city of Jerusalem, and the covenant promises that were related to the Mosaic system of animal sacrifices, ceremonial washings, and the priesthood" in AD 70.[2] Other preterists favor the traditional understanding that this phrase refers to the end of the age at the return of Jesus Christ.[3] For example, Gentry argues that the phrase "appears first in Matthew 24:3 and points to the end of history. It appears in the disciples' questions which are packed with their assumption that the world will end when the temple ends."[4]

---

1 The Greek word translated "end" (συντελείας) in DeMar, *Last Days' Madness*, 68.

2 DeMar, *Last Days' Madness*, 69; Similarly, Sproul, *The Last Days According to Jesus*, 37.

3 Kik, *An Eschatology of Victory*, 89.

4 Gentry, *The Olivet Discourse Made Easy*, loc. 1037-43.

Gentry contends that the apostles' questions arose from their supposed assumptions and misunderstanding of the teachings of Jesus. He conjectures, "Thus, even though he [Jesus] is now nearing the end of over three years of teaching them, their two questions betray their eschatological confusion. They misconstrue matters by uniting the destruction of the temple with the end of the world."[5] Gentry imagines that the apostles "wrongly associated" the destruction of the temple with "the end of the world."[6] J. Marcellus Kik comments, "There is no doubt the disciples believed that the destruction of the temple and the end of the age were one and the same thing."[7] These preterists would have us believe that the disciples incorrectly connected these two events despite having spent three years under the Lord's direct tutelage. But as we will see, this connection is derived from the prophetic timeline as established in the book of Daniel and the Prophets.

While Gentry admits that the disciples' prophetic expectations about timing were "largely due to the famous prophecy in Daniel 9,"[8] he fails to appreciate that the prophet Daniel connected the temple's desolation with "the time of the end" (Dan. 11:31, 45; 12:1-4, 6-12). This will be further demonstrated in subsequent chapters of this work. Daniel also located the Son of Man's coming with clouds at the time of several eschatological events, including the destruction of the final beast's kingdom, the consummate arrival of Christ's kingdom, and judgment day (Dan. 7:9-27; cf. Matt. 24:30). Contrary to Gentry's claims, the apostles (and Jesus Himself!) followed Daniel by connecting the destruction of the temple with the time of the end.

---

[5] Gentry, *The Olivet Discourse,* loc. 2150.

[6] Gentry, *The Olivet Discourse,* loc. 993; Similarly, John Calvin, *Commentary on a Harmony of the Evangelists, Matthew, Mark, and Luke.* Trans. William Pringle, vol. 3 (Grand Rapids: Baker, 1984), 117; Kik, *An Eschatology of Victory,* 88.

[7] Kik, *An Eschatology of Victory,* 88.

[8] Gentry, *The Olivet Discourse,* loc. 1347

WHICH TEMPLE DESTROYED?

Preterists correctly note that Jesus prophesied the dismantling of the Second Temple, the holy edifice that was before their eyes ("these great buildings … not be left here one stone" Mark 13:2; "As for these things that you see" Luke 21:6).[9] However, they incorrectly argue that this proves that Christ did not also speak about a future rebuilt temple, in other words, a third temple. DeMar contends that the Lord could not have had a future temple in mind because it "would have to be rebuilt with the same stones that made up the temple that was destroyed. Not just any stones will do. Jesus said that 'not one stone *here*'."[10] Gentry laments that futurists "create another suppressed premise" by positing that Jesus referred to a future rebuilt temple in Matthew 24:16.[11] DeMar echoes these sentiments:

> To propose that Jesus was describing a *rebuilt* temple must be proven from Scripture. The New Testament mentions *nothing* about a rebuilt temple. There is nothing in Matthew 24 that even hints at the rebuilding of the temple. Why would Jesus confuse His listeners and those of us who read His recorded prophecy by leaving out a crucial detail like a rebuilt temple? It does not make sense.[12]

Admittedly, Jesus did not relay specific details about the destruction of the Second Temple to be followed by the construction and desolation of the Third Temple. Rather, the disciples only understood *in retrospect* that the temple would be destroyed and rebuilt again; this became apparent once it became clear that the desolations of AD 70 did not fulfill the entirety of the Olivet Prophecy. As I will prove in

---

[9] Kik, *An Eschatology of Victory*, 83.

[10] DeMar, *Last Days' Madness*, 52; cf. Chilton, *Paradise Restored*, 87.

[11] Gentry, *The Olivet Discourse*, loc. 1177; Similarly, Kik, *An Eschatology of Victory*, 72.

[12] DeMar, *Last Days' Madness*, 94.

subsequent chapters, Jesus prophesied in the discourse that His Second Coming, the resurrection of the dead, and the repentance of the Jewish nation will occur shortly after the desolation of the temple. Furthermore, the rebuilding of the temple after its destruction in AD 70 is *an inferred necessity* given that the related prophecies connect these events in a very specific chronology. This leaves the interpreter with three options: (1) the skeptical view, which claims that the predictions of Jesus or of the Synoptic writers failed, (2) the preterist approach, which denies that these prophetic events must occur in tandem, or (3) the futurist view, which argues that Jesus had in mind the mystery of the Third Temple.

I contend that the disciples' questions at the Mount of Olives arose because they did not yet have the schema needed to conceive of the temple being destroyed *twice* before Christ returned. Consequently, while Jesus answered their questions by prophesying the destruction of the temple as a proximate herald for His Second Coming, the disciples could only identify this mystery after the Second Temple period ended without anyone witnessing the Lord's return from heaven (cf. Matt. 24:34).

We should consider that the apostles were also ignorant, at that point, of an extended, interadventual period of two thousand years. This period of Christ's present reign from His heavenly throne is concurrent with the revealed mystery about the apostolic Church, that is, that Jews and Gentiles who trust in Him share in the promises given to Israel (e.g., Rom. 11:25-26; Eph. 3:6; Col 1:27). Therefore, it is obvious that the apostles did not foresee such mysteries, since they can only be understood in retrospect of historical circumstances (cf. Dan. 12:4, 8-10, 13). Similarly, they were yet ignorant that the destruction of Jerusalem, which did not occur until AD 70, would take place apart from any hint of consummate redemption. This points to the rebuilding of the temple in our future, a mystery which has been further clarified by events of the modern era, such as the creation of the State of Israel in 1948, Jewish reacquisition of Jerusalem and its Temple Mount in 1967, and the recent preparations for the Third Temple by the Temple Institute.

TWO QUESTIONS AT OLIVET

Jesus was operating within the normal limits of biblical expression by describing "the temple" (without any numeric qualifier) in the Olivet Discourse to speak of the Third Temple. We know that the Jews who lived during the Second Temple period conceived of their own temple as a continuation of Solomon's Temple because the Scriptures describe its construction simply as a rebuilding of "the house" and "the temple" (Ezra 1:3, 5; 5:2, 11, 15, 17; 6:3, 7-8; Hag. 1:2; cf. Matt. 26:61). Similarly, Jesus answered the disciples' questions regarding their own historical circumstances and the looming destruction of their temple by providing a prophecy concerning the desolation of the eschatological temple that will precede His glorious appearance. Preterists are historically anachronistic when they require Jesus to have used the numeric qualifier "third" to reference a third temple, especially given the fact that such an understanding while the Second Temple stood would have undermined the disciples' expectancy and the unknowability of the timing of the Lord's return.

Preterists vehemently reject the apostolic Church's position that the Olivet Discourse is concerned with events that are future to the modern reader. Russell summarized the traditional interpretation:

> The commonly received view of the structure of this discourse, which is almost taken for granted, alike by expositors and by the generality of readers, is, that our Lord, in answering the question of His disciples respecting the destruction of the temple, mixes up with that event the destruction of the world, the universal judgment, and the final consummation of all things. Imperceptibly, it is supposed, the prophecy slides from the city and temple of Jerusalem, and their impending fate in the immediate future, to another and infinitely more tremendous catastrophe in the far distant and indefinite future.[13]

Gentry considers this interpretation of the discourse to be a tragic mistake:

---

[13] Russell, *The Parousia*, 55.

Indeed, the average evangelical approach to the Olivet Discourse is so seriously misconstrued that it places its fulfillment at the wrong place in history, misses Christ's whole point entirely, applies its judgments to the wrong people, and spreads its catastrophes far beyond its intended focus. Thus, the popular conception has the wrong time, purpose, objects, and scope for its judgments.[14]

If preterism is correct, the reader should expect the historical events of the first century to adequately account for the prophetic details of the Olivet Discourse. However, throughout the next several chapters, we will discover that the preterist paradigm fails to account for these details, and that the events surrounding the destruction of the Second Temple did not exhaustively fulfill the Olivet Prophecy. Conversely, the traditional, futurist interpretation of the prophecy satisfactorily accounts for these prophetic details and provides an awe-inspiring rationale of the most explanatory power.

---

14   Gentry, *The Olivet Discourse*, loc. 161.

5

THE BEGINNING OF BIRTH PAINS

ANCIENT RABBIS, following the Old Testament prophets, taught that the birth pains of the Messiah would be a period of increasing distress and tribulation that would come upon the Jewish nation and the world prior to the arrival of God's kingdom.[1] In the Olivet Prophecy, the Lord Jesus began answering the apostles' questions by reminding them that the birth pains must arrive before the end.

> See that no one leads you astray. For many will come in my name, saying, "I am the Christ," and they will lead many astray. And you will hear of wars and rumors of wars. See that you are not alarmed, for this must take place, but the end is not yet. For nation will rise against nation, and kingdom against kingdom, and there will be

---

[1] The Baylonian Talmud, *Sanhedrin 98b and Shabbat 118a;* cf. Isa. 13:1, 6-9, 17-19; 26:17-19; 33:11; 37:3; 66:7-9; Jer. 4:31; 6:22-26; 22:18-23; 48:41; 49:22; 50:41-43; Hosea 13:13; John 16:21; 1 Thess. 5:3.

famines and earthquakes in various places. All these are but the beginning of the birth pains. (Matt. 24:4-8)

See that you are not led astray. For many will come in my name, saying, "I am he!" and, "The time is at hand!" Do not go after them. And when you hear of wars and tumults, do not be terrified, for these things must first take place, but the end will not be at once. . . Nation will rise against nation, and kingdom against kingdom. There will be great earthquakes, and in various places famines and pestilences. And there will be terrors and great signs from heaven. (Luke 21:8-11)

Many events that occurred at the end of the first century AD could be said to represent the conditions that Jesus termed "the beginning of the birth pains." To illustrate, the New Testament and the Jewish historian Josephus related accounts of false christs and false prophets.[2] Several battles, civil wars, and "rumors of wars" raged throughout the Roman Empire.[3] In addition, Saint Luke relayed that a famine plagued the Empire, especially Judea (Acts 11:27-29). Also, during the years leading up to the destruction of Jerusalem, famines occurred in Rome and throughout Greece, and several earthquakes took place.[4] Many Jews within the vicinity of the Jerusalem temple felt an earthquake during this period.[5] Furthermore, two comets streaked across the empire in AD 60.[6] Finally, Josephus recorded the arrival of ominous signs, including a

---

[2] Josephus, *Jewish Antiquities* 20.8.5; 20.97-98; Acts 8:9-11; 13:6; 20:29-31; 2 Cor. 11:13; 12:11; 2 Tim. 2:16-17; 2 Pet. 2:1; 1 John 2:18; 4:1; Rev. 2:2.

[3] Josephus, *Antiquities* 18.6.10; Philo of Alexandria, *Flaccus*, Vol. 25. 3.8; 4.21; Philo of Alexandria, *On the Embassy to Gaius* 31.213; Josephus, *The Wars of the Jews* 2.14.5; 4.9.2. Tacitus recounted several battles in *The Annals of Imperial Rome* as did Suetonius in *The Twelve Caesars*.

[4] Tacitus, *The Annals of Imperial Rome*, Trans. Michael Grant (London: Penguin Books, 1989) 271; Matt. 27:54; 28:2; Acts 16:26.

[5] Josephus, *The Wars of the Jews* 6.5.3.

[6] Tacitus, *Annals* 14.20.

THE BEGINNING OF BIRTH PAINS

star resembling a sword, lightning storms above the temple, and chariots and armor-clad soldiers in the clouds over Jerusalem.[7]

Preterists present this historical evidence as proof of preterism;[8] however, it should be noted that these catastrophic events occur in every period of history. DeMar admits no less, explaining that "wars, earthquakes, famines, and plagues have been a part of the human condition since the Fall... This means that their contemporary manifestation does not necessarily carry any prophetic importance."[9] On one level, the normative nature of these initial portents ("the beginning of the birth pains") evidences that they do not signal the end of the age. Chilton concurred, "In themselves, Jesus warned, they were not to be taken as signals of an imminent end."[10] Gentry argues that Jesus used the phrase "the beginning of birth pains" to warn against "false starts" concerning the end and that this phrase has "no specific referent and is not reserved for final-eschatological events."[11] He explains in detail:

> In my fuller analysis of the text, I will show that early in the Discourse he warns them not to become confused by preliminary signs, for "that is not yet the end" [Matt.] (24:6b) and "all these things are merely the beginning of birth pangs" (24:8). So in answering their question regarding "when will these things be" he cautions them against being misled by the initial signs. This means he is in fact answering their question as to "when these things will be" but has not arrived at the answer yet.[12]

Jesus warned against a premature identification of these initial signs as prophetic harbingers of the eschaton because these events occur in

---

[7] Josephus, *The Wars of the Jews* 6.5.3.

[8] DeMar, *Last Days' Madness*, ix, 73-86; Gentry, *The Olivet Discourse*, loc. 1337-1534, 1570-1612, 1944-1989; Kik, *An Eschatology of Victory*, 91-97.

[9] DeMar, *Last Days' Madness*, 340, 342.

[10] Chilton, *Paradise Restored*, 90; Similarly, DeMar, *Last Days' Madness*, 179.

[11] Gentry, *The Olivet Discourse*, loc. 1337, 1534-40.

[12] Gentry, *The Olivet Discourse*, loc. 1156; cf. loc. 2081.

every period. Nevertheless, the Scriptures predict an intensification of these labor pains in the years leading up to the end of the age. To illustrate, the Apocalypse predicts a slurry of hail, fire, and blood destroying a third of all trees and all grass, a fiery mountain killing a third of marine life, a falling star poisoning a third of rivers and tributaries, and thick darkness blocking the visibility of the Sun, Moon, and stars for a third of people (Rev. 8:7-12). The apostle John also foresaw that a falling star will open a large shaft in the earth, resulting in smoke darkening the atmosphere (Rev. 9:1-2). In addition, he described a terrifying earthquake of unprecedented magnitude (Rev. 6:12-17; 16:18-21; cf. Rev. 11:13, 19). None of these events took place in the first century, but this has not deterred many preterists from engaging in exegetical gymnastics to argue that they did occur.

Jesus continued His discourse by enumerating other events that would continue the birth pains of tribulation:

> Then they will deliver you up to tribulation and put you to death, and you will be hated by all nations for my name's sake. And then many will fall away and betray one another and hate one another. And many false prophets will arise and lead many astray. And because lawlessness will be increased, the love of many will grow cold. But the one who endures to the end will be saved. (Matt. 24:9-13; cf. Matt. 10:17-22, 34-39)

Preterists correctly note that the book of Acts relates that the apostles and other early disciples were persecuted, which included threats, beatings, legal accusations, flogging, imprisonment, and martyrdom for their faithfulness to the gospel.[13] However, Luke's parallel account of the Olivet Discourse includes the phrase "but before all this" (Luke 21:12), which notifies the reader that this persecution would begin before "the beginning of sorrows" described in the preceding verses (Luke 21:8-11; cf. Matt. 24:4-8). Furthermore, the writings of the holy Church fathers

---

[13] DeMar, *Last Days' Madness*, 120; Gentry, *The Olivet Discourse*, loc. 1570; Acts 5:17-20, 25-26, 30-33, 40-42; 7:58-60; 8:3; 12:1-5; 14:19; 16:22-24; 17:5-6; 18:17; 20:23-25; 21:32-36; 22:24; 24:23; cf. John 21:18-19.

confirm that this persecution continued unabated for many centuries beyond the era of the apostles, and preterists admit that Christians have been intensely persecuted for nearly two thousand years. These facts argue against the limited specificity advocated by preterism, namely, that Jesus spoke only about a limited persecution that occurred prior to AD 70.

The portion of the Olivet Discourse discussed above should be understood as a warning about the persecution and tribulation that Christians have experienced during the interadventual period (Matt. 24:9-13; Mark 13:9-13; Luke 21:12-19). This understanding is strengthened by Jesus' explanation that this tribulation will reach a new level of intensity once "the abomination of desolation" is seen standing in the holy place of the temple (Matt. 24:15-29; Mark 13:14-24), which prohibits the reader from equating this earlier tribulation with the unprecedented and unequaled tribulation that will occur immediately before the end of the age (Matt. 24:21-29; Luke 21:22-23; cf. Dan. 12:1-2).

The apostle John also differentiated between the general tribulation experienced by believers (Rev. 1:9; cf. Rev. 2:9-10) and the great tribulation (Rev. 7:14; 12:7-17; 13:5-8; cf. Rev. 2:22). He saw a vision wherein the souls of the martyrs were instructed to "rest a little longer" until their fellow Christians experienced martyrdom during the great tribulation (Rev. 6:9-11; 7:14; cf. Rev. 20:4). The biblical evidence indicates that the initial labor pains of tribulation will intensify and reach a crescendo as the end approaches, consistent with Christ's statement that "the end will not be at once" (Luke 21:9).

THE GOSPEL TO THE ENTIRE WORLD

Jesus continued His Olivet Discourse by prophesying about a worldwide preaching of the gospel prior to the end. He explained that "this gospel of the kingdom will be proclaimed throughout the whole world as a testimony to all nations, and then the end will come" (Matt.

24:14; cf. Luke 21:26). Preterists argue that the Greek word translated "world" here is a technical term which refers to the civilized world of the Roman Empire.[14] They contend that the apostolic gospel had already been proclaimed throughout "all nations" throughout the Empire, and they support these claims by appealing to the apostle Paul's statements:[15]

> Your faith is proclaimed in all the world. (Rom. 1:8)

> Their [the heavens'] voice has gone out to all the earth, and their words to the ends of the world. (Rom. 10:18)

> For your obedience is known to all ... [The gospel] has been made known to all nations. (Rom. 16:19, 26)

> The gospel, which has come to you, as indeed in the whole world it is bearing fruit and increasing. . . [It] has been proclaimed in all creation under heaven. (Col. 1:5-6, 23)

Several objections can be made to this preterist interpretation of these passages. First, unlike the verse under consideration ("whole world" Matt. 24:14), these Pauline passages simply cannot be understood literally but should be taken hyperbolically.[16] The apostle utilized exaggeration in these verses to emphasize the evangelistic success of the gospel, and his companion Luke also employed similar hyperbolic expressions. For example, Paul explained that devout Jews "from every nation under heaven" were staying in Jerusalem on the day of Pentecost (Acts 2:5). Certainly, the reader should not demand that Jews from Britania or

---

[14] The Greek word translated "world" is *oikomenay* (οἰκουμένη); e.g., Gentry, *The Olivet Discourse*, loc. 1641; James B. Jordan, *The Vindication of Jesus Christ: a Brief Reader's Guide to Revelation* (Monroe, LA: Athanasius Press, 2008), Kindle, loc. 126, 357, 132; Russell, *The Parousia*, 265; cf. Sproul, *The Last Days According to Jesus*, 56.

[15] Chilton, *Paradise Restored*, 91; Gentry, *The Olivet Discourse*, loc. 1662; Thomas Ice and Kenneth L. Gentry, *The Great Tribulation, Past or Future?: Two Evangelicals Debate the Question* (Grand Rapids, MI: Kregel Publications, 1999), 45; Kik, *An Eschatology of Victory*, 99-100; Sproul, *The Last Days According to Jesus*, 44.

[16] F. F. Bruce, *The Epistles to the Colossians, Philemon and to the Ephesians* (Grand Rapids: Eerdmans, 1984), 42-43, 79.

THE BEGINNING OF BIRTH PAINS

Armenia, much less, the Han Dynasty, were in town for the festival. Similarly, unbelieving Jews accused Paul and his traveling companions of turning "the world upside down" with the gospel (Acts 17:6). In these passages, it is inappropriate to render these expressions literally.

The apostle Paul used hyperbole in the above verses, a point that becomes more apparent when we consider that he employed a different Greek term than Jesus did in Matthew 24:14 in all but one of these references.[17] First, Paul substituted "world" for "earth/land" in Colossians 1:5-6, and this is an allusion to Genesis 1:28 (LXX), a verse that speaks of God's command for mankind to multiply and subdue the entire created world, that is, the earth.[18] In other words, this verse is not limited to a limited geographical region. Instead, the apostle alluded to this text in the Colossians passage to show that the gospel was spreading vastly and successfully wherever it was being proclaimed. Second, scholars dispute the meaning of the phrase that is often translated "to all the nations" in Romans 16:26. Many suggest that the preposition in this verse, often translated "to," expresses purpose or intent and more accurately conveys the meaning "for all the nations."[19] The idea is that the gospel is not limited to the nation of Israel or to a particular group of nations. This means that the intended scope of the gospel is *all nations*, and it does not suggest that it had already accomplished this purpose in the first century. Third, while the Greek word "world" (*oikomenay*) can refer to the Roman Empire (Luke 2:1; Acts 11:28; 17:6; 19:27; 24:5), it does not denote such a limited geographical region in Romans 10:18.[20] Rather, this verse is an allusion to Psalm 19:4 (LXX) which was written during the reign of King David, not during the time of any civi-

---

17   The Greek noun *cosmos* (κόσμος) instead of *oikomenay* (οἰκουμένη).

18   He substituted *cosmo* (κόσμῳ - "world") for *gais* (γῆς - "earth").

19   The Greek eis (εἰς); e.g., Mark A. Seifrid in G. K. Beale and D. A. Carson, *Commentary on the New Testament Use of the Old Testament* (Grand Rapids: Baker Academic, 2007), 693.

20   The Greek word *oikomenay* (οἰκουμένη).

lized empire. This psalm speaks of the heavens and the celestial bodies declaring God's glory to "all the earth" and to "the end of the world." As such, the apostle borrowed the language of this psalm to express the idea that the heavenly message of the gospel is intended for everyone under heaven, including Jews and Gentiles (Rom. 10:12, 18). Fourth, the phrase translated "which has been proclaimed" (Col. 1:23) is in the aorist tense, which often carries a continuous aspect, and in this case, is better translated "which is proclaimed." John Piper explains the implications for this meaning of the verse:

> The fact that the [substantival] participle "proclaimed" is aorist tense does *not* mean the proclamation has already happened in the past. That is not the way aorists in substantival participles work, as Daniel Wallace makes clear. . . The aorist tense in such uses denotes no specific time. . . So the simplest reading of Colossians 1:23 is that Paul is *defining* the gospel as the kind of gospel that is unbounded and global in scope, and therefore is preached, by definition, in all the creation. There is no statement here that it has already happened. So I would translate it . . . *the gospel which is proclaimed in all creation under heaven.* I happily note that N.T. Wright suggests the same interpretation.[21]

The figurative language employed by Paul and his travelling companion, Luke, to describe the non-discriminant intent and victory of the gospel contrasts with the literal meaning of Jesus' words in Matthew 24:14. There is no compelling reason to interpret the Master's words in the latter in a hyperbolic manner. Instead, the gospel will be proclaimed to all nations, that is, to all ethnic groups throughout the world, in order to provide them with legal testimony prior to the judgment at the end of the age (Matt. 24:14), a judgment which will include all nations (Matt. 25:32).[22] The book of Revelation also conveys the concept that

---

21 John Piper, "Has the Gospel Been Preached to the Whole Creation Already?" On March 14, 2017. *Desiring God.* http://www.desiringgod.org/articles/has-the-gospel-been-preached-to-the-whole-creation-already.

22 Two phrases translated "all the nations" (πᾶσιν τοῖς ἔθνεσιν; πάντα τὰ ἔθνη).

THE BEGINNING OF BIRTH PAINS

the everlasting gospel must be proclaimed to "every nation and tribe and language and people" prior to the glorious revelation of Jesus Christ (Rev. 14:6).

On the other hand, the preterist approach to Matthew 24:14 imports an unintended meaning upon the words of Jesus and thereby distorts the very basis for worldwide evangelism. This is further supported by the fact that the preterist interpretation of Matthew 24:14 unwittingly undermines the Great Commission (Matt. 28:18-20; cf. Mark 16:15-18) for at least two reasons: First, Jesus promised to be with His disciples in their evangelistic endeavors until "the end of the age" (Matt. 28:20), an age that many preterists believe ended with the destruction of Jerusalem in AD 70. Second, Jesus commanded His disciples to make disciples of "all nations" (Matt. 28:19). Based on their interpretation of "all nations" (Matt. 24:14) and their placement of "the end" in the ancient past, hermeneutical consistency demands that preterists understand this commandment as having been fulfilled no later than AD 70.

In addition, preterists cannot demand that we import the meaning of Pauline passages onto the "all nations" (Matt. 24:14) while arguing that this exact language means something very different when it appears a few chapters later in the same Gospel (Matt. 28:19). Other preterist arguments, such as Kik's contention that Matthew 24:14 is about "witnessing" and the Great Commission is about making disciples, are unconvincing.[23] Even Sproul famously taught that the solitary imperative for Christian evangelism is the commandment of Jesus in the Great Commission. Consequently, a Great Commission, supposedly fulfilled in AD 70, leaves preterists without the primary imperative for worldwide evangelism.

---

23 Kik, *An Eschatology of Victory*, 101.

6

THE ABOMINATION OF DESOLATION

THE PREVIOUS SIGNS that Jesus prophesied were too general to predict the onset of the end of the age. However, He then provided one specific sign—the abomination of desolation—to signify the arrival of the unprecedented tribulation.

> So when you see the abomination of desolation spoken of by the prophet Daniel, standing in the holy place (let the reader understand), then let those who are in Judea flee to the mountains. Let the one who is on the housetop not go down to take what is in his house, and let the one who is in the field not turn back to take his cloak. And alas for women who are pregnant and for those who are nursing infants in those days! Pray that your flight may not be in winter or on a Sabbath. For then there will be great tribulation, such as has not been from the beginning of the world until now, no, and never will be. And if those days had not been cut short, no human being would be saved. But for the sake of the elect those days will be cut short. (Matt. 24:15-22)

DeMar admits that the abomination mentioned by Jesus was the sign demonstrating the arrival of the great tribulation before the end of the age.¹ However, he also asserts that the first disciples had "no doubt" that the setting up of this abomination "was fulfilled in events leading up to the temple's destruction in A.D. 70."² In support of this interpretation of the abomination, Josephus and several ancient and modern rabbis have adopted the view that Daniel's prophecies of the abomination were fulfilled in the destruction of the Second Temple.³

Most preterists teach that the abomination—an idol—stood "in the holy place" of the temple sanctuary, which ultimately resulted in the desolation of Jerusalem in AD 70. Gentry explains this approach:

> Although the "abomination of desolation" involves the destruction of Jerusalem (beginning with its encircling), it culminates in this final abominable act within the temple itself. Thus, the "abomination of desolation" prophecy finds complete fulfillment in AD 70 during the events leading up to and including the August/September destruction of the Temple by the armies of the Roman general Titus.⁴

Many traditional interpreters disagree with this identification while maintaining that the abomination refers to the idol of the final Antichrist that he will erect in the Third Temple in Jerusalem. At this point, I will demonstrate that this assessment finds its basis in several incontrovertible details found in Holy Scripture.

Jesus Christ revealed many details about the abomination of desolation in the Olivet Discourse: First, it will be a visible and identifiable sign ("when you see the abomination of desolation" Matt. 24:15). The "you" here is not restricted to Christ's first-century disciples, although the grammar does not prohibit that interpretation. A preferable interpretation, as the Synoptic Gospels reveal, is that the earliest disciples

---

1   DeMar, *Last Days' Madness*, 179.

2   DeMar, *Last Days' Madness*, 101; Similarly, Gentry, *The Olivet Discourse Made Easy*, loc. 1764.

3   Josephus, *Antiquities* 10:11:7.

4   Gentry, *The Olivet Discourse Made Easy*, loc. 1839.

served as representatives for Christ's disciples more generally, that is, the apostolic Church. This is evident based on a comprehensive word study of the second person plural "you" in the Synoptics, especially the context surrounding the Olivet Discourse and the five primary didactic sections in the book of Matthew.

Second, Jesus specifically instructed His disciples to search the prophecies of Daniel to learn about the abomination of desolation. He explained that this is the very event "spoken of by the prophet Daniel" (Matt. 24:15). The phrase "let the reader understand" is the key to unlocking the meaning of this abomination (Matt. 24:15). This phrase does not mean that Matthew was instructing his readers to "read" and "understand" the words of Christ but that Jesus Himself was telling His disciples to read and understand the prophecies of Daniel. This is evident because this same statement appears in Mark's parallel account.

Third, the abomination will stand in the holy place (Matt. 24:15). In other words, the abomination will be an idol which will be erected inside the holy place, the inner courtyard of the Jerusalem temple, and in all probability, within the most holy place. As we will see, the prophecies of Daniel confirm that the abomination refers to an idol that will set up inside the temple sanctuary.

Fourth, the abomination will start the period of great and unprecedented tribulation ("when you see . . . then there will be great tribulation" Matt. 24:15, 21). This tribulation will be particularly intense ("great") and without duplication ("such as has not been since the beginning of the world until this time, no, nor ever shall be" Matt. 24:21). These words of Jesus show that the great tribulation could never be duplicated because the language prohibits, at least in the plenary sense, any double fulfillment. Jesus quoted Daniel 12:1 almost verbatim in this point in the discourse, demonstrating that He had in mind the unprecedented tribulation described in Daniel 12:1-4 (cf. "spoken of by Daniel the prophet" Matt. 24:15).

As Jesus commanded, we should read about the abomination of desolation in the prophecies of Daniel so that we can understand it. The abomination appears four times in the book of Daniel (Dan. 8:11-13; 9:26-27; 11:31; 12:11), and it always describes a self-exalting ruler who uses military force to desecrate the temple sanctuary with two simultaneous actions: First, he will remove the daily offering of the Jerusalem temple. Three of the four references to this abomination in the book of Daniel clearly identify this offering as the tamid, the burnt offering of lambs which the Levites were commanded to offer every evening and morning on the bronze altar of the temple (Dan. 8:11-13; 11:31; 12:11). Second, this wicked ruler will simultaneously erect the abomination of desolation in the temple sanctuary. The idea is that this self-exalting ruler will forcefully replace the tamid offering with his idol. These four passages read as follows:

> He [the little horn] even exalted himself as high as the Prince of the host; and by him the daily sacrifices were taken away, and the place of His sanctuary was cast down. Because of transgression, an army was given over to the horn to oppose the daily sacrifices; and he cast truth down to the ground. He did all this and prospered . . . How long will the vision be, concerning the daily sacrifices and the transgression of desolation, the giving of both the sanctuary and the host to be trampled underfoot? (Dan. 8:11-13 NKJV)

> The people of the prince who is to come shall destroy the city and the sanctuary. . . Then he shall confirm a covenant with many for one week; but in the middle of the week, he shall bring an end to sacrifice and offering. And on the wing of abominations shall be one who makes desolate, even until the consummation, which is determined, is poured out on the desolate. (Dan. 9:26-27 NKJV)

> And forces shall be mustered by him [the king of the north], and they shall defile the sanctuary fortress; then they shall take away the daily sacrifices, and place there the abomination of desolation. (Dan. 11:31 NKJV)

> And from the time that the daily sacrifice is taken away and the abomination of desolation is set up there shall be one thousand two hundred and ninety days. (Dan. 12:11 NKJV)

Regarding the prophecy of Daniel 9, many commentators have argued that the ruler who will "bring an end to sacrifice and offering" (Dan. 9:27) is the Messiah who would be "cut off, but not for Himself" (Dan. 9:26 NKJV). While it is correct to identify the slain Messiah as Jesus Christ, who died for the sins of the world, it is untenable to equate Him with the prince who will end "sacrifice and offering." Rather, based on the grammar, the nearest antecedent for the one who will end the sacrifice and offering is the coming prince whose people would destroy the temple and its sanctuary (Dan. 9:26-27).[5] This identification becomes certain once a comparison is made between this passage and the other related prophecies in the book which clearly communicate that the evil, self-exalting ruler will forcefully remove the tamid and set up the abomination of desolation (Dan. 8:11-13; 11:31; 12:11).

This coming prince will forcefully stop the temple sacrifices and offerings in the middle of the final "week" of years (Dan. 9:27), that is, three-and-a-half years before the terminus of the prophecy. It should not escape our notice that this period roughly corresponds to the 1,290 days discussed in Daniel 12, the period which will begin with these same events and terminate at the end of the age (Dan. 12:11-13)! Consequently, the final grouping of seven years will end with the final "consummation" which is the answer to Daniel's prayer recorded at the beginning of the chapter, a prayer that God would redeem the Jewish nation and restore Jerusalem and its holy sanctuary (Dan. 9:1-19). This period will "bring in everlasting righteousness" for the prophet's people and for the Holy City (Dan. 9:24).

The other prophecies about the abomination of desolation also contain specific time indicators which demonstrate that they pertain to the time of the end. For example, Daniel was told that "the vision [of Daniel 8] refers to the time of the end" (Dan. 8:17) and "the latter time of the indignation . . . at the appointed time, the end" (Dan. 8:19; cf. Dan. 11:27). In addition, four times in the final vision of Daniel,

---

5 In Hebrew grammar, an antecedent can be found as part of a clause or prepositional phrase.

THE ABOMINATION OF DESOLATION

we are told that the vision would not be completely understood by the nation until the time of the end (Dan. 11:40; 12:4, 9, 13). As such, the exhaustive fulfillment of these prophecies did not occur in history, such as during the period of the Maccabees, with the actions of Antiochus IV Epiphanes, as many commentators argue.

In the Olivet Discourse, Christ mentioned only one abomination of desolation, and He identified it as the particular abomination about which Daniel wrote. Jesus did not say that the abomination would be *similar to* the one mentioned by Daniel, nor did He indicate that it would be an event only foreshadowed by the one described by the prophet. Rather, as we have seen, several verses confirm that Christ had in mind the same abomination of Daniel's prophecies.

N. T. Wright, a preterist and leading New Testament scholar, teaches that Daniel 9:27 is "the crucial determining reference [for the abomination in the Olivet Discourse], with the others [Dan. 11:31; 12:11] being subordinated to it." Gentry affirms this assessment. However, this is a weak argument because Jesus borrowed His phrase "the abomination of desolation" from the final vision of the book of Daniel (Dan. 11:31; 12:11 LXX in Matt. 24:15). This phrase is only similar to the abomination statement in Daniel 9, although there is no doubt that Jesus also had this verse in mind as part of a larger constellation of verses about the same abomination.

CHRONOLOGICAL PROBLEMS

The inability of preterists to definitively identify the abomination of desolation in history is a frequently observed weakness of the entire system. DeMar admits that the preterist community lacks consensus about this identification.[6] Gentry concedes that some prophetic details of Matthew's version of the Olivet Discourse, beginning with the abomi-

---

[6] DeMar, *Last Days' Madness*, 109.

nation, "appear more difficult to assimilate into the preterist approach."[7] However, preterists' inability to conclusively identify the abomination has not deterred them from hunting feverishly through the annals of history to find it, a search forced upon them by their interpretation of the discourse. This weakness is especially troubling for the preterist system because the Lord taught that the abomination will be the climactic event that signifies the arrival of the unprecedented tribulation and the end of the age.

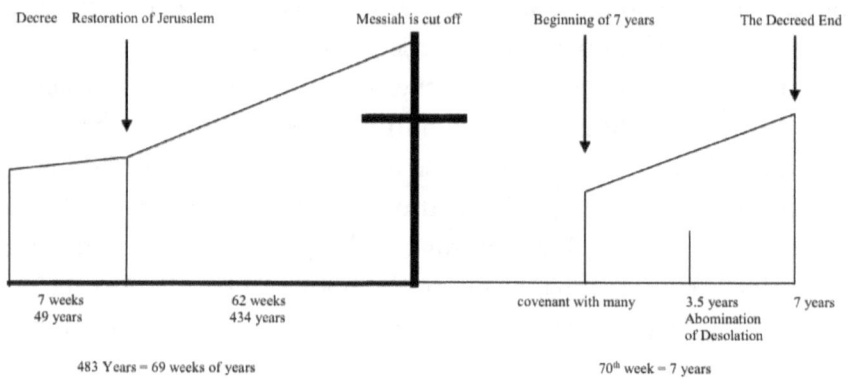

A variety of preterist opinions exist regarding the abomination of desolation. Many preterists attach the label to the revolutionary actions of the Jewish Zealots against the Romans.[8] However, all the Zealots' actions pertaining to the Second Temple occurred *too late* to allow for the specified period of three and a half years (aka forty-two months or 1,260 days) of unprecedented tribulation (cf. Dan. 9:27; 12:1, 11; Rev. 11:2-3; 12:6, 14-17; 13:4-10). Chilton suggested that the abomination "seems to be the occasion when the Edomites (Idumeans), the agelong enemies of Israel, attacked Jerusalem. . . One evening in A.D. 68 the

---

[7] Gentry, *The Olivet Discourse Made Easy*, loc. 1710.

[8] Ice and Gentry, *The Great Tribulation*, 47.

THE ABOMINATION OF DESOLATION

Edomites surrounded the holy city with 20,000 soldiers."[9] This event in AD 68 shares the same difficulty because it also took place much too late to allow for the specified three and a half years of great tribulation. These historical events by the Zealots and Edomites occurred only two years prior to the destruction of Jerusalem in AD 70. In addition, both of these views are at odds with most other preterist interpretations, which see the abomination as referring to the actions of Generals Vespasian and Titus and their Roman legions.[10]

Russell explained that "most [preterist] expositors find an allusion to the standards of the Roman legions in the expression, 'the abomination of desolation,' and the explanation is highly probable."[11] This view suggests that the metallic images of Caesar and the legionary eagles atop the Roman standards constituted a idolatrous desecration (read "abomination") of Jerusalem's holiness. One weakness of this position is that it separates the proposed abomination from the holy place of the temple, whereas the abomination was to involve the desecration of the sanctuary precinct and the removal of the regular burnt offerings *at the beginning* of the tribulation (Dan. 8:12-14; 9:27; 11:31; 12:11; Matt. 24:15; Mark 13:14). This preterist view simply places the abomination far too late chronologically. To illustrate, General Vespasian and his armies arrived to begin their initial assault on Jerusalem in late spring of AD 68, and after a one-year hiatus, General Titus resumed this assault. Titus and his forces eventually entered the temple, but this occurred even later, in the late summer of AD 70.

Preterist N. T. Wright discusses several other pitfalls with this preterist interpretation of the abomination, as it relates to the Olivet Discourse:

---

[9] Chilton, *Paradise Restored*, 92.

[10] E.g., Kik, *An Eschatology of Victory*, 102, 110.

[11] Russell, *The Parousia*, 73; Similarly, Kik, *An Eschatology of Victory*, 103-04.

> This [Matt. 24:15-20] is scarcely to be taken as a reference, after the event, to the actual happenings of AD 66-70. For a start, Titus and his legions were occupying the Mount of Olives and Mount Scopus, the two highest hills overlooking Jerusalem; fleeing to the hills would mean surrender and/or death. For another thing, by the time the Romans took the sanctuary itself it was too late to do anything about running away. Thirdly, the tradition of the Christians getting out of Jerusalem and going to Pella hardly counts as fleeing "to the hills"; to get to Pella they would have had to descend 3,000 feet to the Jordan valley and then travel north for about thirty miles (Pella itself is about three miles east of the Jordan, and twenty miles south of the sea of Galilee). No one in their right mind would describe a flight to Pella as "to the hills."[12]

DeMar is aware of the difficulties with these preterist interpretations of the abomination of desolation. He points out that Luke's parallel account shows that Jerusalem would be "surrounded by armies" (Luke 21:20-21), which he believes is a reference to the saints fleeing the city after the invasion and subsequent withdrawal of the armies of Cestius Gallus in November AD 66. He explains that Jewish "escape [from Judea] was made possible because Cestius and his armies suddenly and without warning withdrew from the temple area."[13] However, this position forces the preterist interpreter to locate the abomination at this particular time. However, these events occurred *far too early* to fit the biblical chronology, as this would place the abomination almost a full four years before the destruction of Jerusalem.

DeMar desperately puts forth four different events as "possible" abominations of desolation, including the actions of the Zealots, Idumeans, Romans, and Jews.[14] He scavenges for any historical occurrence that could potentially be identified as the abomination but to no avail. He even considers the temple sacrifices that the high priests

---

12 Wright, *Jesus and the Victory of God*, 353.

13 DeMar, *Last Days' Madness*, 111.

14 DeMar, *Last Days' Madness*, 104-109.

performed after the crucifixion of Jesus to be the "abomination, a rejection of the work of Christ."[15] This idea, which DeMar attributes to Dr. James B. Jordan, reveals their desperation. By the time of the destruction of the Second Temple, the high priests had been offering sacrifices in the temple for nearly three decades following the crucifixion of Jesus. As such, these sacrifices could not have constituted the particular sign that Jesus said will mark the beginning of the unprecedented tribulation (cf. Matt. 24:15-19; Mark 13:14-20; Luke 21:20-24), especially since priests offered sacrifices in the days immediately after He delivered the Olivet Prophecy.

Preterists ignore the Lord's instruction to the reader that the abomination will be the very event that had been "spoken of by the prophet Daniel" (Matt. 24:15). They seek in vain to identify the primary sign that will signal the unprecedented tribulation because the historical events preceding the destruction of the Second Temple do not fit the details of Daniel's prophecies. DeMar attempts to avoid these chronological problems by arguing that Christ's words ("those days will be shortened" Matt. 24:22; cf. Mark 13:20) imply a foreshortening of the tribulation period.[16] Nevertheless, Jesus did not teach a *premature* termination of the 1,260 days of the tribulation period; rather, He promised to return to save the elect and to preserve humanity ("no flesh would be saved" Matt. 24:22) by preventing the tribulation from continuing unabated *beyond* its appointed days.

Preterists also cast aspersion on the futurist interpretation of the abomination of desolation. Hanegraaff, for example, argues that Jesus could not have predicted a worldwide tribulation because no one could escape it simply by fleeing into the mountains outside Judea.[17] DeMar agrees:

---

[15] DeMar, *Last Days' Madness*, 108.

[16] DeMar, *Last Days' Madness*, 121-22.

[17] Hanegraaff, *The Apocalypse Code*, 31.

People around the globe will have no such advantage [of seeing the abomination] if what Jesus is describing here refers to a worldwide tribulation period. The only ones who can benefit are those who can see the temple. The tribulation period cannot be global because all one has to do to escape is flee to the mountains.[18]

Such musing betrays an ignorance of the futurist position which sees an unprecedented worldwide tribulation as beginning at its epicenter—the Jerusalem temple. Jesus commanded only "those who are in Judea" to flee to the hills (Matt. 24:16), a necessary exodus due to the invading armies of the Antichrist and his abomination that will stand in the holy place (Matt. 24:15; Mark 13:14; Luke 21:20). Furthermore, the apostle Paul implied that those at least as far away as Thessalonica should be able to identify "the man of lawlessness ... [who] takes his seat in the temple of God" (2 Thess. 2:3-4).

Some preterists contend that the abomination of desolation must have been fulfilled in the first century AD because Jesus described first-century living conditions in this section of the Olivet Discourse (Matt. 24:17-20). DeMar explains, "Most roofs in Israel were flat with an outside staircase. . . In these verses, Jesus refers to the strict Sabbath laws that were operating in first-century Israel."[19] This contention fails to consider that these architectural features also exist in modern Israel. Furthermore, based on rabbinic laws, the rebuilding of the Third Temple will undoubtedly be accompanied by the reinstatement of Sabbath requirements for all Jews, the same requirements that Orthodox Jews observe today. Many of these Sabbath laws have already been reinstated and are being enforced in the modern State of Israel.

DeMar also acknowledges that Luke's parallel passage to the Olivet Discourse is concerned with the "days of vengeance" (Luke 21:22; cf.

---

18   DeMar, *Last Days' Madness*, 120-22.

19   DeMar, *Last Days' Madness*, 111.

THE ABOMINATION OF DESOLATION

Isa. 61:2; 63:4), a period that DeMar identifies with Jerusalem's destruction in AD 70.[20] This portion of the discourse reads as follows:

> But when you see Jerusalem surrounded by armies, then know that its desolation has come near. Then let those who are in Judea flee to the mountains, and let those who are inside the city depart, and let not those who are out in the country enter it, for these are days of vengeance, to fulfill all that is written. Alas for women who are pregnant and for those who are nursing infants in those days! For there will be great distress upon the earth and wrath against this people. They will fall by the edge of the sword and be led captive among all nations, and Jerusalem will be trampled underfoot by the Gentiles, until the times of the Gentiles are fulfilled. (Luke 21:20-24)

Contrary to DeMar's claim, this passage does not describe the relatively long period of exile that began with the destruction of Jerusalem in AD 70 but the much shorter exile that will occur during the future tribulation period. This is based a few different lines of evidence: First, the unprecedented tribulation will begin with the appearance of the abomination of desolation in the holy place of the temple (Matt. 24:15-21; Mark 13:14-19), a period which tightly corresponds with Luke's parallel account of the Gentiles trampling Jerusalem after their armies after have surrounded it (Luke 21:20-24). The prophet Daniel consistently described this eschatological period as forty-two months of unprecedented trouble that will begin with the willful ruler forcefully setting up his abomination of desolation and removing the daily burnt sacrifice (Dan. 8:9-12; 9:27; 11:31; 12:1, 7, 11).

Second, the apostle John described this as a period during which the temple's outer court will be "given over to the nations" so that they "trample the holy city for forty-two months . . . 1,260 days" (Rev. 11:2-3). This echoes Christ's language about Jerusalem being "trampled underfoot" by the nations while the Jews remain in exile "among all nations" (Luke 21:24; cf. Zech. 14:1-3). The implication is that the city

---

20 DeMar, *Last Days' Madness*, 25.

will no longer be trampled after this period of Gentile domination ("the times of the Gentiles" Luke 21:24) because of the glorious arrival of the Son of Man.

Third, other prophetic texts demonstrate that the Gentiles will trample the temple sanctuary after a relatively recent return from exile (Isa. 63:18; cf. Isa. 64:10-11; Ezek. 38:8; Zeph. 2:1-2), which does not fit the periods for the destruction of the first or second temples.

THE GREAT TRIBULATION

The prophetic system of preterism pushes many of its adherents to interpret Christ's description of the unprecedented tribulation as mere hyperbole. Hanegraaff represented this opinion when he wrote that Jesus "was not literally predicting that the destruction of Jerusalem would be more cataclysmic than the catastrophe caused by Noah's flood" but was "clearly using prophetic hyperbole."[21] Preterists recognize that they cannot sustain their premise that the great tribulation ended with the destruction of the temple in AD 70 while taking the words of Jesus literally when he described the tribulation with such particularity ("such as has not been from the beginning of the world until now, no, and never will be. And if those days had not been cut short, no human being would be saved" Matt. 24:21-22; cf. Dan. 12:1-2). Arguably, the Jews have experienced many devastations, such as the genocidal pogroms, the Holocaust, and assimilation, which have greatly surpassed the intensity and duration of the First Jewish-Roman War.

Some preterists teach that the Old Testament supports their thesis that Jesus used hyperbole to describe the unprecedented tribulation.[22] For example, Hanegraaff surmises that the prophet Jeremiah employed

---

[21] Hanegraaff, *The Apocalypse Code*, 30, 62.

[22] E.g., Gentry, *The Olivet Discourse Made Easy*, loc. 1925; cf. loc. 1935.

such hyperbolic language to describe the destruction of the First Temple in the sixth century BC.[23] The prophet Jeremiah declared,

> Ask now, and see, can a man bear a child? Why then do I see every man with his hands on his stomach like a woman in labor? Why has every face turned pale? That day is so great there is none like it; it is a time of distress for Jacob; yet he shall be saved out of it. (Jer. 30:6-7)

However, the immediate context of this passage reveals that the prophet did not write about events in his own day but about the future unprecedented tribulation. This is evident from the description of the Messianic birth pains (Jer. 30:6), the ultimate restoration of Judah and Israel to the Promised Land in "quiet and ease . . . and none shall make him afraid" (Jer. 30:3, 10), the Jewish nation obediently serving the risen Christ ("David their king" Jer. 30:9), and the complete destruction of all wicked nations on the day of the Lord (Jer. 30:7-9, 11, 16).

Chilton objected to the futurist understanding of the great tribulation because it seems to require a double fulfillment. He explains that the Olivet Discourse "cannot be made to fit into some 'double-fulfillment' scheme of interpretation; the Great Tribulation of A.D. 70 was an absolutely unique event, never to be repeated."[24] Most traditional interpreters agree with Chilton that the tribulation will be unprecedented, and hence without duplication, but disagree with his assessment that it refers to the period of the First Jewish-Roman War of AD 66-70. However, the futurist position recognizes that the Olivet Prophecy conveys a degree of *versatility of application* sufficient to prompt the first-century Jewish Christians to flee Judea and Jerusalem and so escape the initial onslaught of Roman armies.[25]

---

23 Hanegraaff, *The Apocalypse Code*, 62.

24 Chilton, *Paradise Restored*, 93.

25 Eusebius, *Ecclesiastical History* 3.5.3.

Jesus continued His discourse by warning about false christs ("anointed ones") and false prophets who will make false predictions about messianic appearances during the great tribulation:

> Then if anyone says to you, "Look, here is the Christ!" or "There he is!" do not believe it. For false christs and false prophets will arise and perform great signs and wonders, so as to lead astray, if possible, even the elect. See, I have told you beforehand. So, if they say to you, "Look, he is in the wilderness," do not go out. If they say, "Look, he is in the inner rooms," do not believe it. For as the lightning comes from the east and shines as far as the west, so will be the coming of the Son of Man. Wherever the corpse is, there the vultures will gather. (Matt. 24:23-28)

Some preterists agree with the traditional interpretation that Matthew 24:27 refers to the Second Coming ("so also will the coming[26] of the Son of Man be"). For example, regarding this verse, Gentry writes, "When he [Jesus] does return it will be visible and dramatic as lightning flashing."[27] Gentry then retreats into a diatribe about how Jesus was supposedly contrasting His "dramatic coming in the second advent with the metaphorical coming in AD 70," only to return in the next verse to the "AD 70 judgment."[28] Apparently, Gentry realizes that Christ's coming[29] in Matthew 24:27 is concerned with His personal presence at His return, as also evidenced by the contrasted content in the previous verse ("Look, he is in the wilderness. . . Look, he is in the inner rooms" Matt. 24:26). As we will see in a later chapter, Gentry's futile attempt to disconnect the coming of Jesus from His personal return is not based on exegetical considerations but on concerns to protect his preterist position regarding the Olivet Discourse.

---

26 Greek *parousia* (παρουσία).

27 Gentry, *The Olivet Discourse*, loc.1989; Similarly, Kik, *An Eschatology of Victory*, 124.

28 Gentry, *The Olivet Discourse*, loc. 1989-94; Similarly, Kik, *An Eschatology of Victory*, 124.

29 Greek *parousia* (παρουσία).

THE ABOMINATION OF DESOLATION

Preterist opinions differ as to whether Matthew 24:28 ("Wherever the corpse is, there the vultures will gather") envisions literal vultures feasting on human corpses[30] or is a metaphor to illustrate the idea that Gentry puts forth that "Israel is judicially dead; the Roman armies will devour her carcass."[31] Gentry, following N. T. Wright and others, argues that the vultures, variously translated as eagles, refers to the Roman Eagles.[32] The latter interpretation is unlikely. Admittedly, a potential corresponding prophecy in the Apocalypse depicts birds feasting upon the carcasses of those slain in battle (Rev. 19:17-18, 21; cf. Ezek. 39:17-20). But more to the point, the immediate context of Christ's statement points to the greater likelihood that it serves as a metaphor conveying that no one can miss His glorious return; it is certain, like the arrival of vultures when a carcass is in the vicinity (Matt. 24:28; Luke 17:37).

We have seen that preterists are unable to identify the abomination of desolation in history. Their attempts to identify it fail to account for the prophetic expectations of the book of Daniel and the Olivet Discourse. The historical events of the first century AD do not provide for biblical expectations of an idol being set up in the Jerusalem temple that signals the beginning of a period of unprecedented tribulation lasting three and a half years, that is, forty-two months. Preterists have proposed several candidates for the abomination, including the actions of the Jewish Zealots, the Edomites, Cestius Gallus, General Vespasian, and General Titus, but none of the events associated with these historical players fit the prophetic details of the biblical prophecies.

---

30   Hanegraaff, *The Apocalypse Code*, 33.

31   Gentry, *The Olivet Discourse Made Easy*, loc. 2019; cf. loc. 2004, 2024, 2045; Kik, *An Eschatology of Victory*, 110.

32   Wright, *Jesus and the Victory of God*, 360; Gentry, *The Olivet Discourse Made Easy*, loc. 2024-2029.

TABLE 1: THE ABOMINATION OF DESOLATION IN DANIEL 8, 9, AND 11-12

	Daniel 8	Daniel 9	Daniel 11-12
Time of Fulfillment	[17] the vision refers to the time of the end.	[27] Even until the consummation	[11:35] until the time of the end
	[19] what shall happen in the latter time of the indignation; for at the appointed time of the end		[11:35] because it is still for the appointed time.
	[26] Therefore seal up the vision, for it refers to many days in the future.		[12:9] the words are closed up and sealed till the time of the end.
Evil Agent	[9] a little horn

[23] a king | [26] the prince who is to come | [11:36] the king |
| **Self-Exaltation** | [9] which grew exceedingly great. . .
[10] And it grew up to the host of heaven; and it cast down some of the host and some of the stars to the | — | [11:36] Then the king shall do according to his own will: he shall exalt and magnify himself above every god, shall speak blasphemies |

	stars to the ground, and trampled them. ¹¹ He even exalted himself as high as the Prince of the host ²⁵ And he shall exalt himself in his heart. ... He shall even rise against the Prince of princes		blasphemies against the God of gods, and shall prosper. ³⁷ ... for he shall exalt himself above them all.
His Military Destroys Jerusalem and its Temple Sanctuary	⁹ and toward the Glorious Land. ¹¹ by him ... the place of His sanctuary was cast down. ¹² an army was given over to the horn	²⁶ the people of the prince who is to come shall destroy the city and the sanctuary. The end of it shall be with a flood, and till the end of the war desolations are determined.	11:41 He shall also enter the Glorious Land 11:31 And forces shall be mustered by him, and they shall defile the sanctuary fortress
Removes the Daily Sacrifice (tamid)	¹¹ and by him the daily sacrifices were taken away ¹² Because of transgression, an army was given over to the horn to oppose the daily sacrifices;	²⁷ he shall bring an end to sacrifice and offering.	11:31 then they shall take away the daily sacrifices,
Sets up the Abomination of Desolation	¹³ and the transgression of desolation	²⁷ And on the wing of abominations shall be one who makes desolate	11:31 and place there the abomination of desolation.

He Will Prosper Until the End	[12] and he cast truth down to the ground. He did all this and prospered. [24] And shall prosper and thrive [25] But he shall be broken without human means.	[27] Even until the consummation, which is determined, is poured out on the desolate.	11:36 and shall prosper till the wrath has been accomplished; for what has been determined shall be done. 11:41 yet he shall come to his end, and no one will help him.
Length of the Fulfillment	[13] "How long will the vision be, concerning the daily sacrifices and the transgression of desolation, the giving of both the sanctuary and the host to be trampled underfoot?" [14] And he said to me, "For two thousand three hundred days; then the sanctuary shall be cleansed."	[27] Then he shall confirm a covenant with many for one week; but in the middle of the week he shall bring an end to sacrifice and offering. And on the wing of abominations shall be one who makes desolate, even until the consummation	11:32 Those who do wickedly against the covenant he shall corrupt with flattery 12:11 "And from the time that the daily sacrifice is taken away, and the abomination of desolation is set up, there shall be one thousand two hundred and ninety days.

7

PROPHECY OF THE SEVENTY WEEKS

THE PROPHECY OF THE SEVENTY WEEKS in Daniel 9:24-27 serves a critical purpose in the study of eschatology, largely due to the fact that the Olivet Discourse is widely considered to be an exposition of this prophecy. The angel Gabriel delivered it in response to the prophet's penitential prayer that the Jews be brought back to their homeland after being exiled for seventy years in Babylon (Dan. 9:1-19). Daniel requested that the Lord turn His wrath away from Jerusalem, and show favor to the desolate sanctuary of His holy temple (Dan. 9:16-18). The prophecy continues as follows:

> Seventy weeks are decreed about your people and your holy city, to finish the transgression, to put an end to sin, and to atone for iniquity, to bring in everlasting righteousness, to seal both vision and prophet, and to anoint a most holy place. Know therefore and understand that from the going out of the word to restore and build Jerusalem to the coming of an anointed one, a prince, there shall be seven weeks. Then for sixty-two weeks it shall be built again with

squares and moat, but in a troubled time. And after the sixty-two weeks, an anointed one shall be cut off and shall have nothing. And the people of the prince who is to come shall destroy the city and the sanctuary. Its end shall come with a flood, and to the end there shall be war. Desolations are decreed. And he shall make a strong covenant with many for one week, and for half of the week he shall put an end to sacrifice and offering. And on the wing of abominations shall come one who makes desolate, until the decreed end is poured out on the desolator. (Dan. 9:24-27)

Preterists and traditional interpreters generally agree on several features of the prophecy: First, it is an expansion of Jeremiah's prophecy that predicts the return of the Jews to the land of Israel after seventy years of Babylonian exile (Jer. 25:11-12; 29:10; Dan. 9:2), enumerating the events that would occur during a period of seventy "weeks" (literally "sevens" or "heptads"). These seventy "weeks" are almost universally understood to mean seventy groupings of seven years (70 x 7 years = 490 years; cf. Gen. 29:27-28). Second, the prophecy pertains to the prophet's people—the Jews—and the Holy City (Dan. 9:24). Third, the 490-year period consummates the following divine purposes: "to finish the transgression, to put an end to sin, and to atone for iniquity, to bring in everlasting righteousness, to seal both vision and prophet, and to anoint a most holy place" (Dan. 9:24). Some scholars have attempted, with varying degrees of success, to connect all six redemptive actions to the first advent of Jesus Christ. Fourth, most Christian interpreters understand "an anointed one" who would be "cut off" and "have nothing" after the first sixty-nine weeks (483 years) to refer to Christ and His death on the cross (Dan. 9:26; cf. Isa. 53:8).

However, scholars vehemently disagree regarding the timing and events of the seventieth week, in other words, the final seven years, of the prophecy. Preterists usually view "the prince who is to come" (Dan. 9:26) as Emperor Vespasian or General Titus,[1] whereas many futurists see this figure to be the future Antichrist. Most interpreters see the

---

[1] E.g., Kik, *An Eschatology of Victory*, 108.

destruction of the city in this verse as a reference to the Roman invasion of Jerusalem in AD 70, although some futurists interpret it as referring to the city's future destruction by the Antichrist's forces or as a double entendre.

Many preterists see the one who will "make the strong covenant [alternatively 'strengthen the covenant'] with many for one week, and for half of the week he shall put an end to sacrifice and offering" (Dan. 9:27) as a reference to the ministry and death of Christ (cf. Matt. 26:28).[2] On the other hand, futurists interpret the verse as describing the Antichrist deceptively and strategically confirming the holy covenant with many nations (Dan. 8:25; 11:21-24, 27-28; cf. Isa. 28:14-16, 18; Ezek. 38:8, 11, 14; 1 Thess. 5:3). Then he will violate the international league by setting up the abomination of desolation at the midpoint of the final seven years ("for half of the week he shall put an end to sacrifice and offering. . . on the wing of abominations shall come one who makes desolate" Dan. 9:27). This event will include the forced cessation of the daily sacrifice in the Third Temple (Dan. 9:27; 11:31; 12:11; Matt. 24:15; 2 Thess. 2:4).

Many futurists interpret Daniel's seventieth week as referring to the final seven years prior to the return of Jesus. This requires a gap of nearly two thousand years between the sixty-ninth and seventieth weeks. DeMar summarizes,

> Again, the prophetic scenario is dependent on splitting the seventieth "week" (seven years) from the previous sixty-nine "weeks" (483 years) and inserting a "gap" of nearly two thousand years after the sixty-ninth "week" and before the seventieth "week" of Daniel 9:24-27. There is nothing in Daniel 9:24-27 that even hints that there will be a rebuilt temple.[3]

While the prophecy does not specify a gap, the grammatical construction of the passage divides the 490 years into distinct periods of seven weeks (49 years), sixty-two weeks (434 years), and one week (7

---

2 Kik, *An Eschatology of Victory*, 109.

3 DeMar, *Last Days' Madness*, 95.

years). This allows for the possibility of one or two gaps, especially since the angel specified that certain prophetic events would signal the start and completion of each period.

DeMar argues that futurists have "no biblical warrant" for seeing the first sixty-nine weeks and the seventieth week as non-continuous periods of time: "The idea of separation and the placement of an indeterminable gap between the two sets of weeks is one of the most unnatural and nonliteral interpretations of Scripture found in any eschatological system."[4] He claims that interpreting the prophecy in this manner is a form of "manipulating" Scripture and contriving a novel interpretation so that the passage fits an "already established prophetic system."[5] Kik states that a gap would indicate that "we would still be in our sins."[6] DeMar quotes the axiom that "necessity is the mother of invention" and claims that the idea of a future seventieth week originated in the modern period.[7] He quibbles, "Why is there no mention of this 'great parenthesis' either in the Bible or in nearly nineteen hundred years of church history?"[8]

DeMar's complaint about the traditional interpretation of this passage is verifiably false. The testimony of the holy Church fathers is reason enough to reject his insistence that such teaching is absent from the sacred tradition of the Church. The fathers taught that Jesus is the Messiah who was "cut off" after the sixty-ninth week, and many of them also held the view that the seventieth week, and more particularly the final three and a half years, is reserved for fulfillment in our future. For example, Irenaeus (c. AD 180) saw the final week as pointing to the final

---

[4] DeMar, *Last Days' Madness*, 95; Similarly, Kik, *An Eschatology of Victory*, 107.

[5] DeMar, *Last Days' Madness*, 95; Similarly, Hanegraaff, *The Apocalypse Code*, 54.

[6] Kik, *An Eschatology of Victory*, 108.

[7] DeMar, *Last Days' Madness*, 325, 328.

[8] DeMar, *Last Days' Madness*, 95.

PROPHECY OF THE SEVENTY WEEKS

seven years prior to the return of Christ.[9] Hippolytus (c. AD 200) taught that the final week referred to "the last week that is to be at the end of the whole world."[10] He laid out this futurist view of the prophecy:

> For when the sixty-two weeks are fulfilled, and Christ has come, and the Gospel is preached in every place, the times will then be accomplished. Then, there will remain only one week (the last) . . . And in the middle of it, the abomination of desolation will be manifested. This is the Antichrist, announcing desolation to the world. And when he comes, the sacrifice and oblation will be removed.[11]

DeMar critiques the futurist interpretation of Daniel 9:27, seeing in it the Antichrist (not Jesus, as many preterists argue), who will confirm or strengthen ("make firm") the covenant with many during the final seven years. He mocks this interpretation by exclaiming, "It's not Jesus who 'will put a stop to sacrifice and grain offering' through his shed blood (9:27)—it's the antichrist!"[12] However, as argued in the last chapter, in every reference to the abomination of desolation in the book of Daniel, it is a self-exalting, evil ruler who removes the daily sacrifice from the sanctuary (Dan. 8:11-12; 11:31-32, 45; 12:11).

All eschatological systems, including preterism, must leave room for a gap before Daniel's final "week" of years. Many preterists, following Clement of Alexandria, allow for a gap of forty years between the Messiah who was "cut off" after the sixty-ninth week and the destruction of Jerusalem during the seventieth week.[13] Nevertheless, DeMar and others reject a gap altogether. He places the "cutting off" of the Messiah in the midpoint of the seventieth week instead of immediately

---

[9] Irenaeus 1.553, 1.554, 1.560 in David Bercot, *A Dictionary of Early Christian Beliefs: A Reference Guide to More Than 700 Topics Discussed by the Early Church Fathers* (Peabody, MA: Hndrickson Publishers, Inc, 1998).

[10] Hippolytus 5.213 in Bercot, *A Dictionary of Early Christian Beliefs*.

[11] Hippolytus 5.182 in Bercot, *A Dictionary of Early Christian Beliefs*.

[12] DeMar, *Last Days' Madness*, 328; Similarly, Adams and Fisher, *The Time of the End*, 87.

[13] E.g., Adams and Fisher, *The Time of the End*, 90; Kik, *An Eschatology of Victory*, 109.

after the sixty-ninth week. He claims that the termination of the seventieth week occurred exactly three and a half years after the Lord's crucifixion when the evangelistic effort focused upon Israel supposedly ended and the apostolic preaching to the Gentiles began.[14]

However, this interpretation is incorrect. The prophet Daniel had prayed for the Lord to show mercy to the Jewish nation by turning them from their iniquities and by putting an end to the desolations that had come upon Jerusalem (Dan. 9:1-19). DeMar's interpretation strongly implies that the prophetic answer to these prayers was that the Romans would bring ultimate desolation upon Jerusalem. On the other hand, the futurist position is that the prophetic fulfillment of prophecy must include the final salvation of the Jewish nation, the eschatological redemption of Jerusalem, and the glorious return of Jesus Christ to usher in "everlasting righteousness" for the nation. In addition, DeMar's interpretation necessarily separates the abomination of desolation from the removal of the daily sacrifice, requiring the former event to have occurred four decades after the seventieth week, which contradicts the temporal details of the prophecy (cf. Dan. 9:26-27).

DeMar charges those who accept the traditional interpretation with denying the faithfulness of God: "What would we think of such a deal? Could God ever delay keeping His promise in such a way and still be called a covenant-keeping God? No!"[15] The traditional interpretation teaches that the Lord will fulfill His promise to redeem Daniel's nation, city, and temple, albeit after a mysterious delay. This delay does not mean that God is slack to fulfill His promises but that He is patiently waiting for His people to repent (2 Pet. 3:9). Ironically, the preterist position denies God's faithfulness by placing the terminus ad quem (i.e., the endpoint) of Daniel's prophecy in the first century AD without receiving the answer to his prayers and "pleas for mercy" for his desolate nation, city, and sanctuary (Dan. 9:1-19). While the angel predicted

---

14 DeMar, *Last Days' Madness*, 327.

15 DeMar, *Last Days' Madness*, 331.

specific prophetic events related to the final redemption of the nation (Dan. 9:24; cf. Dan. 12:7; Zech. 12:10; Rom. 11:25-27), DeMar's position teaches the exact opposite; he argues that the prophecy terminated with the final destruction of the Jewish kingdom and the ultimate, permanent rejection of the Jews in AD 70.

Preterists admit that Daniel's prophecy reveals the cyclical nature of divine judgment. Mathison explains this view:

> Jeremiah provided a specific time text [Jer. 25:11-12; 29:10] that was greatly extended in Daniel [9:24-27]. Leviticus 26, especially verse 18, provides the covenantal basis for such extensions of judgment. Leviticus 26 also indicates that this principle of sevenfold judgment can be repeated many times.[16]

DeMar also correctly sees that the seventy years' captivity mentioned in Jeremiah 29:10 provided the pattern for the 490 years of captivity in Daniel 9:24.[17] It is not as apparent to preterists that desolations will continue until the Antichrist destroys Jerusalem and the Third Temple, immediately prior to the national repentance and ultimate salvation of the Jewish nation.

---

[16] Mathison, *When Shall These Things Be?*, 164.

[17] DeMar, *Last Days' Madness*, 330.

8

THE DAY OF JESUS CHRIST

THE LORD JESUS CHRIST taught that specific cosmic phenomena will occur after the great tribulation: "Immediately after the tribulation of those days the sun will be darkened, and the moon will not give its light, and the stars will fall from heaven, and the powers of the heavens will be shaken" (Matt. 24:29). Gentry admits that a literal, straight-forward interpretation of this passage does not support preterism: "A quick reading of this statement seems to undermine the preterist approach I have been presenting. . . And certainly if we were to interpret this passage in a strictly literal sense, it would be difficult to associate these prophetic events with AD 70. But looks are deceiving."[1] Kik admits that this passage "employs such strong and vivid language that many think it can be descriptive of nothing else than the end of the world and the Second Coming of Christ. These descriptive terms would seem to indicate a catastrophic end of the earth."[2] In this chapter, we will examine

---

[1] Gentry, *The Olivet Discourse Made Easy*, loc. 2055-2061; Similarly, Kik, 31-32.

[2] Kik, 127.

preterist claims about this passage and the reasons why this verse does not favor a preterist interpretation.

The language of cosmic phenomena in the Olivet Discourse pertains to the eschatological day of Yahweh—the day of the Lord. In this portion of the discourse, Jesus taught that the darkening of the Sun, Moon, and stars will occur "immediately after" the unprecedented tribulation (Matt. 24:29; Mark 13:24-25; cf. Luke 21:25-26). Equally true, such cosmic phenomena will signal the onset of the day of the Lord, as God declared through the prophet Joel: "And I will show wonders in the heavens and on the earth, blood and fire and columns of smoke. The sun shall be turned to darkness, and the moon to blood, before the great and awesome day of the Lord comes" (Joel 2:30-31; cf. Acts 2:20-21). These prophecies provide the reader with a sequence of events regarding the day of the Lord.

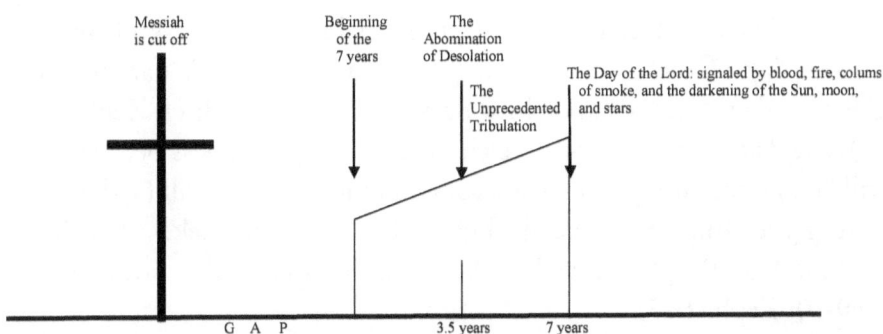

Preterists and traditional interpreters generally agree that Christ's prophecy about stellar darkness (Matt. 24:29; Mark 13:24-25) is not a quotation of a single text but represents a general theme found in multiple Old Testament prophecies (e.g., Isa. 13:10; 34:4; Ezek. 32:7;

Joel 2:10, 31; 3:15; Amos 8:9).³ New Testament scholar, Craig L. Blomberg, explains:

> [The lines of Matt. 24:29] allude to Isa. 13:10, with echoes of 34:4. . . . The closest thing to an actual quotation that we find in Matthew is "the moon will not give its light," with a different Greek word used for "light" than in the LXX. It is Isa. 34:4, though, that actually has the stars being dissolved and falling. . . A constellation of allusions rather than an actual quotation seems to be a more accurate description of Matthew's form.⁴

These Old Testament prophets depicted the darkening of the Sun, Moon, and stars at the day of the Lord (Isa. 13:10; 24:23; 50:3; Joel 2:10; 3:15; Amos 8:9; cf. Rev. 6:12-14). They taught that the heavenly bodies will become darkened so that they no longer shine (Joel 2:10; 3:15; cf. Ezek. 32:7-8). The luminaries will no longer provide light although they will continue to operate within their orbits (Isa. 13:10; cf. Isa. 24:23). The prophet Joel declared, "Let all the inhabitants of the land tremble, for the day of the Lord is coming; it is near, a day of darkness and gloom, a day of clouds and thick darkness!" (Joel 2:2-3; cf. Zeph. 1:15-16) The day of the Lord will be characterized by darkness because God will "make the sun go down at noon" so that the earth will be darkened during the time of "broad daylight" (Isa. 59:9-10; Ezek. 30:3; Amos 5:19-20; 8:9). People will walk "like the blind" so that they stumble (Isa. 59:9-10; Zeph. 1:17).

Consistent with the Old Testament prophets, the apostle John connected the timing of the day of the Lord with six observable phenomena: (1) an unprecedented earthquake, (2) cosmic darkness, (3) stars falling to the earth, (4) the sky receding as a scroll, (5) people

---

3   Chilton, *Paradise Restored*, 99, 133; DeMar, *Last Days' Madness*, 150; Gentry, *The Olivet Discourse Made Easy*, loc. 2009-2121; Hanegraaff, *The Apocalypse Code*, 31, 89; Mathison, *When Shall These Things Be?*, 159; Sproul, *The Last Days According to Jesus*, 52.

4   Craig L. Blomberg in Beale and Carson, *Commentary on the New Testament Use of the Old Testament*, 87.

taking shelter, and (6) the earth dwellers recognizing that the day of the Lamb's wrath has arrived:

> When [the Lamb of God] opened the sixth seal, I looked, and behold, there was a great earthquake, and the sun became black as sackcloth, the full moon became like blood, and the stars of the sky fell to the earth as the fig tree sheds its winter fruit when shaken by a gale. The sky vanished like a scroll that is being rolled up, and every mountain and island was removed from its place. (Rev. 6:12-14)

John saw that the Sun will become "black as sackcloth" and the Moon will appear crimson "like blood" (Rev. 6:12; cf. Joel 2:30-31), similar to Isaiah's prophecy that God will clothe the heavens with black sackcloth, reminiscent of an ancient mourning practice (Isa. 50:3).

In particular, the earthquake will cause every mountain and island to be moved from its geographical location. It should be noted that the atmospheric dust and debris from such an earthquake would be sufficient to darken the daytime sky and create the perception of a blood-red moon, an appropriate heavenly symbol corresponding to the blood spilled on earth at that time (c.f. Joel 2:30). In addition, a massive earthquake is associated with other passages pertaining to the day of the Lord (Isa. 2:13-16; 30:25; 40:4; Ezek. 38:18-20; Amos 8:8; Zech. 14:4-5; Rev. 11:13; 16:18-21). The language of the apostle in Revelation 6 and of related passages strongly favors a literal interpretation.

Saint John's prophecy also depicts the "stars" falling to the earth "as the fig tree sheds its winter fruit when shaken by a gale" and the sky vanishing "like a scroll that is being rolled up" (Rev. 6:13-14). This is an allusion to Isaiah's prophecy that "all the host of heaven shall rot away, and the skies roll up like a scroll. All their host shall fall, as leaves fall from the vine, like leaves falling from the fig tree" (Isa. 34:4). However, the Revelation passage also appeals to Christ's statement that "the stars will fall from heaven, and the powers of the heavens will be shaken" (Matt. 24:29). This motif is consistent with Luke's unambiguous parallel account of cosmic and oceanic phenomena ("signs in the sun and moon and stars, and on the earth distress of nations in perplexity because of the roaring of the sea and the waves" Luke 21:25). The literalness of this description is evident and strongly argues against any symbolic interpretation of the cosmic phenomena depicted in the parallel statement (Matt. 24:29; Mark 13:24-25).

Events of the Day of the Lord
The Battle of Armageddon
A Great Earthquake and Heaven Shaking
Cosmic Darkness—Clouds and Pillars of Smoke
People Taking Shelter
A Massive Hailstorm
A Fiery Inferno
The Return of Jesus Christ

Wright explains that the various descriptions of the day of the Lord "have regularly been seen as predictions of the end of the space-time universe," and he contends that they do not refer to the end of the universe or the final judgment.[5] Hanegraaff chides, "To suppose that stars are literally going to fall from the sky is nonsense. One star alone would obliterate the earth—let alone a hundred billion stars."[6] Such statements contain a fallacy of definition. The Greek word translated "stars" here often does not refer to distant suns from other galaxies. This term can refer to any fiery objects in the sky such as meteors, asteroids,

---

[5] Wright, *Jesus and the Victory of God*, 320, 325, 362.

[6] Hanegraaff, *The Apocalypse Code*, 136; cf. DeMar, *Last Days' Madness*, 142.

or burning debris. Therefore, it is preferable to understand the falling "stars," whatever they consist of, as the direct cause of the great earthquake and the catastrophic atmospheric conditions such as "blood and fire and columns of smoke" (Joel 2:30; variously translated "vapor of smoke" Acts 2:19). Consequently, such passages can be rendered literally without creating a scenario where the planet is vaporized. Second, the traditional futurist position does not advance the idea that the universe will be completely decimated on the day of Christ, only that the present cosmos will experience massive atmospheric changes, not entirely dissimilar from the manner in which the flood in Noah's day destroyed the earth (2 Pet. 3:5-7, 10-13). Nonetheless, the planet will continue to exist into the new heavens and the new earth.

Preterists sometimes obscure the fact that the Apocalypse variously portrays "stars" as literal (e.g., Rev. 6:13; 8:10-12) and figurative (e.g., Rev. 1:20; 2:28; 12:1; 22:16). Futurist commentators understand the casting down of a third of the stars to the earth as symbolic (Rev. 12:4), as evidenced by the fact that this is an allusion to an Old Testament metaphor (Dan. 8:10). Nevertheless, while critiquing futurism, DeMar finds it necessary to point out that the fall of "'a third of the meteorites of heaven' would have a devastating effect on our planet."[7] DeMar fails to regard the fact that the surrounding context of each individual use of the word "stars" ought to guide our interpretation. As a general rule of hermeneutics, any biblical text should be understood literally unless the historical or linguistic context makes such an interpretation unlikely or impossible.

The majority of preterists argue that Christ's language of cosmic darkness symbolizes the end of the nation of Israel in AD 70.[8] For example, Peter Leithart, a preterist scholar, claims that this language is "obviously used to describe an historical event, the collapse of a political-

---

[7] DeMar, *Last Days' Madness*, 143, 146.

[8] DeMar, *Last Days' Madness*, 144, 147; Gentry, *The Olivet Discourse Made Easy*, loc. 2066; Kik, 32; Wright, *Jesus and the Victory of God*, 362.

religious order" by which he means "the end of the Old Covenant order or Judaism by using language of cosmic collapse."[9] Kik agrees, "In the light of prophetic language and pronouncements, this verse is descriptive of the passing away of Judaism. It describes the eclipse of the Old Testament dispensation. It describes the passing away of Jewish privileges and glories."[10] He also writes, "The sun of Judaism has been darkened; as the moon it no longer reflects the light of God; bright stars, as the list of heroes in Hebrews 11, no longer shine in the Israel of the flesh."[11] Gentry explains, "When a national government collapses in war and upheaval, Scripture often poetically portrays it 'as a cosmic catastrophe – an undoing of Creation.' . . . And in a sense it is 'the end of the world' for those nations God judges. So is it with Israel in AD 70."[12] Preterists reason that Jesus employed this cosmic language to speak about the destruction of Israel, since similar prophetic passages depict the downfall of ancient geopolitical civilizations such as Egypt, Babylon, and Edom:

> **David Chilton:** There was a "language" of prophecy, instantly recognizable to those familiar with the Old Testament. . . As Jesus foretold the complete end of the Old Covenant System – which was, in a sense, the end of the whole world – He spoke of it as any of the prophets would have, in the stirring language of covenantal judgment. . . These heavenly lights are used to speak of earthly authorities and governors. . . It must be stressed that none of these events literally took place. God did not intend anyone to place a literalist construction on these statements. Poetically, however, all these things did happen: as far as these wicked nations were concerned, "the lights went out." This is simply figurative language, which would not surprise us at all if we were more familiar with the Bible and appreciative of its literary character. . . The light of Israel

---

[9] Peter J. Leithart, *The Promise of His Appearing: An Exposition of Second Peter* (Moscow, ID: Canon Press, 2004), 2, 5.

[10] Kik, 32, cf. pp. 128, 132, 136-37.

[11] Kik, 128-29.

[12] Gentry, *The Olivet Discourse Made Easy*, loc. 2121-27.

is going to be extinguished; the covenant nation will cease to exist. When the Tribulation is over, old Israel will be gone.[13]

Hank Hanegraaff: Jesus is not predicting the eradication of the cosmos. Nor is he prophesying the end of civilization. . . . Rather, Jesus is employing hyperbolic language that is deeply rooted in Old Testament history.[14]

J. Marcellus Kik: A study of the Old Testament Scriptures discloses to us the fact that there is an apocalyptic language which describes great national disasters. Familiar symbols are used to articulate the destruction of nations.[15]

Keith Mathison: Over and over, the prophets describe the catastrophes that are about to befall Israel and her enemies in terms of the earth being shaken, the stars falling, and the sun and moon being darkened. . . Many of these prophecies describe judgments that occurred centuries ago. This "cosmic judgment language" is a metaphorical way of describing important events surrounding the fall of earthly kingdoms.[16]

James Stuart Russell: It will at once be seen that the imagery employed in this passage [Isaiah 13] is almost identical with that of our Lord. If these symbols therefore were proper to represent the fall of Babylon, why should they be improper to set forth a still greater catastrophe—the destruction of Jerusalem?[17]

R. C. Sproul: The graphic language used by Jesus to describe the attending events is metaphorical and consistent with the poetry of fervor used by Old Testament prophets.[18]

N. T. Wright: [The day of the Lord passages] are, as we have seen from the passages in Isaiah and Jeremiah, . . . typical Jewish imagery

---

13 Chilton, *Paradise Restored*, 98, 99.

14 Hanegraaff, *The Apocalypse Code*, 31.

15 Kik, 129.

16 Mathison, *When Shall These Things Be?*, 162.

17 Russell, *The Parousia*, 80.

18 Sproul, *The Last Days According to Jesus*, 56.

for events within the present order that are felt and perceived as "cosmic" or, as we should say, as "earth-shattering." More particularly, they are regular Jewish imagery for events that bring the story of Israel to its appointed climax. The days of Jerusalem's destruction would be looked upon as days of cosmic catastrophe.[19]

This preterist argument that the Old Testament prophecies about the day of the Lord pointed to national judgments in history simply begs the question. One reason for this is that the downfall of historical civilizations did not exhaustively fulfill the prophetic expectations regarding the day of the Lord. Rather, the prophets warned their immediate audience of coming judgment by employing language that was readily understood as pointing to the eschatological day of the Lord. Furthermore, only futurism accounts for the prophetic expectations of a multinational military invasion of the land of Israel immediately prior to the day of the Lord (Ezek. 38:1-39:24; Joel 3:1-16; Zeph. 1:15-16; Zech. 14:1-5; 12-15; Rev. 16:12-16; cf. Isa. 13:4-6).

Finally, the prophecies reveal that Judah and Jerusalem will be delivered while the nations which invade the land will be destroyed on that day (Ezek. 38:21-23; 39:3-20; Joel 3:1-16; Zech. 14:3, 11-19; cf. Isa. 13:14-16). The exact opposite scenario played itself out during the First Jewish-Roman War in AD 66-70; Judea and Jerusalem were decisively destroyed while the invading Roman legions were victorious! Preterists attempt in vain to explain away this historical fact. For example, James Jordan desperately argues that the Roman Empire "did not cease to exist in AD 70" but ceased to be "a spiritual power energized by the full power of Satan."[20]

---

[19] Wright, *Jesus and the Victory of God*, 362.

[20] Jordan, *The Vindication of Jesus Christ*, loc. 508.

THE DAY OF JESUS CHRIST

THE ALREADY AND NOT YET

The Old Testament prophecies concerning the day of the Lord were fulfilled in part through localized, historical judgments of antiquity. Nevertheless, as explained in a previous chapter, these prophecies collectively form a larger patchwork motif that awaits plenary fulfillment at the day of Jesus Christ—judgment day. The terminology of these prophetic oracles conveyed a firm expectation of judgment for the hearers and urged immediate repentance. Against the backdrop theme of the day of the Lord, these eschatological prophecies allowed for contemporary application while holding out until the end of the age for their exhaustive fulfillment. This is an example of inaugurated eschatology, otherwise known as the "already and not yet" principle of biblical interpretation.

A detailed and comprehensive analysis of this already and not yet pattern regarding Christ's kingdom is beyond the scope of this work. However, this pattern is conceded by many partial preterists. For example, Gentry expounds, "This is akin to there being several historical episodes of 'the day of the Lord' in the Old Testament. . . Each of these anticipate the final 'day of the Lord' event at the end of history (2 Pet 3:10)."[21] Mathison similarly elucidates, "All of these different events that are referred to as 'the day of the Lord' are types of the final day of the Lord—the day on which God will lead his armies into battle, utterly and completely defeating all his enemies."[22] Hanegraaff approves of this evaluation:

> While the near-future catastrophe (demotion of Babylon and destruction of Jerusalem) fulfills the cosmic language, it does not exhaust its meaning. . . While Peter's prophecy [2 Pet. 3:10-13] was fulfilled in the destruction of Jerusalem, the events of AD 70 and the cosmic language Peter used to describe them point forward to an even greater day of judgment when the problem of sin and Satan

---

[21] Gentry, *The Olivet Discourse Made Easy*, loc. 2405.

[22] Mathison, *When Shall These Things Be?* (Phillipsburg, NJ: P & R Publishing, 2004), 159.

will be full and finally resolved! . . . In sum, then, John [in Revelation], like Jesus and the prophets before him, uses the imagery of sun, moon, and stars to refer to the near-future judgment of Jerusalem. While the language finds ultimate fulfillment in the second coming of Christ, it is inaugurated in the Jewish holocaust of AD 70.[23]

Full preterists and many partial preterists teach that the prophecy given by the apostle Peter concerning the day of the Lord was fulfilled in AD 70 (2 Pet. 3:4-13). Peter Leithart represents the sentiments of many preterists that the collapsing universe language in Matthew and elsewhere points to the destruction of the temple in AD 70, which "marked the end of the Old Creation and brought in a New Creation."[24] He then provided a detailed "preterist reading" of 2 Peter, as did John Owen and Chilton.[25] He explains his reason for regarding Peter's prophecy as having been fulfilled in the first century AD:

> If 1 Peter is about a revelation that is "ready" to come, about an "end of all things" that is "at hand," about a judgment that is "ready to begin" at the house of God, then 2 Peter, which is a reminder of things taught in the previous letter, must be about the same topic. . . . Peter wrote his second letter on the theme of the coming of Jesus, which he says was also a theme of his first letter, which is 1 Peter. Since 1 Peter's teaching about the "coming" of Jesus highlights its imminence, 2 Peter must be dealing with the same looming events.[26]

We will now examine the prophecy of 2 Peter 3 and explore some of the dangerous implications of a preterist interpretation of the passage.

They [scoffers] will say, "Where is the promise of his coming? For ever since the fathers fell asleep, all things are continuing as they

---

[23] Hanegraaff, *The Apocalypse Code*, 135-136

[24] Leithart, *The Promise of His Appearing*, 25.

[25] Leithart, *The Promise of His Appearing*, 1; John Owen, *The Works of John Owen*, 16 volumes (London: Banner of Truth, 1965-68), 9:134-135; David Chilton, *The Days of Vengeance: An Exposition of the Book of Revelation* (Horn Lake, MS: Dominion Press, 2006.

[26] Leithart, *The Promise of His Appearing*, 13-14; cf. DeMar, *Last Days' Madness*, 30.

were from the beginning of creation." For they deliberately overlook this fact, that the heavens existed long ago, and the earth was formed out of water and through water by the word of God, and that by means of these the world that then existed was deluged with water and perished. But by the same word the heavens and earth that now exist are stored up for fire, being kept until the day of judgment and destruction of the ungodly. But do not overlook this one fact, beloved, that with the Lord one day is as a thousand years, and a thousand years as one day. The Lord is not slow to fulfill his promise as some count slowness, but is patient toward you, not wishing that any should perish, but that all should reach repentance. But the day of the Lord will come like a thief, and then the heavens will pass away with a roar, and the heavenly bodies will be burned up and dissolved, and the earth and the works that are done on it will be exposed. Since all these things are thus to be dissolved, what sort of people ought you to be in lives of holiness and godliness, waiting for and hastening the coming of the day of God, because of which the heavens will be set on fire and dissolved, and the heavenly bodies will melt as they burn! But according to his promise we are waiting for new heavens and a new earth in which righteousness dwells. (2 Pet. 3:4-13; cf. 1 Pet. 1:8, 13)

In this passage, the apostle Peter foresaw the literal destruction of "the heavens and earth." He appealed to the themes of creation and the worldwide flood to argue against the uniformitarianism of the scoffers who deny that God will full His promise to return and bring a cataclysmic judgment against the world (2 Pet. 3:4; cf. Gen. 1-2; 6-9; Isa. 24). Peter explained that God will destroy the present heavens and earth "by the same word" with which He created the world and later destroyed it by the flood (2 Pet. 3:5-7). The heavens are reserved for a fiery dissolution that will be revealed on the day of the Lord, variously called "the day of judgment" and "the day of God" (2 Pet. 3:7, 10, 12). The apostle confirmed that the created order will be destroyed by fire, and he pointed out a parallel in its antediluvian destruction with water. It should not escape the reader's attention that the same planet continued to exist after it was destroyed by the flood.

Peter reminded his readers of God's promises to create "new heavens and a new earth" (Isa. 65:17-25; 66:22 in 2 Pet. 3:13). D. A. Carson, a premier New Testament scholar, points out a practical implication of this new creation:

> The Isaianic promise of "a new heaven and a new earth" (LXX) is also picked up by Revelation's final vision: Rev. 21:1, with its promise of a new heaven and a new earth, introduces the glorious description of the final state that follows the millennium and the judgment of God. The same vision can be cast without using the same words that Peter uses: the apostle Paul talks about the anticipated liberation of the entire creation from its bondage to decay (Rom. 8:18-25). It is doubtful that either Christian steadfastness or Christian morality, let alone Christian spirituality and Christian eschatology, can long be maintained without the dominance of this vision.[27]

In addition to surrendering Christian ethics and eschatology, many preterists compromise other important doctrines in order to maintain a consistent preterist hermeneutic. For example, they superimpose their preterist interpretation of the cosmic darkness in the Olivet Discourse upon related passages concerning the day of the Lord, such as 2 Peter 3. They conclude that all these passages were fulfilled in the destruction of Jerusalem and its temple in AD 70. Consequently, they deny that the theme of transition from the old creation to the new creation is concerned with the destruction and subsequent renewal and redemption of the material universe. They surmise that the introduction of the new covenant is the totality of the new creation.

This faulty conclusion about the new creation creates uncertainty in the minds of many preterists about the historic interpretation of other new creation passages (e.g., Rom. 8:18-25; Rev. 21:1-22:5). The preterist must then consider whether Christians will be resurrected to enter the heavenly Jerusalem, a city that they suppose has already descended in a mere metaphorical or relational-covenantal fashion in AD 70. This creates doubt as to whether sin, sorrow, pain, and death will be fully

---

[27] Beale and Carson, *Commentary on the New Testament Use of the Old Testament*, 1061.

abolished in the new creation, as God has promised (Rev. 21:4), since this creation supposedly arrived in AD 70.

The apostle Paul warned against preterist teachers who advanced the idea that the day of the Lord was imminent or "at hand" (2 Thess. 2:1-8; cf. 2 Tim. 2:17-18). Some preterists have heeded Paul's warning and do not adhere to a fully-realized interpretation of the day of Christ. For example, Chilton, Gentry, Jordan, and others teach that the new creation is being manifested progressively, having arrived only in a nascent sense in the first century.[28] To illustrate, Chilton described this position as it relates to the new creation in Revelation:

> Salvation is a re-creation . . . "a new heaven and earth." . . . The *primary* significance of that phrase is symbolic, and has to do with the blessings of salvation. John next saw "the Holy City, New Jerusalem." . . . *It is the Church.* . . We are in the New Jerusalem now. Proof? . . . Heb. 12:22-23. . . The highest fulfillment will take place in heaven for eternity. But, *definitively* and *progressively*, it is true now. We are living in the new heaven and the new earth; we are citizens of the New Jerusalem."[29]

While traditional interpretations disagree with the preterist view that the dissolution of the old creation is about the destruction of Jerusalem in AD 70, they generally agree that the new creation exhibits an "already and not yet" aspect of fulfillment. To demonstrate, Jesus Christ was resurrected from the dead to be a firstfruits' offering to God (1 Cor. 15:23), and the regenerating power of the Holy Spirit is a firstfruits' work of our own resurrection (Rom. 8:23). As such, we who belong to Christ also belong to the new creation (2 Cor. 5:17) and to the heavenly Jerusalem which He has prepared for Christians to receive (Heb. 11:10, 16; 12:22; Rev. 21:1-22:5). The new creation has begun in the resurrection of Christ and in His holy Church but this does not mean that this creation has completely and consummately arrived. Admittedly,

---

[28] E.g., Jordan, *The Vindication of Jesus Christ*, loc. 604.

[29] Chilton, *Paradise Restored*, 203-204.

even some partial preterists recognize an "already and not yet" approach to the new creation and correctly teach that its arrival awaits a future fulfillment at the glorious return of Christ.

9

COMING ON THE CLOUDS

THE COSMIC EVENTS of the day of the Lord will culminate in the glorious appearing of Jesus Christ from heaven. In the Olivet Discourse, the Master promised, "Then will appear in heaven the sign of the Son of Man, and then all the tribes of the earth will mourn, and they will see the Son of Man coming on the clouds of heaven with power and great glory" (Matt. 24:30). This verse is a conflation of Daniel 7:13 ("Behold, with the clouds of heaven there came one like a son of man"), Zechariah 12:10 LXX ("they will weep"; "all the tribes"), and possibly Isaiah 11:12 and others. The historic Church has always taught that Matthew 24:30 is an unambiguous reference to the glorious return of Christ.[1]

Matthew 24:30 presents a dilemma for preterists, since they teach that it does not refer to the Second Coming of Jesus, but to first-century events. Chilton explained: "What appears to pose a problem for this

---

[1] Wright, *Jesus and the Victory of God*, 342.

interpretation, however, is what Jesus says . . . Jesus seems to be saying that the Second Coming will occur immediately after the Tribulation. Did the Second Coming occur in A.D. 70? Have we missed it?"[2] Sproul framed the problem for preterism:

> This passage describes the parousia in vivid and graphic images of astronomical perturbations. It speaks of signs in the sky that will be visible and the sound of a trumpet that will be audible. Perhaps no portion of the Olivet Discourse provides more difficulties to the preterist view than this one. This portion leads many interpreters to see a clear historical division between references to the destruction of Jerusalem and references to the parousia of Christ. These interpreters grant that the destruction of the temple and Jerusalem took place within the time-frame of one generation, but insist that Christ has yet to appear in clouds of glory. This is true of interpreters from both the liberal and the conservative ends of the theological spectrum.[3]

Wright claims that the coming of the Son of Man on clouds in this verse has nothing to do with His return but is "a symbol for a mighty reversal of fortunes within history and at the national level."[4] The idea behind the verse, then, would be that the destruction of Jerusalem and the temple in AD 70 was the sign proving that Jesus had been vindicated, exalted, and enthroned as Israel's Messiah.[5] Hanegraaff describes this approach:

> It is important to note that "the sign" is what "shall appear." It is misleading to understand the phrase as meaning "then shall appear the Son of Man in the sky." The Son of Man does not appear; the

---

[2] Chilton, *Paradise Restored*, 97.

[3] Sproul, *The Last Days According to Jesus*, 49.

[4] Wright, *Jesus and the Victory of God*, 341.

[5] Chilton, *Paradise Restored*, 100, 103; DeMar, *Last Days' Madness*, 165; Gentry, *The Olivet Discourse Made Easy*, loc. 2156, 2161, 2187, 2192-2202; Hanegraaff, *The Apocalypse Code*, 26-27, 84; Kik, 137-38; Mathison, *When Shall These Things Be?*, 201; Wright, *Jesus and the Victory of God*, 362.

sign appears. Then Christ defines what the sign signifies: it is the sign that the Son of Man is now in heaven.[6]

The discourse in the other Gospel accounts reveals a significant difficulty for the preterist contention that "the sign of the Son of Man" (Matt. 24:30) is an event that signifies His coming but is distinct from it. To demonstrate, Mark and Luke substituted Matthew's phrase "the sign of the Son of Man will appear in heaven" with the simpler expression "they will see the Son of Man coming" in heaven (Mark 13:26; Luke 21:27). The obvious conclusion is that the later writers understood "the sign" epexegetically, in other words, the sign should be equated with Christ's bodily appearance in the sky.

Most partial preterists teach that the Son of Man's coming (Matt. 24:30; Mark 13:26) refers to Christ's post-resurrection ascension to heaven.[7] Hanegraaff claims that Jesus is "clearly not *descending* to earth in his second coming but rather *ascending* to the throne of the Almighty in vindication and exaltation."[8] As Wright points out, the Greek word translated "coming" in this verse could be rendered "going."[9] The idea is that Jesus ascended to receive His kingdom and to sit at the Father's right hand until His enemies were destroyed in AD 70. Chilton explained that the directionality of Christ "going" away to His Father finds its basis in Daniel's prophecy of the Son of Man (Dan. 7:13-14):

> But notice exactly what Daniel says: Christ is seen going *up*, not *down*! The Son of Man is going to the Ancient of Days, not coming *from* Him! He is not descending in clouds to the earth, but ascending in clouds to His Father! Daniel was not predicting the Second

---

[6] Gentry, *The Olivet Discourse Made Easy*, loc. 2138-2145; Similarly, Kik, 137.

[7] E.g., DeMar, *Last Days' Madness*, 163; Mathison, *When Shall These Things Be?*, 164-65, 181-82, 201.

[8] Hanegraaff, *The Apocalypse Code*, 83; Similarly, Adams and Fisher, *The Time of the End*, 23-24; France, *The Gospel According to Matthew*, 343-44; Jordan, *The Vindication of Jesus Christ*, loc. 215; Kik, 37.

[9] The Greek word *erkomenon* (ἐρχόμενον) in Wright, *Jesus and the Victory of God*, 361.

Coming of Christ, but rather the climax of the First Advent, in which, after atoning for sins and defeating death and Satan, the Lord ascended on the clouds of heaven to be seated on His glorious throne at His Father's right hand.[10]

This preterist interpretation of Christ's statement about His coming is counter-intuitive and fraught with several difficulties. Perhaps the most troublesome is that it requires multiple "comings." As DeMar admits, this view requires that preterists differentiate the Son of Man's "coming"[11] from His "coming on the clouds of heaven" a few verses later (Matt. 24:27, 30). They interpret the former as a "judgment coming" of Jesus in AD 70 and the latter as His ascension (cf. Acts 1:9-11).[12] This interpretation is unlikely and forced, being necessary only to preserve a commitment to a preterist hermeneutic. In addition, the book of Revelation frequently echoes Christ's statement about the Son of Man's coming, and it presents it as a still future event and not to Christ's ascension;[13] I will present this argument in more depth later in this chapter.

Furthermore, many preterists teach that the Son of Man's coming in the Olivet Discourse points to a third coming of Jesus, specifically, His reigning presence. For example, Wright develops the view that the disciples were interested in Christ's arrival in Jerusalem to reign as King and that these verses represent, in a spiritual or figurative sense, His "coming" to Jerusalem as "the vindicated, rightful king."[14] Ironically, such preterist interpreters posit three different "comings" of Christ, yet these strongly contrast with the interpretation of the apostolic Church

---

10   Chilton, *Paradise Restored*, 69; also DeMar, *Last Days' Madness*, 161, 164-65; Wright, *Jesus and the Victory of God*, 361.

11   The Greek word *parousia* (παρουσία).

12   DeMar, *Last Days' Madness*, 71.

13   The apostle John employed the verb *erkomai* (ἔρχομαι - "coming").

14   Wright, *Jesus and the Victory of God*, 342; cf. p. 345.

because they leave no room in the Olivet Prophecy for His glorious return.

One appealing motive for preterists to interpret the Son of Man's coming (Matt. 24:30; Mark 13:26) as His ascension is to avoid what they deem to be a necessary admission of prophetic failure as put forth by higher critics and skeptics.[15] Wright elaborates of this approach:

> As we have seen, neither the godly traditions of the church nor the (sometimes) less godly traditions of scholarship are used to reading the passage in this way. The godly are less likely to accuse me of scholarly trickery, designed to get around what to them seems a clear statement of the future second coming of the Lord. The scholarly are likely to accuse me of pious trickery, getting round the problem that Jesus seems to have been mistaken.[16]

Wright's solution is neither a comfort to the skeptics nor to the godly.

At any rate, Hanegraaff, perhaps uniquely among preterists, claims to recognize some "already and not yet" aspects of Christ's statement about His coming (Matt. 24:30; Mark 13:26). He suggests that this statement contains "final consummation language to characterize a near-future event."[17] Hanegraaff's admission regarding Christ's coming with clouds shows his willingness to understand this as a declaration regarding His return from heaven. Yet, as we will see, Hanegraaff misses the fact that it echoes the language of the Old Testament to describe the Lord's glorious return.

DANIEL 7 IN THE NEW TESTAMENT

Contrary to preterist claims, the prophecy of Daniel 7 does not prove that Jesus spoke about His ascension to God the Father in the Olivet Discourse. The careful reader should notice that the prophecy

---

15 E.g., Sproul, *The Last Days According to Jesus*, 12-16.

16 Wright, *Jesus and the Victory of God*, 342.

17 Hanegraaff, *The Apocalypse Code*, 26.

does not indicate a clear temporal connection between the Son of Man's coming in the clouds and His ascension—His presentation before the Ancient of Days.

> I saw in the night visions, and behold, with the clouds of heaven there came one like a son of man, and he came to the Ancient of Days and was presented before him. And to him was given dominion and glory and a kingdom, that all peoples, nations, and languages should serve him; his dominion is an everlasting dominion, which shall not pass away, and his kingdom one that shall not be destroyed. (Dan. 7:13-14)

This prophecy, consistent with the temporal ambiguity found throughout the Prophets, contains the mystery of the twofold advent of Christ. Notice that the Son of Man receives the kingdom in order that "all peoples, nations, and languages should serve Him" (Dan. 7:14). Later in the vision, these nations receive the kingdom as a possession (Dan. 7:18, 22, 27), a verdict awarded when the books are opened at the judgment (Dan. 7:9-10, 22, 26; Rev. 20:11-15) and Christ slays and throws the Beast into the fiery flame (Dan. 7:11, 24-26; cf. Rev. 19:11-21). It is evident that this vision is bookended on one side by Christ's arrival in heaven, and on the other side, by His glorious return with clouds. To restate this, the prophet foresaw the ascended Jesus' acquisition of the kingdom before His Father *and* His future return in the Father's glory to consummate the kingdom.

The book of Revelation provides clues about the temporal relationship between these two prophetic events. The apostle John described Jesus as having the title "one like a son of man" (Rev. 1:13 quoting Dan. 7:13) and displaying features reminiscent of Daniel's Ancient of Days ("The hairs of his head were white, like white wool, like snow. His eyes were like a flame of fire" Rev. 1:14; cf. Dan. 7:9-12; 10:6 LXX). Elsewhere in the book, the apostle saw the ascended Lamb before His Father's throne, having already ransomed people "from every tribe and language and people and nation" and made them to be "a kingdom and priests to our God" (Rev. 5:9-10; cf. Dan. 7:14; Matt. 28:18-20; Rev. 1:6). However, Jesus promised to later give His people "authority over the nations . . . even as I myself have received authority from my Father" (Rev. 2:26-27; cf. Rev. 3:21). The Son of Man has already received an international kingdom, and He will give it in totality to His people at the day of Christ.

TABLE 2: THRONES OF JUDGMENT

	Daniel 7	Revelation	Matthew
The Son of Man coming with clouds	behold, One like the Son of Man, coming with the clouds of heaven (Dan. 7:13)	behold, a white cloud, and on the cloud sat One like the Son of Man (Rev. 14:14)	When the Son of Man comes in His glory (Matt. 25:31); on the clouds of heaven (Matt. 24:30)
Accompanied by myriads of holy angels	Ten thousand times ten thousand stood before Him (Dan. 7:10)	many angels . . . ten thousand times ten thousand (Rev. 5:11)	all the holy angels with Him (Matt. 25:31)
The Lord seated on a glorious throne	the Ancient of Days was seated [on His throne]; His garment was white as snow (Dan. 7:9)	Then I saw a great white throne and Him who sat on it (Rev. 20:11)	then He will sit on the throne of His glory. (Matt. 25:31)

All nations gathered before Him	all peoples, nations, and languages (Dan. 7:27)	You . . . have redeemed us to God by Your blood out of every tribe and tongue and people and nation and have made us kings and priests (Rev. 5:9-10) And I saw the dead, small and great, standing before God (Rev. 20:12)	all the nations will be gathered before Him (Matt. 25:32)
Thrones established	I watched till thrones were put in place . . . the court was seated (Dan. 7:9-10)	Around the throne were twenty-four thrones, and on the thrones I saw twenty-four elders sitting . . . and they had crowns of gold (Rev. 4:4; cf. Rev. 5:8) And I saw thrones, and they sat on them, and judgment was committed to them (Rev. 20:4)	when the Son of Man sits on the throne of His glory, you . . . will also sit on twelve thrones, judging (Matt. 19:28)
Books opened	and the books were opened (Dan. 7:10; cf. Dan. 12:1)	and books were opened (Rev. 20:12)	

The wicked thrown into everlasting hellfire	The beast was slain, and its body destroyed and given to the burning flame. (Dan. 7:11) some to shame and everlasting contempt (Dan. 12:2)	Then the beast . . . and with him the false prophet . . . were cast alive into the lake of fire burning with brimstone (Rev. 19:20) The devil, who deceived them, was cast into the lake of fire and brimstone . . . and they will be tormented day and night forever and ever. (Rev. 20:10)	Depart from Me, you cursed, into the everlasting fire prepared for the devil and his angels (Matt. 25:41) And these will go away into everlasting punishment (Matt. 25:46)
The righteous inherit the kingdom	Then the kingdom . . . shall be given to the people, the saints of the Most High. His kingdom is an everlasting kingdom (Dan. 7:27; cf. Dan. 7:22; 12:2)	He who overcomes shall inherit all things, and I will be his God and he shall be My son (Rev. 21:7; cf. Rev. 5:9-10; 21:1-22:5)	"Come, you blessed of My Father, inherit the kingdom prepared for you" (Matt. 25:34) but the righteous into eternal life (Matt. 25:46)

The judgment scene with thrones in Revelation 4-5 serves as a detailed retelling of the courtroom scene of Daniel 7.[18] The comparative table above compares these scenes and demonstrates John's dependence upon Daniel. The courtroom judgment scene in the Apocalypse provides the prophetic backdrop of Christ being presented before His Father with

---

[18] Beale and Sean M. McDonough in Beale and Carson, *Commentary on the New Testament Use*, 1098; cf. Dan. 7:2, 6-7, 9 in Rev. 4:1-3, 5.

the holy angels to receive a sealed inheritance scroll (Rev. 5:6-9).[19] The text reveals that Jesus had previously redeemed His saints through death and that He will give the full inheritance of the kingdom to them after opening the seventh seal (Rev. 8:1-2; cf. Rev. 11:15-18). As with Daniel, the apostle later received a vision of the Son of Man coming on a cloud of heaven (Rev. 14:14; cf. Dan. 7:13; Rev. 1:7; 19:11-16).

The apostle John combined Daniel 7:13 and Zechariah 12:10, in the exact manner that Jesus did in the Olivet Discourse, to present Christ's glorious appearance as a future event:[20] "Behold, he is coming with the clouds, and every eye will see him, even those who pierced him, and all the tribes of the earth will wail on account of him" (Rev. 1:7; cf. Matt. 24:30). The next verse shows that this coming is in the future ("who is and who was and *who is to come*" Rev. 1:8, emphasis added).

Elsewhere in the book of Revelation, the apostle presented the coming of Jesus as a future event, using such phrases as "I will come" (Rev. 2:5), "I will come to you soon" (Rev. 2:16), "until I come" (Rev. 2:25), "I will come like a thief. . . I will come" (Rev. 3:3), "I am coming soon" (Rev. 3:11), and "Behold, I am coming like a thief" (Rev. 16:15). As the reader should expect, the climactic event that answers to the book's theme in Revelation 1:7 is the revelation of the returning Christ: "one like a son of man" on a cloud and coming to earth (Rev. 14:14-16; cf. Dan. 7:13) and arriving with His holy angels to slay the individual Beast, throwing him into fiery judgment (Rev. 19:11-21; cf. Dan. 7:11). Using the exact language of Jesus (Matt. 24:30), John's descriptions of the cloud-riding advent of the Son of Man is decidedly future and does not describe His ascension.

The overall message of the Apocalypse demonstrates that Jesus has ascended to receive the kingdom and later will appear on clouds of glory

---

[19] In first-century Greco-Roman culture, inheritance scrolls were sealed with seven seals. Marriage contracts typically had five seals.

[20] G. K. Beale, *The New International Greek Testament Commentary* (Carlisle: Paternoster Press, 1999), 197.

to bring judgment (cf. Luke 19:12). Craig L. Blomberg points out that this observation accords with Christ's words to the Jewish Sanhedrin, when He quoted the prophet Daniel, to reveal this two-stage process of redemption (Dan. 7:13 in Matt. 26:64; Mark 14:62; cf. Luke 22:69).

> Jesus will shortly quote this passage from Daniel again, adding the phrase about "seated at the right hand of power" (i.e., God), in a different position than in the OT text, so that Christ is *first* in God's presence and *then* coming on the clouds, presumably therefore coming from heaven to earth. The picture is one of a theophany, which is always from heaven to the world of humankind.[21]

As an aside, the claim that the Messiah will arrive bodily with clouds, based on the prophecy of Daniel 7, is not unique to Christianity; it was explicitly taught within Judaism. The Babylonian Talmud explains that the Son of Man's coming with heavenly clouds (Dan. 7:13) describes Messiah's actual arrival to the Jewish nation:

> R' Yehoshua ben Levi noted a contradiction: On the one hand it is written: And behold! With the clouds of Heaven, one like a man came, which implies that the Messiah will come swiftly. But on the other hand it is written: a humble man, riding on a donkey, which implies that the Messiah will come sluggishly. . . If [the Jews] are deserving, the Messiah will arrive with the clouds of Heaven. If they are not deserving, he will come as a humble man, riding on a donkey.[22]

The traditional Jewish expectation has always been that the Messiah will arrive bodily in Jerusalem at the end of the age.

Some preterists correctly recognize that the language of Christ's coming in Revelation 1:7 pertains to the Second Coming. For example, Gentry betrays his apprehension about the preterist interpretation of this verse:

---

[21] Craig L. Blomberg in Beale and Carson, *Commentary on the New Testament Use,* 87-88.

[22] The Babylonian Talmud, *Talmud Bavli: Tractate Sanhedrin 98a4*, The Schottenstein ed. vol. III (Brooklyn, NY: Mesorah, 2014).

The initial impression this verse leaves on us today is that John is speaking of the Second Advent. It certainly does involve language quite applicable to the future, glorious, history-ending Second Coming of Christ. The Scriptures speak often of his Second Coming, and even with this sort of cloud-coming judgment language (cf. Acts 1:9-11; 1 Thess. 4:16-17; 2 Thess. 1:7-10)... Yet looks are deceiving.[23]

A LITERAL, VISIBLE RETURN

Many preterists argue that the Lord's phrase "every eye will see him" (Matt. 24:30; Rev. 1:7) is metaphor for comprehension or insight and does not refer to actually seeing the glorified Jesus.[24] This interpretation communicates that many people came to understand that the glorified Christ was seated on His heavenly throne when they witnessed the destruction of the Second Temple. Gentry explains,

> They [those who saw the temple burning] "see" it in the sense we "see" how a math problem works: with the "eye of understanding" rather than the organ of vision... First, *every eye* shall see him" simply means that this will be a public event, not hidden in a corner. The bible frequently uses "all" or "every" in a limited sense far short of global universality.[25]

Nevertheless, other preterists evidence their hesitancy to deny the universal scope of this language in their suggestion that Christ's statement alludes to the universal recognition of His enthronement, which supposedly occurred after the destruction of the Roman Empire several centuries later, and not because of the destruction of Judea and Jerusalem in AD 70.[26]

---

23   Gentry, *The Book of Revelation*, 34.

24   DeMar, *Last Days' Madness*, 168; Hanegraaff, *The Apocalypse Code*, 27; Jordan, *The Vindication of Jesus Christ*, loc. 215.

25   Gentry, *The Book of Revelation*, 45.

26   Kik, 39.

This statement of Jesus is a partial quote of the prophet Zechariah (Zech. 12:10 in Matt. 24:30; Rev. 1:7). A straightforward reading of Zechariah's prophecy reveals that the people of Judea and Jerusalem will gaze at the pierced Lord: "And I [Yahweh] will pour out on the house of David and the inhabitants of Jerusalem a Spirit of grace and pleas for mercy, so that, when they look on Me, on Him whom they have pierced, they shall mourn for Him" (Zech. 12:10).[27] Significantly, the apostle John quoted this verse elsewhere with reference to those who visually looked at Christ's pierced body, and he echoed it again in the account of Thomas trusting in the glorified Jesus after seeing and handling His pierced body (John 19:37; 20:25-29). In other words, in every New Testament occurrence of Zechariah's prophecy, people look upon the crucified, flesh-and-bone body of Jesus Christ.

In addition, Jesus added specific qualifiers to the prophecy of Zechariah that provide the reader with additional details regarding His return. The New Testament scholar, G. K. Beale, explains how these qualifiers function:

> The Zechariah [12:10] text has been altered in two significant ways. The phrases "every eye" and "of the earth" (cf. Zech. 14:17) have been added to universalize its original meaning... The word ge ("earth, land") cannot be a limited reference to the land of Israel; rather, it is a universal denotation, since this is the only meaning that the phrase pasai hai phylai tes ges ("all the tribes of the earth") has in the OT (LXX: Gen. 12:3; 28:14; Ps. 71:17; Zech. 14:17). The phrase "all the tribes of Israel" occurs repeatedly in the OT (approximately twenty-five times), which highlights the different wording of Rev. 1:7b.[28]

As Beale shows, the first qualifier, "all the tribes of the earth" (Matt. 24:30; Rev. 1:7), is a technical expression found throughout the Old Testament (LXX) that denotes *the peoples and nations of the world*. Consequently, this Greek phrase is not restricted to the twelve tribes

---

[27] Capital letters have been added for clarity.

[28] Beale and Sean M. McDonough in Beale and Carson, *Commentary on the New Testament Use*, 1090.

of Israel, as preterists often argue.²⁹ Furthermore, the second qualifier, "every eye will see him" (Rev. 1:7), strongly indicates an optical visualization of the risen Lord, especially against the backdrop of Zechariah 12, as argued above.

A significant weakness of the preterist interpretation of Christ's statement that those who pierced Him would see Him coming on the clouds of heaven (Matt. 26:64; Rev. 1:7; cf. Matt. 24:30) is that all or nearly all the men responsible for His crucifixion, in other words, the elders of the Sanhedrin present at His trial, had died long before AD 70. We can deduce this based on the requisite ages of the chief priests and elders at the time of Christ's trial, which took place nearly four decades before the fall of Jerusalem. In addition, we can evaluate the historical records, including the writings of Josephus, which chronicle many of their deaths. Consequently, the qualifier "even those who pierced him" (Rev. 1:7) extends more universally, beyond the scope of those who condemned and executed Jesus. This fact militates against the preterist view that such verses refer merely to those directly involved with His crucifixion.³⁰ The implicit idea of these verses is that those responsible for the Lord's death, even if they themselves had died, would see His glorious return at the future day of Christ.³¹

DeMar admits that the standard translation "all the tribes of the earth" (Matt. 24:30 and Rev. 1:7) is correct only if the verse where this phrase is found refers to the Second Coming.³² Notwithstanding, the assumption, that the context of this verse is limited to first-century Jeru-

---

29 Chilton, *Paradise Restored*, 101; Kenneth Gentry, *Before Jerusalem Fell: Dating the Book of Revelation: An Exegetical and Historical Argument for a Pre-A.D. 70 Composition*, Revised ed. (Powder Springs, GA: American Vision, 1998, 127-28; Gentry, *The Olivet Discourse Made Easy*, loc. 2208-2225; Gentry, *The Book of Revelation Made Easy*, 39-40; Russell, *The Parousia*, 77, 380.

30 DeMar, *Last Days' Madness*, 168; Gentry, *Before Jerusalem Fell*, 142; Gentry, *The Book of Revelation Made Easy*, 39.

31 Contra Kik, 39.

32 DeMar, *Last Days' Madness*, 166. The word translated "earth" here is *gais* (γῆς).

salem, forces the preterist to revise the translation to "tribes of the land," meaning Israel's twelve tribes.[33] This consideration heavily shapes their translation of the same Greek word wherever it appears in other biblical passages, especially in the book of Revelation. For example, Russell translated it as "land" in other passages instead of accepting the traditional rendering "earth" (e.g., Rev. 6:3-15; 8:7).[34]

Russell even argued that the phrase "all the nations," found later in the Olivet Discourse (Matt. 25:32), should with "great probability" be equated with the tribes of Israel! He wrote, "There is no impropriety in designating the tribes as nations. The promise of God to Abraham was that he should be the father of many nations."[35] Apparently, Russell was ignorant of the fact that the "many nations" of the Abrahamic covenant (Gen. 17:5) is not limited to Jacob's biological offspring and that even in Abraham's lifetime, the patriarch sired other blessed Gentile nations, including the Ishmaelites and Edom.

Another objection to the preterist view is that the overwhelming majority of Judean Jews did not receive "a Spirit of grace and pleas for mercy" at the destruction of Jerusalem in AD 70 (cf. Zech. 12:10; Matt. 24:30). While the context of Zechariah's prophecy includes a military invasion of the land of Israel (Zech. 12:2-6, 11), it also contains the promise that God will subsequently "give salvation to the tents of Judah, . . . protect the inhabitants of Jerusalem, . . . [and] destroy all the nations that come against Jerusalem" (Zech. 12:3-9). These prophetic events did not occur when the Romans destroyed Jerusalem in AD 70, despite preterists' desperate attempts to allegorize the Scriptures to suggest otherwise. The weeping and "pleas for mercy" (Zech. 12:10; cf. Matt. 24:30) should be understood as the humble pleading of national repentance at the return of the glorified Christ, the Lord "whom they have pierced."

---

[33] Kik, 139.

[34] Russell, *The Parousia*, 390, 392, 394, 399, 407; Similarly, Jordan, *The Vindication of Jesus Christ*, loc. 191.

[35] Russell, *The Parousia*, 104.

This exact vocabulary also appears in Jeremiah's new covenant promise, specifically, that God will regather the people of Israel back to their homeland ("with weeping they shall come, and with pleas for mercy I will lead them back" Jer. 31:9; cf. Jer. 50:4).

Partial preterists critique the traditional view of Christ's return in the Olivet Discourse as being "a primitive form of space travel," yet this is a double-edged sword for them because they admit that He will return in our future in the manner that they criticize, that is, by descending with the clouds of heaven! To illustrate, the apostle Paul taught, "For the Lord himself will descend from heaven. . . Then we who are alive . . . will be caught up together with them [the resurrected believers] in the clouds to meet the Lord in the air" (1 Thess. 4:16-17; cf. 1 Cor. 15:23).

Some preterists allegorize the meaning of Paul's words; however, the book of Acts also teaches that the Master will return literally and bodily by descending from heaven.

> And when he had said these things, as they were *looking on*, he was lifted up, and a cloud took him out of their sight. And while they were gazing into heaven as he went, behold, two men stood by them in white robes, and said, "Men of Galilee, why do you stand looking into heaven? This Jesus, who was taken up from you into heaven, will come in the same way as you saw him go into heaven." (Acts 1:9-11)

This passage shows that Christ's descent from heaven will take place in the exact manner that the disciples saw Him ascend into heaven. Unsurprisingly for the futurist, this passage highlights two primary details about His ascension into heaven, specifically, that it was accompanied by a visible cloud and that it was optically visualized by human observers.

CLOUD THEOPHANIES IN THE OLD TESTAMENT

Preterists appeal to multiple Old Testament passages, in addition to Daniel 7, to support their view that the Son of Man's coming is not

His future return (Matt. 24:30; Mark 13:26; Luke 21:27). For example, they argue that Old Testament theophanies[36] of Yahweh coming on a cloud reflected a mere metaphor or symbol for His "presence, judgment, and salvation."[37] They put forth many biblical texts as supposed proof of this symbolic phenomenon of God "riding on clouds" in judgment upon nations.[38] Mathison expresses the common preterist sentiment that "none of these texts is intended to communicate the idea that God is literally going to ride on a cloud into one of these nations."[39] Yet an evaluation of these passages reveals that this contention is misleading, and at times, blatantly false.

The phenomena of the Lord visually appearing with a literal cloud originates in the Pentateuch. The book of Exodus relates multiple narratives of Yahweh appearing to Moses and to the children of Israel in a cloud of glory. God descended in a thick cloud of darkness to protect and accompany the Israelites during the Red Sea crossing ("the pillar of cloud by day and the pillar of fire by night" Exod. 13:21-22; 14:19-20, 24; 2 Sam. 22:10). He also appeared in a cloud atop Mount Sinai to deliver the commandments of the law, descended to fill the tabernacle and to "dwell among" the children of Israel, and went ahead of the camp of Israel to lead them during their desert journeys (Exod. 19:9-11; 20:21; 24:15-18; 33:2, 9-10; 34:5; Num. 11:25; Deut. 33:2). The cloud of His glory also filled the temple when King Solomon dedicated it (1 Kings 8:11-13).

Preterists generally accept the concept that God appeared in a visible cloud during the Old Testament period.[40] Nevertheless, DeMar

---

36 A theophany is an appearance or visible manifestation of God.

37 Chilton, *Paradise Restored*, 102; cf. Hanegraaff, *The Apocalypse Code*, 26, 83-84, 106.

38 DeMar, *Last Days' Madness*, 72, 124, 160-61; Gentry, *Before Jerusalem Fell*, 123; Gentry, *The Book of Revelation Made Easy*, 35, 36; Hanegraaff, *The Apocalypse Code*, 26, 83-84; Kik, 38; Mathison, *When Shall These Things Be?*, 162-63.

39 Mathison, *When Shall These Things Be?*, 162-163; Similarly, Kik, 141.

40 E.g., DeMar, *Last Days' Madness*, 160.

and others object, saying that this evidence is insufficient to support the futurist interpretation of Matthew 24:30 because God was not seen as physically present in those encounters.[41] This objection is verifiably false because, as argued above, such Old Testament passages communicate that God personally arrived to Moses and to the nation, and He was accompanied by a visible cloud. But more importantly, the divine Angel of the Lord, in other words, Yahweh in human form—the pre-incarnate Christ—appeared in the clouds. For example, this Angel descended from heaven upon Mount Sinai, visibly appeared to Moses "in a flame of fire out of the midst of a bush," and introduced Himself as God and as I AM (Exod. 3:2-16). This divine Angel was corporeally present, contrary to DeMar's argument, in the pillar of fire and cloud that accompanied the congregation throughout the desert:

> Then the angel of God who was going before the host of Israel moved and went behind them, and the pillar of cloud moved from before them and stood behind them, coming between the host of Egypt and the host of Israel. And there was the cloud and the darkness. (Exod. 14:19-20)

Other passages also portray the Lord as appearing in clouds as a glorified *man* (e.g., Exod. 24:10-11; Isa. 6:1-5, 8; Ezek. 1:26-28; 10:1; Dan. 7:13; 8:15). Finally, as argued previously, the New Testament expects Jesus to bodily and visibly descend from heaven when He returns (Acts 1:9-11; 1 Thess. 4:16-17). Based on these considerations, the reader should understand that Jesus had in mind His glorious return as the incarnate, resurrected Son of Man when He prophesied that He would be seen "coming on the clouds of heaven" (Matt. 24:30).

Preterists point to a variety of other Old Testament passages to support their allegorical interpretation of Christ coming on the clouds (Matt. 24:30; Mark 13:26; Luke 21:27). However, contrary to these claims, some of these passages do not describe cloud-coming theophanies but depict the clouds of darkness that will be visible on the day of

---

[41] DeMar, *Last Days' Madness*, 124, 160.

the Lord (e.g., Ezek. 30:3; Joel 2:1-2; Zeph. 1:14-15). Other passages are found in the Psalms and prophetic portions of the Prophets, and they recast the Exodus cloud theophanies in a poetic fashion. For example, the psalmist described God as coming with a cloud to deliver David from the hands of King Saul (Ps. 18:6-17). Similarly, the prophet Nahum warned of divine judgment against Nineveh by quoting and alluding to the Exodus narrative (Exod. 20:5 in Nah. 1:2 and Exod. 34:6-7 in Nah. 1:3). He portrayed the Lord with clouds under His feet and "rebuking the sea" to make it dry land (Nah. 1:3-4), reminiscent of the Red Sea crossing (Exod. 14:21-22). The prophet Micah utilized themes from the day of the Lord to warn of Samaria's looming destruction (Mic. 1:3-5; cf. Ps. 97:1-6); he saw God descending "out of his place" to "tread upon the high places of the earth" so that mountains melt before His arrival (Mic. 1:3-4). Unlike Christ's prophecy about His coming with clouds, these passages are found in poetic portions of Scripture, and even then, they reinforce the fact that God appeared in plain sight in His glory cloud during the exodus from Egypt.

The classic example cited by preterists of the Lord's cloud coming is found in the prophecies of Isaiah (Isa. 19:1-4).[42] The passage begins "Behold, the Lord is riding on a swift cloud and comes to Egypt" (Isa. 19:1), and it continues with a prophecy concerning Egypt's destruction by civil war, harsh servitude, and drought. Preterists and many futurists interpret this passage as referring to the imminent Assyrian invasion of Egypt in the late-seventh century BC.[43] Gentry contends that it contains "apocalyptic language" and that "no interpreter believes the Egyptians saw God Almighty sitting on a cloud and descending among them in judgment."[44] However, the background of this passage calls to mind the exodus narrative, where God actually appeared in a

---

[42] DeMar, *Last Days' Madness*, 161; Gentry, *The Book of Revelation Made Easy*, 35, 36; Kik, 38.

[43] Mathison, *When Shall These Things Be?*, 162-63.

[44] Gentry, *The Book of Revelation Made Easy*, 35, 36.

visible cloud to destroy Pharaoh's Egypt. Furthermore, the surrounding context shows that this passage is ultimately eschatological and will find its culmination in the day of the Lord, when Egypt and Assyria will join Israel in the worship of the one true God (Isa. 19:23-25). The cumulative evidence from the passage does not deny a literal cloud coming but affirms it from history and predicts it in eschatology.

THE GATHERING OF THE ELECT

The Lord continued the Olivet Discourse: "And he [the Son of Man] will send out his angels with a loud trumpet call, and they will gather his elect from the four winds, from one end of heaven to the other" (Matt. 24:31). Preterists consistently put forth the notion that the angels are human "messengers" (c.f. Luke 7:24; 9:52) who would preach "the trumpet call" of the gospel throughout the nations after the destruction of Jerusalem in AD 70.[45] Some preterists, such as Gentry, do not appear to be entirely comfortable with their reinterpretation of this passage and admit that it could refer to angelic "supernatural power which lies behind such preaching."[46] According to the preterist interpretation, the gathering of the elect (Matt. 24:31; Mark 13:27) means that Jesus would spiritually bring the elect Gentiles into the holy Church (e.g., John 11:52). For example, R. T. France argues that the destruction of Jerusalem was "the cue for the establishment of the universal reign of the Son of Man and the gathering of a new people of God from the ends of the earth."[47] According to Chilton and others, the desolation

---

[45] Chilton, *Paradise Restored*, 103; DeMar, *Last Days' Madness*, 174, 278; Gentry, *The Olivet Discourse*, loc. 2313-18, 2363; Kik, 148.

[46] Gentry, *The Olivet Discourse*, loc. 23, 63.

[47] R. T. France, *The Gospel of Matthew, The New International Commentary on the New Testament* (Grand Rapids: William B. Eerdman's Publishing, 2007), 911.

of Jerusalem made the Church the "New Synagogue . . . the true, the super-Synagogue."[48]

One difficulty of the preterist interpretation of this verse is that Christ had previously taught in the Olivet Discourse that the worldwide preaching of the gospel must occur *before* the end of the age (Matt. 24:14). This anachronism is seen most clearly in the preterist claim that the gospel had already gone to "the entire world" and to "all the nations" prior to AD 70 (cf. Matt. 24:14; Mark 13:10). One wonders, then, how the gospel could have been proclaimed to all the nations before AD 70 while the destruction of Jerusalem signaled the beginning of this same event! Gentry, perceiving this weakness in the preterist argument, suggests that the language of Jesus "highlights AD 70 as the ultimate spark to the worldwide mission. Indeed, the events of AD 70 finally separate Christianity from Judaism."[49] He remarks that the worldwide gathering of the Gentiles began "in earnest" at AD 70.[50] Similarly, DeMar attempts to qualify Jesus' statement by positing that the gospel went "to the Jew first" prior to AD 70 and thereafter went "to the Gentiles in new fullness and with the expectation that the *nations*—Gentiles—would be discipled (Matt. 28:18-20)."[51] However, such elastic use of words does not avoid the anachronism.

Preterist attempts to explain away the clear meaning of the angelic gathering of the elect (Matt. 24:31) also gloss over other well-attested passages of Scripture that clearly describe Christ's return. Kik admits, "This [Matt. 24:31], some maintain, is a description of the final resurrection at the second coming of the Lord. That there is some ground for

---

[48] Chilton, *Paradise Restored*, 104-05.

[49] Gentry, *The Olivet Discourse Made Easy*, loc. 2374.

[50] Gentry, *The Olivet Discourse Made Easy*, loc. 1697.

[51] DeMar, *Last Days' Madness*, 176.

such an interpretation one cannot deny. The trumpet is associated with the resurrection of the dead in several passages."[52]

One passage that exemplifies Christ's teaching about the gathering of the elect at the angelic trumpet call (Matt. 24:31) is the apostle Paul's exposition of the passage. The apostle taught that the descent of Jesus from heaven will be accompanied by at least one angel, the sound of a trumpet call, and the gathering of His elect "in the clouds" (1 Thess. 4:16-17). In his correspondence with the Corinthians, Paul also connected the return of Jesus with the last trumpet and the resurrection of the dead (1 Cor. 15:20-23, 50-54; cf. Rev. 11:15-18). Other passages describe the revealing of the Lord Jesus from heaven, with the accompaniment of mighty angels, to render judgment (Matt. 13:41; 16:27; 2 Thess. 1:8).

Jesus provided the interpretation of a parable about the angelic end-time gathering in the Synoptic Gospels. These words clarify the meaning of Matthew 24:31 by identifying the angels and their role in the harvest gathering:

> The harvest is the end of the age, and the reapers are angels. Just as the weeds are gathered and burned with fire, so will it be at the end of the age. The Son of Man will send his angels, and they will gather out of his kingdom all causes of sin and all law-breakers, and throw them into the fiery furnace. In that place there will be weeping and gnashing of teeth. Then the righteous will shine like the sun in the kingdom of their Father. He who has ears, let him hear. (Matt. 13:39-43)

This passage identifies the angels as heavenly beings by describing their role of separating out the evildoers and throwing them into the fiery furnace of hell, hardly the function of earthly preachers of the gospel! Admittedly, Jesus did not formally depict the gathering of the elect in these verses, yet in the original parable, He mentioned that He will "gather the wheat [the righteous]" into His barn (Matt. 13:30). In addition, He mentioned that "the righteous will shine like the sun in the

---

[52] Kik, 145.

kingdom," an allusion to the resurrection prophecy of Daniel ("many of those who sleep in the dust of the earth shall awake . . . and those who are wise shall shine like the brightness of the sky above; and those who turn many to righteousness, like the stars forever and ever" Dan. 12:3). Based on these facts, we see that Christ's parable directly connects this angelic harvest gathering with the resurrection of the dead at the end of the age.

In the "Isaiah Apocalypse," the prophet Isaiah also connected the same eschatological events that Jesus later predicted in the Olivet Discourse (Isa. 24-27). For example, Isaiah prophesied that the day of the Lord would be characterized by devastations upon the earth, an unprecedented earthquake, the darkening of the Sun and Moon, Yahweh's reign in Jerusalem, and the divine punishment of rebellious angels and "the kings of the earth" (Isa. 24, esp. Isa. 24:19-23; 26:21). After the national birth pains of tribulation, the Lord Himself will return from heaven to destroy the sea beast and to "swallow up death forever" and "wipe away tears from all faces" through the resurrection of the dead (Isa. 26:17-27:1; cf. 1 Cor. 15:54; Rev. 7:17; 21:4). He will save those who have waited for Him and will provide a luxurious banquet for them in Mount Zion (Isa. 25:6-9; Rev. 19:7). Like one who gleans grain at the harvest, God will gather the people of Israel back to their own land at the blast of the "great trumpet":

> In that day from the river Euphrates to the Brook of Egypt the LORD will thresh out the grain, and you will be gleaned one by one, O people of Israel. And in that day a great trumpet will be blown, and those who were lost in the land of Assyria and those who were driven out to the land of Egypt will come and worship the LORD on the holy mountain at Jerusalem. (Isa. 27:12-13)

TABLE 3: COMMON ELEMENTS OF MATTHEW 24, 1 THESSALONIANS 4, AND 1 CORINTHIANS 15

	Matthew 24:30-31	1 Thessalonians 4:16-17	1 Corinthians 15:22-23, 51-53
Jesus Christ Appearing in/from Heaven	Then the sign of the Son of Man will appear in heaven . . . and they will see the Son of Man coming	For the Lord Himself will descend from heaven	[I]n Christ all shall be made alive . . . afterward those who are Christ's at His coming
Clouds	on the clouds of heaven	in the clouds . . . the Lord in the air	——
Angel(s)	And He will send His angels	with the voice of an archangel	——
A Trumpet	with a great sound of a trumpet	with the trumpet of God	in a moment, in the twinkling of an eye, at the last trumpet. For the trumpet will sound
Gathering of the Righteous	and they will gather together His elect from the four winds, from one end of heaven to the other. (cf. "from the farthest part of earth to the farthest part of heaven" Mark 13:27)	And the dead in Christ will rise first. Then we who are alive and remain shall be caught up together with them in the clouds to meet the Lord in the air.	Behold, I tell you a mystery: We shall not all sleep, but we shall all be changed . . . and the dead will be raised incorruptible, and we shall be changed.

10

THE OLIVET DISCOURSE IN

1 THESSALONIANS 4-5

THIS CHAPTER WILL DEMONSTRATE that the apostle Paul derived his material for 1 Thessalonians 4-5 from the Olivet Discourse. The following excerpt contains the apostle's encouraging instruction for the Thessalonian Christians:

> But we do not want you to be uninformed, brothers, about those who are asleep, that you may not grieve as others do who have no hope. For since we believe that Jesus died and rose again, even so, through Jesus, God will bring with him those who have fallen asleep. For this we declare to you by a word from the Lord, that we who are alive, who are left until the coming of the Lord, will not precede those who have fallen asleep. For the Lord himself will descend from heaven with a cry of command, with the voice of an archangel, and with the sound of the trumpet of God. And the dead in Christ will rise first. Then we who are alive, who are left, will be caught up together with them in the clouds to meet the Lord in the

air, and so we will always be with the Lord. Therefore encourage one another with these words.

Now concerning the times and the seasons, brothers, you have no need to have anything written to you. For you yourselves are fully aware that the day of the Lord will come like a thief in the night. While people are saying, "There is peace and security," then sudden destruction will come upon them as labor pains come upon a pregnant woman, and they will not escape.

But you are not in darkness, brothers, for that day to surprise you like a thief. For you are all children of light, children of the day. We are not of the night or of the darkness. So then let us not sleep, as others do, but let us keep awake and be sober. For those who sleep, sleep at night, and those who get drunk, are drunk at night. But since we belong to the day, let us be sober, having put on the breastplate of faith and love, and for a helmet the hope of salvation. For God has not destined us for wrath, but to obtain salvation through our Lord Jesus Christ, who died for us so that whether we are awake or asleep we might live with him. Therefore encourage one another and build one another up, just as you are doing. (1 Thess. 4:13-5:11)

The statement "For we declare to you by a word from the Lord" (1 Thess. 4:15) requires some consideration of the syntax. Gordon Fee, a New Testament scholar, explains,

> Almost everyone considers all of [1 Thess. 4:15-17] to be a recital of what Paul here calls "the Lord's word." Thus he begins, "for this we tell you with/by a/the word of the Lord, namely that . . ." The slashes indicate areas of considerable debate in terms of understanding what Paul is referring to.[1]

Due to these difficulties, the reader must consider other factors in order to determine the meaning of the apostle's statement. The idea that "the word of the Lord" (1 Thess. 4:15) refers to a logion, an authentic saying from the mouth of Jesus, has much to commend it. As noteworthy supporting evidence for this claim, the apostle Paul always referred to

---

1 Gordon D. Fee, *The First and Second Letters to the Thessalonians* (Grand Rapids: William B. Eerdmans Publishing, 2009), 182-84.

THE OLIVET DISCOURSE IN 1 THESSALONIANS 4-5

Christ when he used the title "the Lord," except when quoting the Old Testament (LXX).[2] In addition, the apostle habitually identified the source of his teaching when he spoke by direct revelation from the Holy Spirit and was not quoting Jesus (1 Cor. 2:12-16; 7:40; 2 Cor. 13:3; Gal. 4:12; 1 Thess. 2:13). Finally, when the apostle identified "the Lord" as the source of his teachings, the content of the teaching also appeared in statements spoken by Jesus (e.g., 1 Cor. 7:10-11, 25; 9:14; 11:23-25). As we will soon see, this is also the case in 1 Thessalonians 4:13-5:11.

Several biblical scholars teach that the Olivet Discourse is "the word" of Christ to which Paul referred in his teaching to the Thessalonians (1 Thess. 4:15).[3] Several observations about this Thessalonian letter reveal the likelihood of this assertion. For example, many scholars have demonstrated the thematic unity of 1 Thessalonians 4 with 5.[4] Gordon Fee notes that the eschatological content of 1 Thessalonians 5 is "quite closely related to what preceded" and that 1 Thessalonians 5:10-11 summarize important ideas from 4:13-18. He explains that Paul did not mention the return of Jesus again in 1 Thessalonians 5 because he was relating how the disciples should live prior to His return.[5] Similarly, G. K. Beale justifies a thematic unity between these two chapters:

> The probability is that [the verses of 1 Thess.] 4:15-17 describe generally the same end-time scenario as 5:1-11. Specifically, Paul narrates the resurrection at the end of the age and then recapitulates in chapter 5 by speaking about the timing of this event and about the

---

[2] The Greek word for Lord here is *kurios* (κύριος).

[3] Béda Rigaux, *The Letters of St. Paul, Modern Studies* (Chicago: Franciscan Herald, 1968), 539; Lars Hartman, *Prophecy Interpreted: The Formation of Some Jewish Apocalyptic Texts and of the Eschatological Discourse Mark 13 Par* (Lund: Gleerup 1966), 187-90; Niels Hyldahl, "Auferstehung Christi – Auferstehung der Toten (1 Thess. 4:4, 13-18)," In: *S. Pedersen [Hrsg.]. Die Paulinische Literatur und Theologie* (TeolSt 7) (1980), 130; Kim Seyoon, *"The Jesus Tradition in 1 Thess 4.13-5.11,"* New Testament Studies 48 (2002), 231-42.

[4] T. L. Howard, *"The Literary Unity of 1 Thessalonians 4:13-5:11,"* GTJ 9 (1988): 163-90; G. K. Beale, *1-2 Thessalonians*, The IVP New Testament Commentary Series (Downers Grove, IL: Inter Varsity Press, 2003), 130, 142-43; Fee, *The First and Second Letters to the Thessalonians*, 182-84.

[5] Fee, *The First and Second Letters to the Thessalonians*, 182-84.

judgment on unbelievers, which will also happen at the same time. That both 4:15-18 and 5:1-11 explain the same events is discernible from observing that both passages actually form one continuous depiction of the same narrative in Matthew 24.[6]

Beale, following J. Bernard Orchard and others, contends that the apostle Paul paraphrased the Olivet Discourse in 1 Thessalonian 4:13-5:11.[7] Beale demonstrates this dependency in a comparison table that provides numerous parallels between the two passages,[8] and many other scholars have noted the literary parallels between the two passages.[9] Undoubtedly, the linguistic signature of the Olivet Discourse finds duplication in 1 Thessalonians 4:16-5:9. The power of this argument rests in the thematic parallels, a similar sequence of events, and the appearance of "now concerning" at the same point within the sequence.[10]

The comparative table on the next two pages of this book demonstrates these features, proving beyond a reasonable doubt that Saint Paul borrowed heavily from the Olivet Discourse for his teaching in 1 Thessalonians 4-5. The table provides persuasive evidence that the apostle appealed to the discourse for his material in 1 Thessalonians 4-5. He followed the discourse in a sequential manner and alluded to Christ's teachings that appear in the discourse before and after the supposed transition verse of Matthew 24:36. This further militates against dividing the discourse at this verse, as many partial preterists do. This

---

[6] Beale, *1-2 Thessalonians*, 136-38.

[7] Beale, *1-2 Thessalonians*, 130, 142-43; J. Bernard Orchard, *"Thessalonians and the Synoptic Gospel,"* Biblica 19 (1938): 19-42; William E. Bell, "A Critical Evaluation of the Pretribulational Rapture Doctrine in Christian Eschatology," Th.D. dissertation (New York University, April 1967), 249-50.

[8] Beale, *1-2 Thessalonians*, 137.

[9] G. Henry Waterman, *"The Sources of Paul's Teaching on the 2nd Coming of Jesus in 1 and 2 Thessalonians,"* JETS 18 (1975): 105-13 1975, 105-13; I Howard Marshall, *1 and 2 Thessalonians* (Grand Rapids: Eerdmans, 1983), 126.

[10] The Greek phrase is *peri de* (περὶ δὲ - "now/but concerning").

same argument prohibits anyone from dividing the discourse anywhere after Matthew 24:29.

The apostle's use of the Olivet Discourse at this point demonstrates that Christ's statement about His glorious coming, the trumpet blast, and the angelic gathering of the elect (Matt. 24:30-31; cf. Mark 13:26-27; Luke 21:27) is concerned with the resurrection of the righteous dead, a connection that severely undermines preterism.

TABLE 4: PARALLELS BETWEEN THE OLIVET DISCOURSE AND 1 THESSALONIANS 4-5:[11]

Matthew 24	1 Thessalonians 4:16-5:9
24:30 "[T]hey will see the Son of Man coming on the clouds of heaven."	4:16, 17 "For the Lord Himself will descend from heaven . . . in the clouds."
24:31 "His angels with a great sound of a trumpet, and they will gather together His elect from the four winds, from one end of heaven to the other" (cf. Mark 13:27 "from the farthest part of the earth to the farthest part of heaven").	4:16-17 "[W]ith the voice of an archangel, and with the trumpet of God. And the dead in Christ will rise first. Then we who are alive and remain shall be caught up together with them in the clouds to meet the Lord in the air."
24:36 "But of that day and hour no one knows."	5:1-2 "But concerning the times and the seasons, brethren, you have no need that I should write to you."

---

[11] The linguistic signature of the Olivet Discourse finds duplication in this prophecy of Paul. The careful reader should notice the thematic parallels, the similar sequence of events, and the appearance of "now concerning" (περι δε) at the same point within each sequence.

24:39 "And did not know until the flood came and took them all away, so also will the coming of the Son of Man be" (cf. Luke 21:34, 36 "unexpectedly . . . pray always that you may be counted worth to escape").	5:3 "For when they say, "Peace and safety! Then sudden destruction comes upon them . . . and they shall not escape."
24:8 "sorrows"	5:3 "labor pains"
24:42-44 "Watch therefore, for you do not know what hour your Lord is coming. But know this, that if the master of the house had known what hour the thief would come, he would have watched and not allowed his house to be broken into. Therefore, you also be ready, for the Son of Man is coming at an hour you do not expect."	5:2, 4-7, 8, 10 "For you yourselves know perfectly that the day of the Lord so comes as a thief in the night...But you, brethren, are not in darkness, so that this day should overtake you as a thief. You are all sons of light and sons of the day. We are not of the night nor of darkness. Therefore, let us not sleep, as others do, but let us watch and be sober. For those who sleep, sleep at night . . . . But let us who are of the day . . . whether we wake or sleep."
24:49 "drinks with the drunkards"	5:7-8 "[T]hose who get drunk are drunk at night. . . . be sober."
25:6 "[A] cry was heard . . .'go out to meet him.'"	4:16-17 "with a shout . . . to meet the Lord."

Major Premise: 1 Thessalonians 4:16-17 describes the same events as Matthew 24:30-31 (as shown in the table).

Minor Premise: 1 Thessalonians 4:16-17 is about the return of Jesus Christ and the resurrection of the righteous.

Conclusion: Therefore, Matthew 24:30-31 is about the return of Jesus Christ and the resurrection of the righteous.

THE OLIVET DISCOURSE IN 1 THESSALONIANS 4-5

France and Wright object to the argument that Paul borrowed from the Olivet Discourse in 1 Thessalonians 4-5 on the grounds that it is eisegesis.[12] Their concern that such an interpretation prohibits Matthew and Mark from "having their own voices" sounds reasonable, but evades a more important consideration—that the striking parallels between these passages increase the likelihood that they describe the same prophetic events. The Thessalonian letters provides definitive answers as to the identity of "the elect" and the exact manner of the mystery of their "gathering together" in the Olivet Discourse (Matt. 24:31; Mark 13:27; cf. 1 Cor. 15:51; 2 Thess. 2:1). Kim Seyoon effectively argues that Paul's purpose for addressing the topic of the resurrection of the dead at this point was to clarify Christ's statement in Matthew 24:30-31.[13]

Furthermore, since the coming of the Son of Man accompanied by angels (Matt. 24:30-31) is an allusion to Daniel's prophecy of the same (Dan. 7:13-14), as both France and Wright acknowledge, it follows that these angels in the Olivet Discourse are *heavenly beings*, as in Daniel's vision, and not human "messengers" who proclaim the gospel, as France posits (as we saw in a previous chapter). The angelic entourage in both passages is consistent with the presence of the archangel at Christ's glorious return in 1 Thessalonians 4:16 (cf. 2 Thess. 1:8).

Jesus' expectation that the resurrection of the dead would occur "immediately after the [unprecedented] tribulation" (Matt. 24:29-31; Mark 13:24-27) is the logical antecedent to Paul's own teaching on this subject (1 Thess. 4:16-17). This is also consistent with Daniel's later vision, which includes the concept that the resurrection of the dead will occur at the time of the unprecedented tribulation (Dan. 12:1-3); this is argued more fully in a subsequent chapter of this book. Despite the futile

---

[12] R. T. France, *The Gospel of Mark: a Commentary on the Greek Text* (Grand Rapids: W.B. Eerdmans, 2002), 503; N. T. Wright as quoted in Carey C. Newman, "In Grateful Dialogue." *Jesus & the Restoration of Israel: a Critical Assessment of N.T. Wright's Jesus and the Victory of God* (Downers Grove, IL: InterVarsityPress. 1999), 244-77.

[13] Seyoon, *"The Jesus Tradition in 1 Thess 4.13-5.11,"* 231-42.

attempts of DeMar and others to deny a literal rapture,[14] Paul's rapture passage explains that the living saints will experience a mysterious transformation when Jesus returns (1 Thess. 4:13-18), by which the dead and living saints will receive glorified, incorruptible bodies. Neither group will need wait any longer for kingdom glory, so that "what is mortal may be swallowed up by life" (2 Cor. 5:4, 1 Thess. 4:13-18; cf. 1 Cor. 15:50-57). The apostle called this translation of the living "a mystery" (1 Cor. 15:51; cf. Rev. 10:7).

DOUBLE VISION

In the Olivet Discourse, the Lord Jesus taught that He will gloriously appear at the end of the age and will send His angels "with a loud trumpet call . . . [to] gather his elect from the four winds" (Matt. 24:31; cf. Matt. 24:6, 13-14, 34). The Lukan version of the discourse presents this as the time when God's kingdom will arrive (Luke 21:31-32). Similarly, the apostle John connected the final angelic trumpet blast with the "mystery of God," the consummate arrival of Christ's kingdom, and the time for judging and rewarding the dead:

> In the days of the trumpet call to be sounded by the seventh angel, the mystery of God would be fulfilled, just as he announced to his servants the prophets. . . Then the seventh angel blew his trumpet, and there were loud voices in heaven, saying, "The kingdom of the world has become the kingdom of our Lord and his Christ, and he shall reign forever and ever. . . You [the Lord] have taken your great power and begun to reign. The nations raged, but your wrath came, and the time for the dead to be judged, and for rewarding your servants, the prophets and saints, and those who fear your name, both small and great, and for destroying the destroyers of the earth." (Rev. 10:7; 11:15, 17-18)

---

14   DeMar, *Last Days' Madness,* 159; DeMar admits that the passage does "indicate the rapture" (p. 277).

Partial preterists teach that all these events occurred in AD 70, a view that ultimately requires *two* last trumpets signaling *two* consummate arrivals of the kingdom of God, because the apostle Paul explicitly connected Christ's glorious return from heaven with the time of "the end," the sounding of the final trumpet, the resurrection of the righteous dead, and the arrival of the kingdom (1 Cor. 15:23-26, 50-55). He elsewhere associated the timing of Jesus' return from heaven with an angelic command, the sounding of "the trumpet of God," and the resurrection and rapture of God's people (1 Thess. 4:16). However, partial preterists teach that God's kingdom arrived in AD 70 (cf. Luke 21:31-32; Rev. 11:15). This paradigm requires God's kingdom, recently inaugurated in the early Christian Church, to have arrived in some consummated sense in AD 70, only to await another consummate arrival at Christ's future return!

Partial preterists also paint themselves into a corner by contending that the biblical period of "the last days" does not end with "the last day." They insist that "the last days" refers to the period that ended the Jewish kingdom in AD 70. However, they agree with the futurist position that the resurrection of the dead will occur in our future on "the last day" (John 6:39-40, 44, 54; 11:24; 12:48). This preterist framework *implicitly* requires *two* days called "the last day," one in AD 70 that ended "the last days" period of the first century AD and another "last day" at the return of Jesus, when the dead will be resurrected.[15] This logic can be taken a step further. Partial preterists must necessarily allow for an additional period of "last days" leading up to "the last day" in our future, which is, at best, confusing.

Partial preterists also unwittingly create two periods of the end times. The prophet Daniel prophesied that the unprecedented tribulation will occur at the divinely-appointed "time of the end" (Dan. 8:17-19; 11:27, 35, 40; 12:1- 9). Preterists teach that this appointed time refers to the destruction of Jerusalem and the temple in AD 70. However, many

---

15 See admission in Sproul, *The Last Days According to Jesus*, 168, 170, 183

preterists also believe that planet Earth will be dissolved or destroyed in our future. One wonders how these preterists can escape the conclusion that such an event would not constitute the time of the end.

THE PARTIAL PRETERIST MODEL

The partial preterist paradigm requires a spiritual or judgment "coming" of Christ in AD 70, followed by a third coming, that is, His future return![16] Many preterists postulate three distinct "comings" of Jesus in addition to "the coming of the Son of Man" (Matt. 24:30; Mark 13:26), which they interpret as His ascension. Therefore, they need at least three to five eschatological "comings" of Jesus Christ:

- His "coming" to the earth in the first advent

- His "coming/going" to the Father at the ascension, based on their erroneous interpretation of Matthew 24:30

- His supposed judgment "coming" against the Jewish kingdom in AD 70

- His spiritual "coming," that is, the arrival of His reigning presence at Jerusalem in AD 70, as taught by Wright and others

- His glorious return in our future

Partial preterism requires at least *two* last trumpets, which signal *two* "comings" of Jesus on *two* distinct judgment days, at *two* different times of the end, which result in *two* distinct gatherings of the elect, *two* arrivals of Christ's kingdom, and *two* very different dissolutions of *two* sets of heavens and earths. This "double vision" transforms the powerful

---

[16] For an admission of two parousias, see Sproul, *The Last Days According to Jesus*, 169.

testimony of biblical eschatology into a maze of confusion. Clearly then, preterists have invented artificial divisions within the eschatological framework of the Bible. Such models of eschatology demand that the Scriptures conform to preterist presuppositions about the historic past. By force fitting historical events of the first century into the biblical prophecies, they obscure their proper contexts and betray their straightforward, consistent interpretation.

11

NERO AND THE MARK

THE APOSTLE JOHN provided the reader with an important clue to identify the person known as the Beast in the book of Revelation: "This calls for wisdom: let the one who has understanding calculate the number of the beast, for it is the number of a man, and his number is 666" (Rev. 13:18). Most preterists argue that the Jewish practice of gematria demonstrates that the apostle had Emperor Nero in view.[1] Gematria is a Jewish alphanumeric code in which Hebrew or Aramaic letters and words are assigned specific numerical values.[2] Gentry explains how gematria could be used to identify Nero as 666:

> When Nero Caesar's name is transliterated into Hebrew, we get *Neron Kesar* (*nrwn qsr*: Hebrew has no letters to represent vowels).

---

[1] Adams and Fisher, *The Time of the End*, 55-56; Chilton, *Paradise Restored*, 181; DeMar, *Last Days' Madness*, 257; Hanegraaff, *The Apocalypse Code*, 146; Russell, *The Parousia*, 462-65; Sproul, 203.

[2] "Gematria," *Wikipedia*, on May 23, 2017. https://en.wikipedia.org/wiki/Gematria.

It has been documented by archaeological finds that a first century Hebrew spelling of Nero's name provides us with precisely the value of 666. Jastrow's lexicon of the Talmud contains this very spelling.[3]

Chilton believed that John's original readers would have immediately guessed the identification of Nero and "those who understood Hebrew probably grasped it instantly."[4] DeMar teaches that John's readers would have decoded this enigmatic number "with relative ease."[5] Hanegraaff insists that the apostle's original audience would have been "absolutely certain" that their calculations identified Nero as the Beast.[6] Hanegraaff concludes, "Obviously no amount of wisdom would have enabled a first-century audience to figure out the number of a twenty-first-century Beast."[7] Other preterists disagree. Jordan declares, "666 does *not* have anything to do with Nero Caesar."[8]

The preterist contention that the number of the Beast should be identified with Nero is rife with difficulties. Gentry admits that the preterist view requires a rare spelling of Nero Caesar that is decidedly "not the most common one" and that it must include an additional Hebrew letter.[9] Hanegraaff points out that the calculation only fits the Greek name Nero Caesar[10] only if it is first transliterated into Hebrew.[11] Simon Kistemaker summarizes the many fallacies with the preterist calculation of 666:

---

[3] Gentry as quoted in DeMar, *Last Days' Madness*, 258.

[4] Chilton, *Paradise Restored*, 181.

[5] DeMar, *Last Days' Madness*, 257.

[6] Hanegraaff, *The Apocalypse Code*, 144.

[7] Hanegraaff, *The Apocalypse Code*, 8.

[8] Jordan, *The Vindication of Jesus Christ*, loc. 427.

[9] This additional letter is נ (transliterated nun). Gentry, *Before Jerusalem Fell*, 199.

[10] The Greek is *Nerone Kaisar* (Νερων Καισαρ).

[11] Hanegraaff, *The Apocalypse Code*, 146.

A popular interpretation of many scholars is that the number 666 has the numerical value of the name Nero Caesar... But the choice of Nero's name creates many difficulties. First, to arrive at the number 666 as the numerical value of Nero's name, one has to add the name Caesar. But even then, the expanded name Nero Caesar has the numerical value of only 616. Only when one adds an extra letter *n* to the name Nero, resulting in Neron Caesar, is the full number 666 achieved. But then one has to resort to the Hebrew spelling of Neron Caesar, which is *nun* = 50, *resh* = 200, *waw* = 6, *nun* = 50, *qoph* = 100, *samech* = 60, *resh* = 200, for a total of 666. But the normal spelling of the transliterated Hebrew word for "Caesar" is *qysr*, which includes the letter *yodh*. This letter, with the numerical value of 10, makes the total 676; therefore, proponents of this numerical scheme have searched for a manuscript that lacks the extra letter *yodh*. Among the literature of the Dead Sea Scrolls, archaeologists have discovered a fragment that has the Hebraic (Aramaic) spelling of the name Neron. The next word *qysr* has two damaged consonants after the letter *q*, but there is no room for a vowel. Nevertheless, the questions must be asked, "Why would the author not use a Greek form instead of a Hebrew form?"[12]

While it is possible that the apostle John intended a calculation for the Beast using gematria, it is more likely that he had the Greek method of isopsephy in mind. Many first-century Greek writings attest to the widespread use of isopsephy throughout the Roman Empire, and John's original audience, the seven churches of Asia that were comprised predominantly of Greek-speaking Jews and Gentiles, would have understood the practice. Obviously, this is a problem for the preterist interpretation because isopsephy does not fit the view, as Hanegraaff notes. He explains that the Greek isopsephism for Nero totals 1,005 instead of the 666 required by John's calculation.[13]

The discerning Christian should understand that the calculation of the Beast's number 666, using either gematria or isopsephy, does not

---

12   Kistemaker in Mathison, *When Shall These Things Be?*, 228-29.

13   Hanegraaff, *The Apocalypse Code*, 146

result in the formal name Nero Claudius Caesar Augustus Germanicus or any of its derivatives. As many preterist teachers admit, they must reject the usual spelling for Nero and choose an extremely rare form of his name, which has been reconstituted from a damaged manuscript that may have originally included an extra Hebrew letter. This is nothing short of exercising selection bias and conforming data to fit a predetermined conclusion.

A CONFUSED CHRONOLOGY

Most preterists teach that Emperor Nero was the Beast who would speak blasphemies and "make war on the saints and . . . conquer them" for forty-two months (cf. Rev. 13:5-10).[14] The relevant prophecy reads as follows:

> And the beast was given a mouth uttering haughty and blasphemous words, and it was allowed to exercise authority for forty-two months. It opened its mouth to utter blasphemies against God, blaspheming his name and his dwelling, that is, those who dwell in heaven. Also it was allowed to make war on the saints and to conquer them. And authority was given it over every tribe and people and language and nation, and all who dwell on earth will worship it, everyone whose name has not been written before the foundation of the world in the book of life of the Lamb who was slain. If anyone has an ear, let him hear: If anyone is to be taken captive, to captivity he goes; if anyone is to be slain with the sword, with the sword must he be slain. Here is a call for the endurance and faith of the saints. (Rev. 13:5-10)

Preterists interpret this forty-two-month period of the Beast as the Neronian persecution that began with the emperor's persecution of Christians in Rome, from approximately November AD 64 until his suicide in June AD 68. Gentry comments, "The fit [with Nero] is both

---

[14] Adams and Fisher, *The Time of the End*, 55; Chilton, *Paradise Restored*, 179; Hanegraaff, *The Apocalypse Code*, 148; Jordan, loc. 324; Russell, *The Parousia*, 512.

relevant and remarkable."[15] However, the proposed chronology of Nero cannot account for the prophecy that the Son of Man will appear and subsequently kill the Beast and his armies (Rev. 19:19-21; cf. 2 Thess. 2:8). Preterists teach that "the coming of the Son of Man" occurred in conjunction with Jerusalem's destruction in AD 70; however, the fall of Jerusalem took place more than two years after Nero's death! This may explain why Hanegraaff erroneously places the Year of the Four Emperors (AD 69) and the destruction of Jerusalem during the Neronian persecution.[16] Russell recognized the anachronism regarding Nero's death:

> No doubt there is here something of an anachronism. The death of Nero is placed in the vision subsequent to the judgment of Jerusalem, whereas it actually preceded that event by two years or more. As we have before remarked, something must be conceded to poetic license. In an epic, a drama, or a vision, it is unreasonable to require strict chronological sequence. . . There is, however, another answer to the charge of anachronism. It deserves consideration whether this whole scene of the great battle and victory of Christ the King, and the punishment of the beast and his armies, may not be properly conceived as taking place in the spirit, not in the flesh? That is, whether it may not be the representation of transactions in the unseen state; the judgment of the dead, and not of the living.[17]

Russell's proposals that this anachronism can be explained as "poetic license" or as taking place in the unseen realm are hardly satisfying. Gentry opts for the explanation that the 1,260 days is a symbolic figure.[18] The preterist evasion of the literalness of this time period is problematic. Preterists generally acknowledge that the Bible equates the various references to "time, times, and half a time" (Dan. 7:25; 12:7;

---

[15] Gentry, *The Book of Revelation Made Easy*, 68, 69; Hanegraaff, *The Apocalypse Code*, 144; Russell, *The Parousia*, 460.

[16] Hanegraaff, *The Apocalypse Code*, 144.

[17] Russell, *The Parousia*, 512; cf. Kistemaker in Mathison, *When Shall These Things Be?*, 224.

[18] Chilton, *Paradise Restored*, 179.

Rev. 12:14), "half of the week" (Dan. 9:27), forty-two months (Rev. 11:2; 13:5), and 1,260 days (Rev. 11:3; 12:6).[19] Also, "the man clothed in linen" told the prophet Daniel about a mysterious extension of this period that nearly every commentator regards as literal: "And from the time that the regular burnt offering is taken away and the abomination that makes desolate is set up, there shall be 1,290 days. Blessed is he who waits and arrives at the 1,335 days" (Dan. 12:11-12; cf. Dan. 8:14). A symbolic interpretation hardly suits the precision of the specific designations 1,260 days, 1,290 days, and 1,335 days. The specificity of these numbers demonstrates the literalness of the intended meaning.

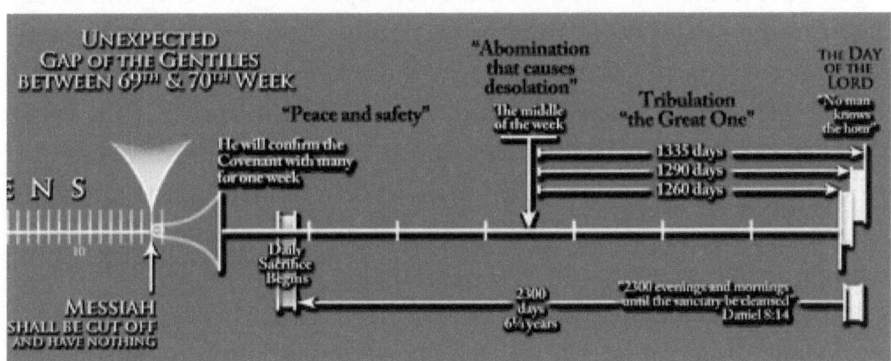

No preterist proposal for the abomination of desolation fits the prophetic timeline of events as found in the books of Daniel and Revelation. Preterists often point out that the First Jewish-Roman War broke out approximately forty-two months before Jerusalem's destruction,[20] and many preterists begin their calculation with Emperor Nero's commission of Vespasian to squash the Jewish rebellion in the winter of AD 66-67. Gentry supposes that this calculation of forty-two months should begin with the time that Rome began "to get into a position to

---

19   Gentry, *Before Jerusalem Fell*, 253; Russell, 429, 453.

20   Gentry, *Before Jerusalem Fell*, 250, 252; Hanegraaff, 61; Russell, 429, 453.

destroy the Temple."²¹ Nevertheless, it took Vespasian's legions months to arrive in Palestine (February/March AD 67), and their first assault on Jerusalem began several months later. The holy temple was not destroyed until July or August AD 70. None of these events in Judea and Jerusalem occurred early enough to allow for forty-two months, and no other proposed actions of Nero, Vespasian, or Titus in "the holy place" (cf. Matt. 24:15) allows for a period of at least forty-two months.

As demonstrated in a previous chapter, the forty-two months of unprecedented tribulation will begin when the residents of Judea see "the abomination of desolation . . . standing in the holy place" of the Jerusalem temple, as foretold by the prophet Daniel (Matt. 24:15). As argued previously, all four Danielic references to this end-time event describe the self-exalting ruler as forcefully removing the daily sacrifice and erecting the abomination in the temple sanctuary (Dan. 8:11; 9:27; 11:31; 12:11). Consistent with this motif, the apostle Paul wrote about the Man of Lawlessness who "takes his seat in the temple of God, proclaiming himself to be God," prior to being killed by the returning Christ (2 Thess. 2:1-10; cf. Dan. 11:36-37), and the apostle John foresaw that the temple's outer court will be trampled underfoot by the Gentiles for forty-two months (Rev. 11:2).

Many preterists recognize that the abomination must include the desecration of the holy temple, so they argue that these prophecies must refer to the invasion of the temple by the Zealots and Idumeans.²² This invasion took place in the early winter of AD 68 which is much too late to allow for a period of forty-two months prior to the destruction of Jerusalem in AD 70. In addition, this interpretation does not adequately account for the role of an individual who is variously called a former "little horn" (Dan. 8:9-11), the prince (Dan. 9:26), the king (Dan. 11:36), and the Man of Lawlessness (2 Thess. 2:3). No first-century individual proudly exalted himself above all gods and sat in the

---

[21] Gentry, *Before Jerusalem Fell*, 250, 252-53.

[22] Russell, 427.

temple, only to be killed by the Son of Man at His glorious appearance (2 Thess. 2:1-10; cf. Isa. 11:4 LXX; Dan. 7:11; 11:36; Rev. 19:20-21). As well, they speculate that this event must have occurred during the First Jewish-Roman War, but the historian Josephus recorded that the perpetual daily sacrifice—the tamid offering—continued to be offered in the Jerusalem temple until the summer of AD 70.[23] This removal of the daily sacrifice took place only one or two months before the temple was destroyed, thus not permitting the full forty-two months required by the biblical prophecies.

SEVEN HEADS AND TEN HORNS

Many of the same difficulties plague the preterist interpretation of the seven heads and ten horns of the Beast. The larger passage reads as follows:

> Why do you marvel? I will tell you the mystery of the woman, and of the beast with seven heads and ten horns that carries her. The beast that you saw was, and is not, and is about to rise from the bottomless pit and go to destruction. And the dwellers on earth whose names have not been written in the book of life from the foundation of the world will marvel to see the beast, because it was and is not and is to come. This calls for a mind with wisdom: the seven heads are seven mountains on which the woman is seated; they are also seven kings, five of whom have fallen, one is, the other has not yet come, and when he does come he must remain only a little while. As for the beast that was and is not, it is an eighth but it belongs to the seven, and it goes to destruction. (Rev. 17:7-11)

Almost universally, preterists identify the seven mountains of this passage as Rome, the City of Seven Hills,[24] and classify the seven kings

---

23 Josephus, *War of the Jews* 6.2.1; 6.94.

24 Chilton, *Paradise Restored*, 188; Gentry, *Before Jerusalem Fell*, 149; Gentry, *The Book of Revelation*, 59; Hanegraaff, 113; Sproul, 159; Contra Jordan, loc. 535.

as consecutive Caesars of the Roman Empire.[25] Many preterists offer the explanation that the fatal head wound refers to Nero's suicide in AD 68 that effectively ended the Julio-Claudian dynasty and the healing of the wound as Vespasian's rise to power to "resurrect" the destabilized Empire (cf. Rev. 13:3, 12-15; 17:8).[26] Some view the eighth king as Emperor Otho who was thought by some contemporaries to be the revived Nero,[27] a theory consistent with the Nero Redivivus myth.[28] Nevertheless, Otho had a relatively uneventful and short-lived reign. He did not persecute Christians in the manner of Nero, and he died long before the destruction of Jerusalem. Chilton, along with some other preterists, have avoided the problems with this theory by suggesting the unlikely notion that the Roman Empire was fatally wounded with "the sword of the gospel."[29] Kik posits the idea that the healed head wound refers to the supposed death of the Roman Empire in AD 476 and its "revival" under Charlemagne, the Holy Roman Emperor, in AD 800.[30]

Kistemaker summarizes the chronological problems with preterist attempts to identify the eight kings of the Beast as the first eight Roman Caesars (cf. Rev. 17:11):

> Although Julius Caesar was the first emperor, he is not part of New Testament history. If we begin with Augustus (Luke 2:1), then Nero is number five on the list. But where do we place Galba, Otho, and Vitellius? Are they excluded because of their short-lived reigns? And if we eliminate them, is Vespasian number six, Titus seven, and Domitian eight? There are at least nine different ways of counting these Roman emperors, and a lack of consensus is evident. It is

---

[25] Chilton, *Paradise Restored*, 188; Hanegraaff, 114.

[26] Gentry, *Before Jerusalem Fell*, 144; Gentry, *The Book of Revelation Made Easy*, 71; Hanegraaff, 149-50.

[27] Gentry, *Before Jerusalem Fell*, 308; Gentry, *The Book of Revelation Made Easy*, 71.

[28] Gentry, *Before Jerusalem Fell*, Chapter 18.

[29] Chilton, *Paradise Restored*, 178.

[30] Kik, 250.

impossible to declare with any degree of certainty that John had in mind either Nero or Vespasian as the ruling king when Revelation was composed.[31]

Gentry, like many preterists, begins his count of the emperors with Julius Caesar and claims that Galba, Otho, and Vitellius are the three kings subdued by the little horn of Daniel (cf. Dan. 7:8, 20, 24).[32] He then critiques the common preterist explanation for omitting these three emperors from the count:

> To find the objectors citing Suetonius as evidence that the three emperors of Rome's Civil War were not really considered emperors is somewhat surprising. After all, Suetonius does include them in his book *Lives of the Twelve Caesars*! Furthermore, these three are considered emperors by Tacitus, Josephus, Sibylline Oracles, and 4 Ezra, as well.[33]

Gentry posits that the apostle John deliberately skipped Otho and Vitellius (but not Galba!) in his enumerated list of eight kings (cf. Rev. 17:10-11). He reasons that the indefinite article (*"an* eighth" Rev. 17:11) appears to show that Vespasian was not the immediate successor of Galba but simply reigned sometime after Galba's reign. He claims that Vespasian "is not in the specified enumeration, but possesses the quality of an eighth, a resurrection."[34] The careful reader must wonder if Gentry has an ulterior motive for regarding Galba as the seventh king instead of skipping him, as he does the other two deposed kings. This motive is seen in his admission that the seventh king would reign for "only a little while" (Rev. 17:10) and therefore could not refer to Vespasian, who

---

[31] Kistemaker as quoted in Mathison, 231.

[32] Gentry, *Before Jerusalem Fell*, 157.

[33] Gentry, *Before Jerusalem Fell*, 161.

[34] Gentry, *Before Jerusalem Fell*, xxx, xxxi.

reigned as emperor for more than a decade.[35] In fact, Vespasian's reign continued nine years beyond the destruction of Jerusalem.

Another significant difficulty for preterists is identifying the ten horns or kings of the Beast. The pertinent prophecy reads as follows:

> And the ten horns that you saw are ten kings who have not yet received royal power, but they are to receive authority as kings for one hour, together with the beast. These are of one mind, and they hand over their power and authority to the beast. They will make war on the Lamb, and the Lamb will conquer them, for he is Lord of lords and King of kings, and those with him are called and chosen and faithful. (Rev. 17:12-14).

Russell correctly recognized that the ten kings must rule contemporaneously in the future ("who have not yet received royal power, but they are to receive authority as kings for one hour, together with the beast" Rev. 17:12).[36] Consequently, he rejected the common preterist notion that these kings were from the Herodian Dynasty, rulers who reigned over Judea from 47 BC to 100 AD, with only Agrippa II reigning during the First Jewish-Roman War.[37] He favored the view that the ten kings were the Roman procurators of Judea during the periods of Claudius and Nero.[38] Similarly, DeMar has suggested that they refer to monarchs who ruled Rome's first-century imperial provinces.[39] However, these suggestions fail to account for the fact that *more than twenty* provinces existed at the outbreak of the war. This means that preterists must omit most of the provincial governors to make the data fit their theory regarding the ten kings of the Beast.

---

[35] Gentry, *Before Jerusalem Fell,* 161.

[36] Russell, 500, 502.

[37] Jordan, loc. 535.

[38] Russell, 500.

[39] DeMar, *Last Days' Madness,* 370, 372.

THE MAN OF LAWLESSNESS

As preterists divorce the resurrection of the righteous from the cosmic darkness of the day of the Lord, the glorious coming of the Son of Man, and the angelic gathering of the elect in the Olivet Discourse (Matt. 24:29-31; Mark 13:24-27; Luke 21:26-27), they attempt the same estrangement with 2 Thessalonians 1-2. The latter passage reads as follows:

> Now concerning the coming of our Lord Jesus Christ and our being gathered together to him, we ask you, brothers, not to be quickly shaken in mind or alarmed, either by a spirit or a spoken word, or a letter seeming to be from us, to the effect that the day of the Lord has come [lit. "is at hand"]. Let no one deceive you in any way. For that day will not come, unless the rebellion comes first, and the man of lawlessness is revealed, the son of destruction, who opposes and exalts himself against every so-called god or object of worship, so that he takes his seat in the temple of God, proclaiming himself to be God. Do you not remember that when I was still with you I told you these things? And you know what is restraining him now so that he may be revealed in his time. For the mystery of lawlessness is already at work. Only he who now restrains it will do so until he is out of the way. And then the lawless one will be revealed, whom the Lord Jesus will kill with the breath of his mouth and bring to nothing by the appearance of his coming. The coming of the lawless one is by the activity of Satan with all power and false signs and wonders, and with all wicked deception for those who are perishing, because they refused to love the truth and so be saved. Therefore, God sends them a strong delusion, so that they may believe what is false, in order that all may be condemned who did not believe the truth but had pleasure in unrighteousness. (2 Thess. 2:1-12)

Preterists attack the traditional interpretation of this passage in various ways. For example, DeMar declares, "There is no doubt that Jesus' 'coming' in 2 Thessalonians 2:1 should be attributed to the first century since the time indicators ('has come,' 'now,' 'already') leave no room in this passage for a coming in the distant future."⁴⁰ DeMar fails to understand that the apostle Paul used the term "at hand" to warn the Thessalonian saints that they should reject the faulty notion that the day of the Lord was imminent and without preceding signs (2 Thess. 2:2). In addition, most futurists view "the restrainer" as an archangel or spirit who prevented this man from being revealed in the first century (2 Thess. 2:6-7). Traditional interpreters agree with DeMar that this "mystery of iniquity" was already working among the disobedient when Paul wrote his letter (2 Thess. 2:6-7; cf. 1 Tim. 3:16; 1 John 4:3). However, many futurists also maintain that the restrainer will prevent the incarnation of Satan—the Antichrist—until "his [appointed] time" (2 Thess. 2:6), that is, when Michael the archangel casts the devil out of heaven forty-two months before Christ's return (Rev. 12:6, 9-17).

The Man of Lawlessness would arrive with "the activity of Satan with *all* power and false signs and wonders, and with *all* wicked deception" (2 Thess. 2:9-10). Clearly then, not just any antichrist figure is in view, but one who will arrive with the full deceptive power of Satan—*the* Antichrist—the individual seed of the serpent (Gen. 3:15; Rev. 12:9; 13:3). Regardless of the identity of the restrainer, no first-century figure meets this description of the wicked one.

DeMar also claims that "the coming of our Lord Jesus Christ and our being gathered together to him" (2 Thess. 2:1) cannot refer to the rapture because "gathered together"⁴¹ is not the same Greek word that the apostle used for the rapture in 1 Thessalonians 4.⁴² However, it is closely related to the verb translated "will gather" that Jesus employed in the Olivet Discourse, a verse about His return and the angelic gathering of the righteous at the resurrection (Matt. 24:31), as I demonstrated

---

40   DeMar, *Last Days' Madness*, 277, 278.

41   The Greek word is *episunagōgḗs* (ἐπισυναγωγῆς).

42   DeMar, *Last Days' Madness*, 277-78.

previously.[43] The most satisfying option is to understand both Thessalonian chapters as connected thematically, especially given the fact that the apostle used the introductory formula "now concerning" (2 Thess. 2:1) that he often used to alert the reader that he was expounding on previous teachings (e.g., 1 Cor. 7:1, 25; 8:1; 12:1; 16:1, 12).

Due to their close proximity and thematic relationship between 2 Thessalonians 1 and 2, preterists predictably deny that the first chapter is about the return of Christ. This passage reads as follows:

> This is evidence of the righteous judgment of God, that you may be considered worthy of the kingdom of God, for which you are also suffering—since indeed God considers it just to repay with affliction those who afflict you, and to grant relief to you who are afflicted as well as to us, when the Lord Jesus is revealed from heaven with his mighty angels in flaming fire, inflicting vengeance on those who do not know God and on those who do not obey the gospel of our Lord Jesus. They will suffer the punishment of eternal destruction, away from the presence of the Lord and from the glory of his might, when he comes on that day to be glorified in his saints, and to be marveled at among all who have believed, because our testimony to you was believed. (2 Thess. 1:5-10)

Chilton argued that the revealing and coming of Jesus Christ in this passage cannot refer to His return because those who had been persecuting the Thessalonian saints were to be the recipients of God's retributive wrath at that time.[44] This position is also taken by other preterists, but it is an unnecessary contrivance because the righteous dead are often described as patiently waiting until they receive vindication and their persecutors receive condemnation (e.g., Rev. 6:9-11; 14:13). Consequently, these prophetic events do not require the persecuted saints to remain alive until the time of their vindication.

Russell pointed out the striking parallels between the Beast in the Apocalypse and the Man of Lawlessness in 2 Thessalonians 2 to demon-

---

43 The Greek verb is *episunagó* (ἐπισυνάγω).

44 Chilton, *Paradise Restored*, 120.

strate beyond reasonable doubt that they are one and the same man. However, he did not hesitate to argue that Nero, whom he believed was the Beast, was also the Man of Lawlessness. Those who take this approach typically see Emperor Claudius as the restrainer of 2 Thessalonians 2, whose reign temporarily prevented Nero from obtaining the throne.[45] As DeMar correctly points out, this interpretation contains an obvious error, since Nero "never sat in the temple" as the prophecy requires (2 Thess. 2:4).[46] Chilton simply glossed over this requirement and implied that Nero took his seat in *pagan* temples![47] Gentry interprets the phrase figuratively and quotes Scullard:

> [A] statue [of Julius Caesar] was placed in the temple of Quirinius (deified Romulus), another near those of the kings of Rome, and yet another showed him with a globe beneath his feet; his chariot was set up opposite the temple of Juppiter [sic]. As a *triumphator* he was granted the right to a gilded chair.[48]

These interpretive options are illegitimate because several eschatological prophecies connect the evil ruler with bringing desolation upon the temple in Jerusalem (Dan. 8:11-14; 9:27; 11:31; 12:11; Matt. 24:15-21; Mark 13:14-19; Luke 21:20-24; cf. Rev. 11:2).

The inherent weaknesses of the aforementioned arguments have led many preterists to propose alternative candidates for the Man of Lawlessness. DeMar claims, "There are at least three possible first-century, pre-A.D. 70 candidates: a political figure (Nero or a representative of the Roman government), a religious figure (Phannias or another member of the priesthood), or a zealot (John Levi Gischala)."[49] This list is speculative at best, a mere "grasping at straws." DeMar later suggests Titus as

---

[45] Russell, 182, 505.

[46] DeMar, *Last Days' Madness*, 291.

[47] Chilton, *Paradise Restored*, 177.

[48] Scullard as quoted in Gentry, *Before Jerusalem Fell*, 265.

[49] DeMar, *Last Days' Madness*, 290; Similarly, Jordan, loc. 341.

a candidate, an interpretation that is slightly more appealing because he entered the Jerusalem temple in AD 70.[50] DeMar even considers the possibility that the Man of Lawlessness was the office of the high priests who served in the temple during the period between Christ's atoning death and the destruction of Jerusalem in AD 70. He explains that the high priests are good candidates because they

> offered "strange" sacrifices that violated the provisions of the New Covenant that is now defined by Jesus' blood and no longer by the blood of "bulls and goats" (Hebrews 10:4). The sin of the high priest was akin to that of Nadab and Abihu. He was the man of lawlessness as defined by the provisions of the New Covenant.[51]

The reader is left to wonder if DeMar understands that these sacrifices were already being made when Saint Paul penned the Thessalonian letters. His suggestion undermines the apostle's entire argument, namely, that the day of the Lord cannot arrive until this Man of Lawlessness has been revealed.

The Man of Lawlessness must take his seat in the Jerusalem temple (2 Thess. 2:4) and remove the daily sacrifice (Dan. 8:11-14; 9:27; 11:31; 12:11; cf. Matt. 24:15). This is the strength of one of DeMar's candidates, as he notes, "John Bray offers another first-century candidate . . . John Levi of Gischala. . . And he was the cause of the ceasing of the daily sacrifices three-and-one-half years after Vespasian came against the city."[52] The primary weakness with this approach is that John of Gischala was not killed at "the appearance of his [Jesus'] coming" (2 Thess. 2:8; cf. Rev. 19:17-20), an event that most preterists believe occurred in AD 70. This weakness plagues many preterist theories about the Man of Lawlessness and the Beast of the Apocalypse.

---

50   DeMar, *Last Days' Madness*, 291.

51   DeMar, *Last Days' Madness*, 299; cf. pp. 301-02.

52   DeMar, *Last Days' Madness*, 302.

TABLE 5: COMMON ELEMENTS OF THE MAN OF SIN AND THE BEAST

The Man of Sin in 2 Thessalonians 2	The Beast in the Book of Revelation
the son of destruction (v. 3)	and go to destruction (Rev. 17:8) it goes to destruction (Rev. 17:11)
who opposes and exalts himself against every so-called god or object of worship, so that he takes his seat in the temple of God, proclaiming himself to be God. (v. 4)	they worshipped the beast . . . And the beast was given a mouth uttering haughty and blasphemous words, and it was allowed to exercise authority for forty-two months. It opened its mouth to utter blasphemies against God, blaspheming his name and his dwelling . . . and all who dwell on earth will worship it (Rev. 13:4, 5-6, 8; cf. Rev. 11:1-3)
the mystery of lawlessness is already at work. (v. 7)	the mystery . . . of the beast (Rev. 17:7)
And then the lawless one will be revealed, whom the Lord Jesus will kill with the breath of his mouth and bring to nothing by the appearance of his coming. The coming of the lawless one is by the activity of Satan with all power and false signs and wonders, (vv. 8-9)	From his mouth comes a sharp sword with which to strike down the nations . . . And the beast was captured, and with it the false prophet who in its presence had done the signs by which he deceived . . . These two were thrown alive into the lake of fire that burns with sulfur. And the rest were slain by the sword that came from the mouth of him who was sitting on the horse . . . (Rev. 19:15, 20, 20-21; cf. Rev. 17:14)

and with all wicked deception for those who are perishing, because they refused to love the truth and so be saved. Therefore God sends them a strong delusion, so that they may believe what is false, (vv. 10-11)	And to it the dragon gave his power . . . It performs great signs, even making fire come down from heaven to earth in front of people, and by the signs that it was allowed to work in the presence of the beast it deceives those who dwell on the earth (Rev. 13:2, 13-14)
in order that all may be condemned who did not believe the truth but had pleasure in unrighteousness. (v. 12)	If anyone worships the beast and its image and receives a mark . . . he also will drink the wine of God's wrath, poured full strength into the cup of his anger, and he will be tormented with fire and sulfur in the presence of the holy angels and in the presence of the Lamb. (Rev. 14:9-10)

In addition, DeMar, like other preterists who do not identify Nero as the Man of Lawlessness, struggles to identify "the restrainer" (2 Thess. 2:6-7). DeMar wonders if the restrainer could be the Roman government, specifically Herod Agrippa, who served as a civil restrainer of Jewish persecution against Christians. He also suggests that the "strong delusion" (2 Thess. 2:11-12) refers to the enticement for the first-century Jewish kingdom to revolt against Rome.[53] DeMar ultimately admits that the restrainer is a "mystery" and warns that he can "only offer an educated guess" because "we may never know who Paul had in mind.[54]

---

[53] DeMar, *Last Days' Madness*, 304, 305-06, 308.

[54] DeMar, *Last Days' Madness*, 303.

THE ANTICHRIST

A common preterist objection to traditional, futurist eschatology is that the solitary figure of the Antichrist is not found in the Olivet Discourse or the book of Revelation. For example, Chilton taught that "the term *antichrist* is used in a very specific sense, and is essentially unrelated to the figure known as 'the Beast' and '666'. . . . The term *antichrist*, therefore, cannot be simply a designation of one individual."[55] Russell also denied that the Antichrist refers to a solitary individual.[56] DeMar makes a similar claim with the added statement that the epistles of John (1 John 2:18-27; 4:3-5; 2 John 1:7) corrected a rumor that the early Church had accepted, specifically, that one man would arise as *the* Antichrist.[57]

In contrast to DeMar's claim, the apostle John did not deny the doctrine of a final wicked ruler—the Antichrist—but he affirmed that *additional* antichrists would also appear (1 John 2:18, 22; 4:3; 2 John 7; cf. Matt. 24:24-26). Furthermore, John's individual Beast and Paul's Man of Lawlessness will display antichristian qualities in an unprecedented manner; this establishes the biblical precedent for expecting the individual whom the holy Church fathers called "the Antichrist." Finally, the immediate context of John's teaching above shows that when Jesus "appears," those who have avoided the deception of these antichrists will "have confidence and not shrink from him in shame at his coming" (1 John 2:28; cf. 1 John 3:2; 4:17). This "appearance" is the bodily return of Christ, a fact demonstrated by John's use of this particular Greek word, often translated "appear" or "manifested," which occurs elsewhere throughout the epistle with clear reference to Christ's *bodily* presence (1

---

55 Chilton, *Paradise Restored*, 109-10; cf. DeMar, *Last Days' Madness*, 103, 267, 269.

56 Russell, 333.

57 DeMar, *Last Days' Madness*, 267, 269.

John 1:2; 3:5, 8; 4:9).[58] This is the glorious arrival of Jesus Christ, when, at the resurrection of the last day, "we shall be like him, because we shall see him as he is" (1 John 3:2).

The holy Church has always held a firm conviction in a future revelation of the personal Antichrist, specifically, forty-two months before the glorious return of Jesus Christ. Also, the Church fathers equated the Beast, the Man of Lawlessness, and the Antichrist, teaching that this man will be destroyed by the returning Christ. For example, Justin Martyr (c. AD 160) wrote that Jesus will return from heaven when this "man of apostasy" speaks blasphemies "against the Most High" and persecutes Christians.[59]

Similarly, Saint Irenaeus of Lyons (c. AD 180) believed that the Antichrist should be equated with the "lawless one" and "the son of perdition" who will seek "to be worshipped as God" (cf. 2 Thess. 2:3-4). According to Irenaeus, this wicked man will be "endowed with all of the power of the devil" and will arise from a ten-nation confederacy to "reign over the earth for three years and six months" and to "sit in the temple at Jerusalem" until the Lord returns from heaven in clouds.[60] Irenaeus saw at least the final half of the last "week" of the Prophecy of the Seventy Weeks as referring to the final years prior to Christ's return (Dan. 9:27).

Saint Hippolytus of Rome (c. AD 200) taught that the *entirety* of the final seven years of this prophecy of Daniel refers to "the last week that is to be at the end of the whole world."[61] He also identified the Beast as the future Antichrist who will seek to be worshipped as God.[62] Hippolytus believed that the Antichrist would reign for "a time, times,

---

58 The Greek word is *phanerōthē* (φανερωθῇ).

59 Justin Martyr 1.253, 254 in Bercot, *A Dictionary of Early Christian Beliefs*.

60 Irenaeus 1.553, 1.554, 1.560 in Bercot, *A Dictionary of Early Christian Beliefs*.

61 Hippolytus 5.213 in Bercot, *A Dictionary of Early Christian Beliefs*.

62 Hippolytus 5.214, 5.215 in Bercot, *A Dictionary of Early Christian Beliefs*.

and a half," which he explained means three and a half years, and that he would rebuild Jerusalem and "restore the [temple] sanctuary" while "exalting himself above all kings and above every god."⁶³ He also taught that the Antichrist will reveal the abomination of desolation and remove "sacrifice and oblation" in the middle of the final seven years.⁶⁴

Additionally, Tertullian (c. AD 210) taught that the resurrection of the dead would occur immediately after "the destruction of the Antichrist."⁶⁵ Origen (c. AD 248) referenced Daniel 11:31 to teach that the Antichrist would establish the abomination of desolation at the temple so that he "sits in the temple of God, showing himself that he is God" (cf. 2 Thess. 2:4).⁶⁶ Finally, Cyprian, Victorinus, and Lactantius (c. AD 250-280) agreed that the future Antichrist will persecute God's holy people. Victorinus believed that 666 referred to the name of the Antichrist. Lactantius taught that Christ will return to destroy the Antichrist, who will be the wicked man requiring worship of himself, calling himself God, and performing demonic signs and wonders. He explained that the Antichrist will also attempt to destroy the temple of God and persecute the righteous during the forty-two months of "distress and tribulation, such as there never has been from the beginning of the world" (Matt. 24:21).⁶⁷

The Holy Scriptures and the consensus of the holy Church fathers harmonize to teach the future revelation of the final, individual Antichrist. These witnesses demonstrate that the Antichrist is the Beast, the Man of Lawlessness, and the one identified by 666. Applying the term "Antichrist" to this individual appropriately summarizes his character

---

63   Hippolytus 5.190, 5.184 in Bercot, *A Dictionary of Early Christian Beliefs*.

64   Hippolytus 5.182 in Bercot, *A Dictionary of Early Christian Beliefs*.

65   Tertullian 3.565 in Bercot, *A Dictionary of Early Christian Beliefs*.

66   Origen 4.593-94 in Bercot, *A Dictionary of Early Christian Beliefs*.

67   Cyprian 5.346, 349, 556; Victorinus 7.456; Lactantius 4.593-95; 5:204-19; 7.215 in Bercot, *A Dictionary of Early Christian Beliefs*.

and corroborates the clear teaching of the Bible and the testimony of the fathers. In addition, the tradition of the fathers provides evidence of a future restored Jerusalem and Third Temple, which will be made desolate by the Antichrist. This evidence argues strongly against various preterist theories that certain first-century individuals were the Antichrist or that these prophetic events were fulfilled in the period of the Second Temple.

12

NO TRANSITION TO THE DISTANT FUTURE

AT MATTHEW 24:36

MANY PARTIAL PRETERISTS SEE A BREAK in the Olivet Discourse, beginning with Matthew 24:36 (cf. Mark 13:32), that marks a shift from first-century events to events in our future.[1] This verse reads, "But concerning that day and hour no one knows, not even the angels of heaven, nor the Son, but the Father only." Preterist J. Marcellus Kik explains that the earlier portion of the discourse is about "the subject of the destruction of Jerusalem, or his [Christ's] judgment against the Jewish nation," while the latter portion relates to events of His "second coming at the end of the age when he would judge the world."[2] This

---

1   Kik, 158; Similarly, R. T. France, Kenneth Gentry, and Alistair I. Wilson.

2   Kik, 69; cf. pp. 60, 67.

approach is appealing because it seeks to find linguistic and syntactical evidence for dividing the discourse. However, it crumbles upon critical examination.

France, the foremost champion of this position, posits five exegetical reasons for dividing the Olivet Discourse in the aforementioned manner:[3] First, the proposed transition verse begins with "but about" (Matt. 24:36), a phrase that Christ used earlier in Matthew's gospel to denote a subject change (cf. Matt. 22:31).[4] The apostle Paul employed this phrase as a rhetorical formula to change subjects. Second, Jesus suddenly shifts from describing the plural time indicator "those days" (Matt. 24:19, 22, 29) to the singular "that day and hour" (Matt. 24:42, 44, 50; 25:13). Third, the timing of the events described prior to the supposed transition verse can be discovered based on signs (Matt. 24:15, 34), whereas the timing of Christ's return is "unknown and unknowable" and occurs "without prior warning." Fourth, prior to the transition verse, Jesus employed a specific participle to predict His coming as the Son of Man, as described in Daniel's vision (Dan. 7:13-14), whereas after this verse, He used a different participle, also translated "coming," to speak of His future return (Matt. 24:37, 39); the latter does not reflect any elements from Daniel's vision.[5] Fifth, the verses prior to the transition verse contain temporal indicators, whereas later verses do not.

THE MEANING OF "BUT CONCERNING"

We will now examine each of France's arguments in detail. His first contention that the Greek phrase translated "but about," variously "now concerning," always introduces a new topic is verifiably false.[6] Outside

---

[3] France, *The Gospel of Matthew*, 340-41, 936-38.

[4] The Greek phrase is *peri de* (περὶ δὲ).

[5] The Greek words are *erkhómenos* (ἐρχόμενον) and *parousia* (παρουσία).

[6] The Greek phrase is *peri de* (περὶ δὲ).

of Pauline literature, the biblical writers *never* used this phrase to introduce a new topic.[7] Rather, the phrase typically has a resumptive force: it emphasizes the fact that the speaker is returning to a point that he presented previously.[8]

In Matthew's Gospel, this phrase is *always* resumptive and *never* introduces a new subject. It first appears in Christ's parable of the workers of the vineyard (Matt. 20:1-16), which is about a "master of the house" who hired workers to tend his vineyard at various hours of the day (Matt. 20:2-6). The phrase concludes an unbroken series of chronological events and functions to emphasize that the master hired certain workers at the end of the day and scandalously paid them the same amount as the other workers (Matt. 20:6, 12).

The phrase also appears two chapters later (Matt. 22:30; Mark 12:26), and it functions to transition from a particular statement about certain individuals receiving resurrection (Matt. 22:29-30; Mark 12:24-25) to a general statement about the resurrection (Matt. 22:31-32; Mark 12:26); but more to the point, the same eschatological theme occurs before and after the phrase.

The expression appears again near the end of Matthew's Gospel (Matt. 27:46). The author explained that the sky was darkened from the sixth hour to the ninth hour during Christ's crucifixion, and he included the phrase to highlight the final hour (Matt. 27:45-46). Once again, the same subject appears before and after the expression, and it functions to consummate an uninterrupted sequence of actions.

Gentry surmises that Christ's phrase "but concerning" in the Olivet Discourse (Matt. 24:36) is resumptive and that He used it to cue the disciples that He was starting to answer their question in verse

---

[7] E.g., Acts 21:25; 1 Cor. 7:1, 25; 8:1; 12:1; 16:1, 12; 1 Thess. 4:9; 5:1. Paul employed the phrase throughout 1 Corinthians, and possibly in Acts 21:25 and 1 Thessalonians 4:9, as a literary device that functions to introduce a new topic.

[8] Gen. 15:12; 17:20 41:32 (LXX); Matt. 20:6; 22:30; 27:46; Mark 12:26; John 16:11.

three about "the sign of your coming and of the end of the age?"[9] This argument is problematic because the Lord had already begun answering this question in the preceding verses (Matt. 24:27-35). Furthermore, the argument creates an artificial distinction between the end of the age (Matt. 24:3) and the period of the destruction of Jerusalem and its temple. Although Gentry interprets "the end" in verse six as referring to the destruction of the temple, he fails to recognize that its antecedent is "the end of the age" in verse three. In addition, the Septuagint of the book of Daniel employs the same Greek noun to refer to "the end," the period of the unprecedented tribulation and resurrection of the dead (Dan. 12:1-13 LXX).

"THOSE DAYS" AND "THE DAY"

France again overplays his hand with his second proposal that a subject change occurs beginning with the proposed transition verse, as evidenced by the switch from the plural "those days" to the singular "the day" and "the hour." This red herring becomes apparent upon close examination of the analogy that follows this verse (Matt. 24:37-39). There Jesus compared the flood in Noah's day with the day of His return: "For as were the days of Noah, so will be the coming of the Son of Man" (Matt. 24:37; cf. Luke 17:26; Isa. 54:9). The period of "those days" of Noah were characterized by an unsuspecting populace who engaged in normal daily activities until "the day" when he and his family entered the ark and the flood came upon the remainder of the world (Matt. 24:38). The period of "those days" were contiguous with and culminated in "the day" that the flood arrived. The force of this statement is easily overlooked, but it is prima facie evidence that no gap will separate "those days" of the unprecedented tribulation from "the day" of Christ's return. In addition, "those days" of Noah and "the day"

---

[9] Gentry, *The Olivet Discourse Made Easy*, loc. 2480, 2490, chapter eight.

of the flood all transpired in Noah's days, suggesting that those who endure the great tribulation will witness the return of Jesus.

France encounters further difficulties when the evidence from Luke's parallel account is considered. In Luke's Gospel, the analogy of Noah (Luke 17:26-27) is immediately followed by the analogy of Lot (Luke 17:28), both of which contain several of the same elements. The passage reads as follows:

> Likewise, just as it was in the days of Lot—they were eating and drinking, buying and selling, planting and building, but on *the day* when Lot went out from Sodom, fire and sulfur rained from heaven and destroyed them all—so will it be on *the day* when the Son of Man is revealed. On *that day*, let the one who is on the housetop, with his goods in the house, not come down to take them away, and likewise let the one who is in the field not turn back. Remember Lot's wife. (Luke 17:28-32, emphasis added)

Several observations reveal the fallacy of France's argument: The Genesis narrative does not allow for a gap between "the days" of the daily activities of Sodom's people and "the day" that the angels gathered Lot and his family to flee before the fiery destruction. In addition, the fire from heaven burned up the city on "the [very] day" that this righteous man fled, which is analogous to the preservation of the elect and the fiery destruction of the wicked on the day of Christ (2 Pet. 3:7, 10, 12-13; Rev. 18:8-10). Finally, Jesus used "the day" to indicate the day when the Son of Man comes (Luke 17:24, 29), the exact phrase that France correctly maintains must refer to the future return of Jesus Christ. These parallels further demonstrate that "the day" of Christ's return will take place immediately after "those days" of unequaled tribulation (cf. Matt. 24:29-30). The Olivet Discourse simply does not allow for an intervening time gap beginning at this verse (Matt. 24:36; Mark 13:32) or at any other location.

NO TRANSITION TO THE DISTANT FUTURE

"THOSE DAYS" AND "THE DAY" BASED ON THE ANALOGIES OF LOT AND NOAH

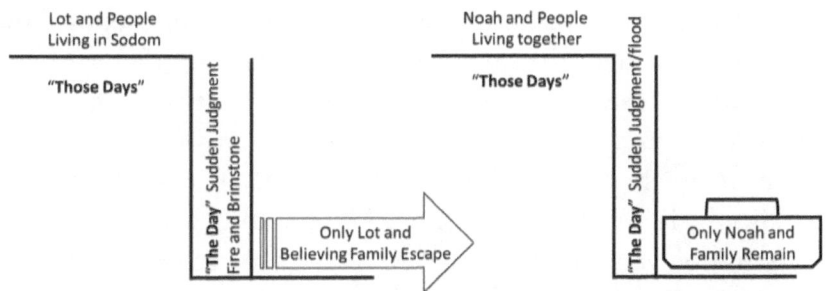

France's third and fifth reasons for dividing the Olivet Discourse contend that the timing of the events described before the proposed transition verse can be predicted by signs and time indicators, whereas the timing of the return of Jesus cannot be predicted. This is a non sequitur for at least two reasons: First, the signs in the early part of the prophecy will herald the *beginning* of the labor pains of tribulation (Matt. 24:4-14); however, the sign of the abomination of desolation will signal the arrival of the unprecedented tribulation (Matt. 24:15-29), the tribulation which will prove that Christ's coming is "near, at the very gates" (Matt. 24:33). The necessity of paying attention to this specific sign proves that the *precise* timing, the exact "day and hour" of His return, is unknown (Matt. 24:36). Second, the statement "that day and hour no one knows" (Matt. 24:36) modifies the previous statement that "this generation" would remain until the end (Matt. 24:34-35). The antecedent for "that day and hour" is undoubtedly the coming of the Son of Man mentioned in the preceding verses (Matt. 24:29-35). Also, the absence of any other referent strongly suggests that Jesus did not switch topics beginning with the proposed transition verse (Matt. 24:36).

DEBUNKING PRETERISM

DIFFERENT WORDS FOR THE LORD'S COMING?

France's fourth reason for dividing the Olivet Prophecy is that the participle translated "coming" that appears prior to the proposed transition verse is different than the participle that appears afterward. This is demonstrably false. The disciples' original question pertained to the sign of Christ's "coming" (Matt. 24:3), and the Lord answered with an explanation about "the coming of the Son of Man" (Matt. 24:27); this answer contains the latter participle "coming" (παρουσία), and it appears *before* the transition verse. In addition, several cognates of the Greek verb "to come" (ερχομαι) also appear *after* the transition verse where the subject is Christ's return (Matt. 24:42-44; 25:6, 19, 31; cf. Mark 13:36), but France attempts to maneuver around this by demanding that the specific participle appears. This hardly suffices, especially since the participial form occurs only once in the entire discourse (Matt. 24:30). Furthermore, the early disciples employed the Greek word parousia (translated "coming") elsewhere to refer to Christ's coming that most preterists teach occurred in AD 70. James used this exact word in his declaration that "the coming of the Lord is at hand" (James 5:7-8), as did Paul when he reminded the Christians in Thessalonica that the Man of Lawlessness would be destroyed at Christ's glorious "coming" (2 Thess. 2:1, 8).

France's claim that the details of Christ's return after the proposed transition verse "do not reflect any elements from Daniel's vision" is also false. To the contrary, the vision of Daniel 7 shares many thematic overlaps with the latter part of the Olivet Discourse: The Son of Man appears in heavenly glory with the angels (Dan. 7:10-14; Matt. 25:31), the Lord sits on the throne as judge (Dan 7:9, 26; Matt. 25:31), the everlasting kingdom is given to all nations (Dan. 7:14, 22, 27; Matt. 25:32, 34, 46), and the wicked are punished by fire (Dan 7:11; Matt. 25:41-46; cf. Ezek. 34:17, 20). A detailed comparison of these similarities was provided previously in this book.

NO TRANSITION TO THE DISTANT FUTURE

GENTRY'S ARGUMENTS FOR DIVISION

Gentry provides additional arguments in favor of dividing the Olivet Prophecy beginning with the proposed transition verse (Matt. 24:36). He contends that the first part of the discourse answers the disciples' first question concerning the timing of "these [prophetic] things," that is, the destruction of the temple (Matt. 24:4-31), while the latter part of the discourse answers the second question about the sign of Christ's return (Matt. 24:36-46).[10] Contrary to Gentry's argument, Jesus' answers highlighted the sign of His return in the verses prior to the proposed transition verse (especially Matt. 24:27-30) and concentrated on the *timing* of His return in the latter part of the discourse. This is further supported by the fact that Mark combined the disciples' final two questions ("Tell us, when will these things be, and what will be the sign when all these things are about to be accomplished?" Mark 13:4), suggesting that they did not ask questions about temporally-separated events but recognized that the destruction of the temple would be chronologically connected with Christ's glorious arrival.

Gentry also argues that Jesus' statement concerning "this generation" serves as a concluding statement (Matt. 24:34):

> Why would such a statement be inserted one-fourth of the way through the discourse if it were dealing in its entirety with events that were to occur in "this generation"? Such would not make sense. That would be like someone giving a speech, and after fifteen minutes saying, "In conclusion," then continuing the speech for another forty-five minutes.[11]

While this verse functions as a kind of concluding statement (Matt. 24:34), this does not indicate that Jesus introduced an *entirely new topic* at the proposed transition verse. One reason for this is that Matthew

---

[10] The Greek word *parousia* (παρουσία); Gentry, *The Olivet Discourse Made Easy*, chapter eight.

[11] Gentry, *The Olivet Discourse Made Easy*, loc. 2460, chapter eight.

combined two different source materials at this point in the Olivet Discourse, which is seen by the fact that this material is divided into two different sections in Luke's Gospel (Luke 17:26-37; 21:25-33). Matthew included the statement about "this generation" here because the latter material explains the timing of Christ's return (Matt 24:36-25:46), a topic that He introduced previously (Matt. 24:27-30).

Gentry argues that temporal progress indicators, such as "then" and "immediately after," do not appear after the transition verse, which suggests that the latter portion of the discourse is not part of the historical sequence of events described in the earlier portion.[12] However, it is more favorable to view the temporal indicators as connecting the specific signs of the great tribulation with Christ's return, followed by *a shift in emphasis,* beginning with the transition verse, to the unknowability of the exact timing of His return. In addition, it is unthinkable that the latter portion of the discourse would lack clear temporal indicators if Christ had intended to temporally disconnect His return from the events described in the preceding material.

OTHER PROBLEMS WITH DIVIDING THE OLIVET DISCOURSE

Many preterists equivocate on the meaning of Jesus' teaching that the wicked will be thrown into the fiery furnace or outer darkness where "there will be weeping and gnashing of teeth" (Matt. 8:12; 13:42, 50; 22:13; 24:51; 25:30; Luke 13:28; cf. Matt. 21:33-43). This phrase appears throughout the Synoptic Gospels in passages that preterists believe predicted the destruction of Jerusalem in AD 70. For example, it appears in Christ's parable of the great banquet, a parable about a king who prepared a wedding for his son (Matt. 22:1-14; cf. Luke 14:16-24). In the parable, the king sent his servants to invite guests to the wedding feast, but those who had been invited abused and killed the servants

---

[12] Gentry, *The Olivet Discourse Made Easy,* loc. 2504, chapter eight.

NO TRANSITION TO THE DISTANT FUTURE

(Matt. 22:3-6). This made the king angry, so he "sent his troops and destroyed those murderers and burned their city" (Matt. 22:7; cf. Matt. 8:12). Preterists interpret this verse as referring to the Roman invasion of Judah and the subsequent burning of Jerusalem's temple in AD 70.[13]

In Matthew's Gospel, Jesus taught that His angels will gather the wicked and cast them into the fiery furnace where "there will be weeping and gnashing of teeth," and He explicitly stated that this event will take place at "the end of the age" (Matt. 13:39-43, 49-50). This is problematic for preterists who insist on dividing the Olivet Prophecy, because they correctly teach that this "end" refers to the future return of Christ and not to AD 70. This problem is highlighted by the fact that the phrase appears twice after the proposed transition verse of the discourse, in the section that these preterists teach refers to the return of Jesus in our future (Matt. 24:51; 25:30; cf. Luke 19:27). It is unlikely that Christ used this same expression to refer to both the temporal destruction of Jerusalem by fire in AD 70 and to the eternal destruction of hellfire at the future day of Christ (cf. Matt. 25:41, 46).

Partial preterists who attempt to divide the Olivet Discourse encounter another significant difficulty. To illustrate, Jesus predicted at least two specific prophetic events that appear in the discourse before the supposed transition verse in Matthew's version *and* in a pericope[14] found in Luke's version (Luke 17:26-37):

> Let the one who is on the housetop not go down to take what is in his house, and let the one who is in the field not turn back to take his cloak. (Matt. 24:17-18; Luke 17:31)

> Wherever the corpse is, there the vultures will gather. (Matt. 24:28; Luke 17:37)

Preterists dig themselves into a hole by arguing that the events described in the early portion of the discourse (Matt. 24:15-35) were

---

[13] E.g., Kik, 77.

[14] Pericopes are distinct extracts or sections of material in the Bible.

fulfilled in the First Jewish-Roman War, while maintaining that the latter portion of the discourse (Matt. 24:36-41), a section of text that shares common source material with Luke's pericope above (Luke 17:26-37), will occur at the future return of Jesus. Preterists who argue that the pericope in Luke was fulfilled in AD 66-70 must also admit that Jesus predicted these same events in a passage that they believe is about our future (Matt. 24:37-41). Both passages include the detailed comparison between "the days of Noah" and "the days of the Son of Man" (Matt. 24:37-39; Luke 17:26-30), as well as the statement "one will be taken and the other left" (Matt. 24:40-42; Luke 17:35-37). On the other hand, those who try to escape this problem by arguing that Luke's passage is about our future must allow for a future Jewish flight from Judea and a banquet for vultures, as futurism maintains.

It is highly unlikely that Jesus used the same descriptions to depict two distinct events, which are separated by thousands of years, without providing clear temporal indications to warrant such an approach. The only real solution is to understand the entire Olivet Discourse, along with Luke's parallel material, as predicting events within one specific time frame. A comparative table of the pertinent texts is presented hereafter.

NO TRANSITION TO THE DISTANT FUTURE

TABLE 6: PARALLELS BETWEEN MATTHEW 24 AND LUKE'S GOSPEL

Matthew 24	Luke 21, 17, 12
Matthew 24:1-14	Luke 21:5-19
24:15 "So when you see the abomination of desolation spoken of by the prophet Daniel, standing in the holy place (let the reader understand),…"	21:20 "But when you see Jerusalem surrounded by armies, then know that its desolation has come near."
24:16 "…then let those who are in Judea flee to the mountains."	21:21 "Then let those who are in Judea flee to the mountains, and let those who are inside the city depart, and let not those who are out in the country enter it,…"
24:17-18 "Let the one who is on the housetop not go down to take what is in his house, and let the one who is in the field not turn back to take his cloak."	*See below for the parallel account.*
24:19-22	21:22-24
24:23, 27	17:22-25
24:28 "Wherever the corpse is, there the vultures will gather."	*See below for the parallel account.*
24:29 "Immediately after the tribulation of those days the sun will be darkened, and the moon will not give its light, and the stars will fall from heaven,…" "…and the powers of the heavens will be shaken."	21:25-26 "And there will be signs in sun and moon and stars, and on the earth distress of nations in perplexity because of the roaring of the sea and the waves, people fainting with fear and with foreboding of what is coming on the world. For the powers of the heavens will be shaken."
24:30 "Then will appear in heaven the sign of the Son of Man, and then all the tribes of the earth will mourn, and they will see the Son of Man coming on the clouds of heaven with power and great glory."	21:27 And then they will see the Son of Man coming in a cloud with power and great glory
24:31-35	21:29-33

Matthew 24	Luke 21, 17, 12
24:36 "But concerning that day and hour no one knows, not even the angels of heaven, nor the Son, but the Father only."	
24:37 "For as were the days of Noah, so will be the coming of the Son of Man."	17:26 "Just as it was in the days of Noah, so will it be in the days of the Son of Man."
24:38 "For as in those days before the flood they were eating and drinking, marrying and giving in marriage, until the day when Noah entered the ark,…"	17:27 "They were eating and drinking and marrying and being given in marriage, until the day when Noah entered the ark,…" and the flood came and destroyed them all
24:39 "…and they were unaware until the flood came and swept them all away, so will be the coming of the Son of Man."	17:30 "…so will it be on the day when the Son of Man is revealed."
See above for the parallel account.	**17:31 "On that day, let the one who is on the housetop, with his goods in the house, not come down to take them away, and likewise let the one who is in the field not turn back…"**
24:40 "Then two men will be in the field; one will be taken and one left."	
24:41 "Two women will be grinding at the mill; one will be taken and one left."	17:35 "There will be two women grinding together. One will be taken and the other left."
See above for the parallel account.	17:37 "And they said to him, 'Where, Lord?' **"He said to them,"** 'Where the corpse is, there the vultures will gather.'
24:42 "Therefore, stay awake, for you do not know on what day your Lord is coming."	
24:43-51	12:39-46

NO TRANSITION TO THE DISTANT FUTURE

As we have seen, the inseparability of the Olivet Discourse is based upon the internal consistency of its contents, the weaknesses of the arguments for dividing it, and the appearance of common source material before and after the proposed transition verse. The late eighteenth-century preterist Nehemiah Nisbett sounded the alarm against those seeking to divide the discourse:

> Some men of great learning and eminence have thought that our Lord is here [Matt. 24:36] speaking, not of the destruction of Jerusalem, but of that more solemn and awful one of the day of judgment. But I can by no means think that the Evangelists are such loose, inaccurate writers, as to make so sudden and abrupt a transition, as they are here supposed to do; much less to break through the fundamental rules of good writing, by apparently referring to something which they had said before; when in reality they were beginning a new subject, and the absurdity of the supposition will appear more strongly, if it is recollected that the question of the disciples was, "When shall these things be?"[15]

---

15 Nehemiah Nisbett, *An Attempt to Illustrate Various Important Passages in the Epistles, &c. of the New Testament: From Our Lord's Prophecies of the Destruction of Jerusalem, and from Some Prophecies of the Old Testament* (London, 1787), 38-39.

13

ALREADY AND NOT YET

THE "ALREADY AND NOT YET" principle is foundational to a proper understanding of New Testament eschatology. The classic example of this principle is called inaugurated eschatology, the doctrine that God's kingdom has been set in motion by Jesus Christ's first advent and will be consummated when He returns. By the energies of Christ and the dynamic activities of the Holy Spirit within the apostolic Church, the future age to come has penetrated "this present evil age" (Gal. 1:4).

George Eldon Ladd correctly described the kingdom of heaven as Christ's reign which people "can and must receive in the present" (e.g., Matt. 6:33; 11:11; 12:28; 21:31; 23:13; Mark 10:15; Luke 11:52; 12:31; 16:16; 17:21), but he also emphasized that this reign will be "eschatologically manifested in the future."[1] He identified different aspects of the kingdom as the providential reigning authority of Jesus (Luke 19:12, 15; 23:42; John 18:36) and the realm of His reign, the latter being further

---

[1] George Eldon Ladd, *The Presence of the Future* (Grand Rapids: Eerdmans, 1974), 138; cf. p. 123.

subdivided into the proleptic present ("already") and future ("not yet") aspects. He demonstrated that Christ equated His future kingdom reign with the age to come (Matt. 8:11; Mark 9:47; 10:23-25; 14:25; Luke 13:28).

The Gospel of John contains several examples of this "already and not yet" phenomenon. For example, the Lord Jesus employed the phrase "the hour is coming and is now here" to highlight this concept (John 4:23; 5:25; 16:32). The phrase "an hour is coming" predicts the eschatological time when the dead will hear His voice and be resurrected, and He taught that the resurrection, in one sense, had already arrived ("and is now here") (John 5:25, 28). Christ maintained the traditional Jewish teaching that the resurrection unto eternal life would occur on the last day (John 6:39-44, 54; cf. Dan. 12:1-3) and that those who trust in Him have already received eternal life (John 3:36; 5:24; 6:40, 47, 54; cf. 1 John 5:11, 13). He explained that He would soon go away to the Father and that His disciples would no longer see Him (John 14:2-3, 12; 16:5, 7, 10, 28; cf. John 16:20-24), but He promised to come to them again "in a little while" (John 16:16-19).

In one sense, Christ's promise to come again was fulfilled when He appeared to the first disciples after His resurrection; however, it also points to His return "in that day," that is, at the day of Christ (John 14:18-20, 23, 28-29; 16:16-19, 20-24). A similar versatility can be seen in Jesus' declaration that His crucifixion was when ("now is") Satan was cast from heaven (John 12:31; 16:11; cf. Luke 10:18); however, the apostle John prophesied that Satan would be cast from heaven at the beginning of the unprecedented tribulation (Rev. 12:4-17). While Christ's crucifixion is the ground and basis for Satan's ultimate downfall, the devil will be cast down to the earth at the beginning of the great tribulation, during which time Christians will "conquer him by the blood of the Lamb and by the word of their testimony, for they loved not their lives even unto death" (Rev. 12:11). Similarly, those who crucified Jesus gazed at His pierced body hanging upon the cross, and John understood this as a fulfillment of Zechariah's prophecy ("They will look on him whom they have pierced" John 19:37; cf. Zech. 12:10). Nevertheless, the exhaustive fulfillment of this prophecy will occur when the surviving inhabitants of Judah and Jerusalem (and all the tribes of the earth!) mourn after they look upon the pierced and risen Savior returning in glory (Zech. 12:10; cf. Matt. 24:30; Rev. 1:7).

Some preterists are open to the likelihood that the New Testament reveals an "already and not yet" pattern of fulfillment. For example, Mathison freely acknowledges such aspects of New Testament eschatology. He identifies this pattern in the present and future aspects of resurrection and in the divine judgment of Satan (John 5:24-26; 12:31). He also correctly teaches that the redemption of individuals is an "already and not yet" aspect of the new creation (2 Cor. 5:17). Also, he cites the Immanuel prophecy of Isaiah as an example of "a prophecy with multiple fulfillments" (Isa. 7:14-16).[2]

Most Christian commentators posit a double fulfillment of the Immanuel prophecy primarily because the apostle Matthew relayed that Christ's virgin birth fulfilled it, coupled with Isaiah's explicit prediction that Damascus and Samaria would be plundered before Immanuel ("God is with us"), the chosen Son, was old enough to distinguish right from wrong (Isa. 7:15-16). For example, the New Testament scholar Craig L. Blomberg commends this interpretation:

> Better than both of these approaches, however, is the concept of double fulfillment. . . Matthew recognized that Isaiah's son fulfilled the dimension of the prophecy that required a child to be born in the immediate future. But the larger, eschatological context especially of Isa. 9:1-7, depicted a son, never clearly distinguished from Isaiah's, who would be a divine, messianic king.[3]

As demonstrated in previous chapters, Gentry embraces an "already and not yet" fulfillment of many biblical prophecies. He teaches that many of the Savior's teachings contain an "eschatological orientation"

---

[2] Mathison, 167, 169, 171, 173-74, 203.

[3] Craig L. Blomberg in Beale and Carson, *The New Testament Use*, 5.

in which proximal events in history prefigure distant, eschatological events.[4] He argues that Christ's teaching that unbelieving Jews will be cast "into outer darkness to endure weeping and gnashing of teeth (Matt 8:12) certainly points to God's ultimate judgment. But it also directly pictures the AD 70 judgment when God horribly judges Israel and removes her temple forever. That judgment is a harbinger of the final judgment itself."[5]

Elsewhere, Gentry speaks about the Master's contemporary audience: "Their prideful boasting will be judged on judgment day at the end of history. But in addition, this [Matt. 23:12] seems also to highlight the approaching AD 70 judgment (which also is eschatological, being a pointer to the final judgment)."[6] He provides insights into this perspective:

> Theologically, a redemptive-historical link does in fact connect AD 70 with the second advent. This could easily confuse the disciples. That is, the AD 70 episode is an anticipatory foreshadowing of the larger event, the second advent. As Carson expresses it: "The near event, the destruction of Jerusalem, serves as a symbol for the far event, i.e., the second coming."[7]

Despite Gentry's admission, many preterists recoil at the notion that the destruction of Jerusalem and its temple in AD 70 functions typologically to point to the much greater eschatological event in the future.

---

[4] Gentry, *The Olivet Discourse Made Easy*, loc. 727-32.

[5] Gentry, *The Olivet Discourse Made Easy*, loc. 360.

[6] Gentry, *The Olivet Discourse Made Easy*, loc. 727-32.

[7] Gentry, *The Olivet Discourse Made Easy*, loc. 1004-09.

DEBUNKING PRETERISM AND THE DAY OF VENGEANCE

Many eschatological passages in the Old Testament do not clearly differentiate between the "already" and "not yet" aspects of Christ's kingdom; this phenomenon is known as the prophetic perspective. However, the mystery of the two advents of Christ was revealed to the holy apostles, and the New Testament assists the reader to identify the portions of the Old Testament prophecies that have been fulfilled and those that will be fulfilled at the end of the age. One classic example of this phenomenon is recorded in the Luke's Gospel (Luke 4:18-21). The passage explains that Jesus opened the scroll of Isaiah the prophet and read the following passage:

> The Spirit of the Lord is upon me, because he has anointed me to proclaim good news to the poor. He has sent me to proclaim liberty to the captives and recovering of sight to the blind, to set at liberty those who are oppressed, to proclaim the year of the Lord's favor." . . . Then he claimed, "Today this Scripture has been fulfilled in your hearing." (Luke 4:18-21)

Notably, Christ quoted the portion of Isaiah's prophecy that He was presently fulfilling (Isa. 61:1-2a), but He stopped midsentence instead of finishing the remaining portion of the prophecy:

> and the day of vengeance of our God; to comfort all who mourn; to grant to those who mourn in Zion—to give them a beautiful headdress instead of ashes, the oil of gladness instead of mourning, the garment of praise instead of a faint spirit; that they may be called oaks of righteousness, the planting of the LORD, that he may be glorified. They shall build up the ancient ruins; they shall raise up the former devastations; they shall repair the ruined cities, the devastations of many generations. (Isa. 61:2b-4)

Christ did not recite the remainder of the prophecy because He intends to fulfill those aspects at the Second Coming. This latter portion of the prophecy is concerned with "the day of vengeance of our God" (Isa. 61:2), also known as the day of the Lord (cf. Isa. 34:8). In the Olivet Discourse, Jesus used a variant of Isaiah's phrase "the day of vengeance" (i.e., "days of vengeance" Luke 21:22). The prophet Isaiah revealed that this solitary day is when God will comfort Zion's mourners so that they find everlasting gladness and rebuild "the ancient ruins . . . the former devastations . . . the ruined cities" of Israel (Isa. 61:2-4; cf. Isa. 58:12; 60:21; Amos 9:14; Zech. 12:10-14; Matt. 5:4). These prophetic events do not match any first-century events but represent the "not yet" of prophetic fulfillment.

THE KING OF THE NORTH

The final vision in the book of Daniel also displays the "already" and the "not yet" of biblical prophecy (Dan. 10-12). Most futurist commentators categorize the various sections of Daniel 11 as follows: the transition from Medio-Persian rule to Macedonian rule under Alexander the Great (Dan. 11:2-3), the Seleucid and Ptolemaic dynasties, with a special emphasis on Antiochus IV Epiphanes (Dan. 11:4-35), and the future Antichrist (Dan. 11:36-45). Preterist commentators differ widely, with many seeing the proud king beginning in 11:36 as Vespasian, Titus, one of the kings of the Herodian dynasty, or some other first-century figure. It was demonstrated in other chapters of this book that the future unprecedented tribulation and the resurrection of the dead are thematically and temporally inseparable. This argument sets forth the futurist position that the Antichrist is in view in the latter portion of Daniel 11, thus prohibiting a preterist paradigm that disallows a future Antichrist. It will now be demonstrated that the Antichrist is in view beginning as early as 11:21.

Mathison correctly noted that a change in the subject does not occur at Daniel 11:36:

> Daniel 11:36-12:3 does not provide any indication that the subject has changed, but, unlike the preceding verses, the events described in 11:36-12:3 do not correspond to any known events in the life of Antiochus IV—or anyone else, for that matter. Some suggest that these verses were fulfilled in the first century. Others suggest that

they have not yet been fulfilled. In either case, their fulfillment did not occur when the prophecies of Daniel 11:21-35 were fulfilled. The two events were telescoped by Daniel into one continuous prophecy, and no one reading it before any of it was fulfilled would have been able to detect a change of subject at verse 36.[8]

A strong case can be made that Antiochus IV Epiphanes (175-164 BC) fulfilled many of the prophetic details of "the king of the north" (Dan. 11:21-35). This interpretation is well established, with much in its defense, and will not be reiterated here. However, the futurist position that the future Antichrist will completely fulfill these verses is highly defensible. This interpretation is based on several incontrovertible pieces of evidence.

First, Daniel referred to the invasion of the ships of Kittim (Dan. 11:30), which is an allusion to Balaam's prophecy, which identifies this event as occurring in "the latter days" (Num. 24:14, 23-24). This period of the latter days does not fit with the reign of Antiochus IV Epiphanes in the second century BC.

Second, the events of the unprecedented tribulation mentioned in Daniel 12 refer back to events that were detailed previously in the same prophetic vision (Dan. 11:30-36). These events include the northern king's forcible removal of the daily burnt offering, known as the tamid, and his setting up "the abomination that makes desolate" (Dan. 11:31; 12:11). They also include the refining, purifying, and whitening of the wise and understanding (Dan. 11:33-35; 12:10). The careful reader should consider that Daniel 10-12 comprises a single prophecy, detailed in the first two chapters of the vision and prophetically elucidated by "the man clothed in linen" in the final chapter.

---

[8] Mathison, 167.

TABLE 7: PARALLEL PASSAGES OF DANIEL 11

	Daniel 11	Parallel Passages
Ships of Cyprus Arrive	For ships from Cyprus shall come against him; therefore, he shall be grieved, and return in rage against the holy covenant, and do damage. (Dan. 11:30)	Come, I will advise you what this people will do to your people in the latter days. . . . But ships shall come from the coasts of Cyprus, And they shall afflict Asshur and afflict Eber (Num. 24:14, 24)
King of the North Removes the Tamid and Sets Up the Abomination of Desolation	And forces shall be mustered by him, and they shall defile the sanctuary fortress; then they shall take away the daily sacrifices, and place there the abomination of desolation. (Dan. 11:31)	And from the time that the daily sacrifice is taken away, and the abomination of desolation is set up (Dan. 12:11)
The Wise Will Understand and Be Refined, Purified, and Made White	And those of the people who understand shall instruct many . . . And some of those of understanding shall fall, to refine them, purify them, and make them white, until the time of the end; because it is still for the appointed time. (Dan. 11:33, 35)	Many shall be purified, made white, and refined, but the wicked shall do wickedly; and none of the wicked shall understand, but the wise shall understand. (Dan. 12:10)

The Lawless One Will Exalt Himself Above Every Deity	Then the king shall do according to his own will: he shall exalt and magnify himself above every god, shall speak blasphemies against the God of gods (Dan. 11:36)	[T]he man of sin is revealed, the son of perdition, who opposes and exalts himself above all that is called God or that is worshiped, so that he sits as God in the temple of God, showing himself that he is God. (2 Thess. 2:3-4)

Third, the antecedent for "the king" (Dan. 11:36) is "the vile person"[9] that was introduced much earlier in the vision (Dan. 11:21). The subject of the vile man is maintained by usage of the third person singular pronouns ("he/him") throughout the interposing verses, without any indication of any change in the subject (Dan. 11:21-35). Then, Daniel 11:36 mentions "the king" without any indication of a subject change. As Mathison points out in his quote above, this use of the noun would be oddly out of place if a subject change had occurred at this point. This lack of subject change is sharply contrasted with the many subject changes prior to Daniel 11:21.

Fourth, this king will speak blasphemies and "exalt himself and magnify himself above every god" (Dan. 11:36). The apostle Paul alluded to this prophecy with reference to the Man of Lawlessness, the Antichrist, who will enter the temple prior to being killed by Christ, who will return to gather the faithful at the day of Christ (2 Thess. 2:1-8; cf. 1 Thess. 4:13-18; Rev. 13:5-6).

Therefore, in one sense, the historical actions of Antiochus IV Epiphanes function as a historical distractor that divinely conceals the true identity of the king—the Antichrist. This identity will become most evident when the prophecy is unsealed and the vision fulfilled. As

---

[9] This phrase is variously translated "the contemptible person."

demonstrated in previous chapters, Jesus alluded to Daniel's abomination of desolation in the Olivet Prophecy (Matt. 24:15-16; Mark 13:14; cf. Dan. 9:27; 11:31, 45; 12:11), and He spoke of it as awaiting a future fulfillment at the end of the age. This means that the abomination did not find exhaustive fulfillment in Antiochus' desecration of the Jerusalem temple in 168 BC.

Some preterists argue that the Olivet Prophecy represents a double fulfillment of this event of Daniel's prophecies,[10] but the temporal relationship of the abomination with the unprecedented tribulation and the resurrection of the dead evidences this argument as special pleading (Dan. 12:1-3, 11). As I have demonstrated, the ultimate, plenary fulfillment of these prophecies will include the Antichrist setting up the abomination in the Third Temple. The partial fulfillment of Daniel's prophecies by Antiochus IV Epiphanes and the complete fulfillment by the Antichrist illustrate the "already and not yet" pattern characteristic of many biblical prophecies.

Such prophecies demonstrate pattern eschatology, that is, cycles of typological fulfillment evidenced throughout redemptive history. In other words, the actions of many historical figures, such as Pharaoh, King Nebuchadnezzar, Antiochus IV Epiphanes, Emperor Caligula, General Titus, Emperor Domitian, and Adolf Hitler, prophetically foreshadow those of the Antichrist. The pattern consists of a self-exalting tyrant who functions as the instrument of covenant discipline against the Jews; he forces assimilation, outlaws the observance of the commandments, desecrates holy places, demands a cult following, mandates idolatrous worship, and attempts to destroy the holy people. However, these enemies of the Jewish people only partially fulfilled the prophetic expectations which pertain to the ultimate enemy—the Antichrist—whose actions will exhaustively fulfill these prophecies.

---

10   E.g., Mathison, 167.

DEBUNKING PRETERISM

ELIJAH AS "ALREADY AND NOT YET"

The prophet Elijah provides an excellent case study depicting the "already and not yet" principle. First of all, the end of Elijah's life on earth was most exceptional; he was taken to heaven in a whirlwind (2 Kings 2:1, 11). However, the prophet Malachi prophesied about his return:

> Behold, I [Yahweh] will send you Elijah the prophet before the great and awesome day of the LORD comes. And he will turn the hearts of the fathers to their children and the hearts of children to their fathers, lest I come and strike the land with a decree of utter destruction. (Mal. 4:5-6; cf. Mal. 3:1-2; 4:1-3; Matt. 11:9-10; Mark 1:2; Luke 7:27)

The prophecy demonstrates that Elijah would deliver a message of intergenerational repentance so that the Lord spares the land of Israel from utter destruction on the day of the Lord. Malachi also prophesied that the Lord would "suddenly come to his temple" after Elijah has purified and refined the Levites so that they bring Him "offerings in righteousness" (Mal. 3:1, 3).

In the New Testament, an enigmatic linkage exists between Elijah and John the Baptizer. Many preterists argue that John exhaustively fulfilled the above prophecies of Malachi.[11] On the other hand, futurists teach that John was a typological, partial fulfillment of the prophecies, and that Elijah will return to prepare the Jewish nation for the day of Christ. Significantly, Jesus never denied the future return of Elijah, but He taught, "Elijah does come first to restore all things. . . I tell you that Elijah has come" (Mark 9:12-13). He also taught that those with spiritual discernment could perceive the truth that John the Baptizer was Elijah (Matt. 11:14-15).

On the other hand, the Baptizer rejected any self-identification as Elijah (John 1:21). This apparent contradiction is easily reconciled

---

11   Gentry, *The Olivet Discourse Made Easy*, loc. 380; Similarly, Russell, 4.

when we understand that John had been given "the spirit and power" of Elijah (Luke 1:17, 76). This is similar to Elisha the prophet receiving the prophetic spirit and prophetic abilities of Elijah, after his master had been caught up to heaven (2 Kings 2:9, 15). The transference of Elijah's "spirit and power" to John (and to a lesser degree, to Elisha) is evidenced by the fact that they performed similar actions at the Jordan River, wore similar clothing, preached a message of repentance to the theocratic kingdom, and were persecuted by a wicked king.

The preterist view that the Baptizer exhaustively fulfilled Malachi's prophecies about Elijah is defective because the former did not fulfill the prophetic expectation by purifying the sons of Levi so that they could offer acceptable sacrifices, nor did he usher in national repentance so as to prevent their utter destruction at the day of the Lord. To the contrary, preterists point out that the land of Israel was utterly destroyed in AD 70. Wright recognizes that John's audience understood his prophetic warnings about "a great national disaster, to be interpreted as the judgment of the covenant god."[12] Yet the nation eventually persecuted and murdered John and Christ, a penultimate rejection of the Lord Himself that resulted in covenantal curses against the land and its people. Chilton admitted that the nation refused to repent, so God cursed the land and "placed [it] under the ban, completely devoted to destruction" by the Roman armies in AD 70.[13]

Many futurists teach that many within the Jewish nation will accept Elijah's message of repentance in preparation for the Lord's return at the day of Christ. The national rejection of John and Jesus contrasts sharply with some of the nation's repentance at the preaching of the coming Elijah prior to the glorious return of Jesus. Many traditional interpreters, following the teaching of the Church fathers, teach that the prophet Elijah (or another Elijah-like prophet) will be one of the two witnesses depicted in the Apocalypse (Rev. 11:3-13). Craig L. Blomberg explains,

---

[12] Wright, *Jesus and the Victory of God*, 326.

[13] Chilton, *Paradise Restored*, 138.

"Whether one sees John as the complete fulfillment of the prediction [of Malachi] depends in large part on one's understanding of the two witnesses in Rev. 11, depicted as mirroring the ministries of Moses and Elijah."[14] The teachings of the Scriptures and their patristic interpretation support the concept that John the Baptizer partially fulfilled Malachi's prophecies while the future arrival of Elijah will completely fulfill them. As such, the prophetic ministry of the two witnesses for three and a half years will usher in the day of Jesus Christ.

THERE ARE SOME STANDING HERE

The Lord prophesied about His return in another passage found in the Synoptic Gospels:

> For the Son of Man is going to come with his angels in the glory of his Father, and then he will repay each person according to what he has done. Truly, I say to you, there are some standing here who will not taste death until they see the Son of Man coming in his kingdom. (Matt. 16:27-28; cf. Mark 8:38-9:1; Luke 9:26-27)

Russell regarded this prophecy as the most important for any discussion about eschatology. He considered it to be "the key" that unlocks the correct interpretation about the meaning of the Son of Man's coming in the Synoptics and "the master key" that opens "many other dark sayings in the prophetic oracles."[15] As DeMar argues, most preterists consider this prophecy "a crucial time text" in favor of preterism.[16] However, we will see that this passage is a fitting example of the "already and not yet" arrival of Christ's kingdom.

Gentry summarizes the preterist position that the prophecy "must point to the AD 70 destruction of the temple which occurs forty years

---

[14] Blomberg in Beale and Carson, *The New Testament Use*, 40.

[15] Russell, 29, 46.

[16] Gary DeMar, *Last Days' Madness*, viii.

later."[17] Preterists posit that the text clearly conveys that most, but not all, of the disciples with Christ when He uttered this prophecy had to die prior to His glorious coming.[18] They reason that the prophecy cannot be about the Second Coming because all these disciples died nearly two millennia ago.[19] Chilton saw no alternative to the preterist interpretation: "Was Jesus right or wrong? . . . And this was no slight miscalculation: Jesus missed the mark by thousands of years! Can we trust him as Lord and Savior, and still hold that he was wrong, or that somehow his prophecy got derailed?"[20] Russell explained the preterist rationale for rejecting the futurist interpretations of this prophecy, specifically, those which understand Christ's "coming in His kingdom" to refer to His post-resurrection appearances or to the subsequent activities of the Holy Spirit within the apostolic Church:

> How can we suppose that Christ, speaking of an event which was to take place in about twelve months, would say [these words = Matt. 16:27-28]? . . . The very form of the expression shows that the event spoken of could not lie within the space of a few months, or even a few years: it is a mode of speech which suggests that not *all* present will live to see the events spoken of; that not *many* will do so; but that *some* will. It is exactly such a way of speaking as would suit an interval of thirty or forty years, when the majority of the persons then present would have passed away, but some would survive and witness the event referred to.[21]

Preterists emphatically reject the traditional interpretations and believe that this entire passage refers to a supposed judgment "coming" of Jesus in AD 70. J. Marcellus Kik explains, "This [Matt. 16:28] could not possibly refer to the second, personal, visible coming"; however, he

---

17 Gentry, *The Olivet Discourse Made Easy*, loc. 428-433, 1550; Similarly, Kik, 64.

18 Gentry, *The Olivet Discourse Made Easy*, loc. 1259, 1269.

19 Hanegraaff, 17.

20 Chilton, *Paradise Restored*, 70.

21 Russell, 30-31.

later argues that the previous verse confirms that "the final judgment takes place at the second coming of Christ" (Matt. 16:27).[22]

On the other hand, many traditional interpreters correctly argue that the first verse of the prophecy in Matthew's Gospel refers to Christ's glorious return with His angels to render rewards of judgment (Matt. 16:27). This interpretation is certain because the introductory participle "for" thematically connects this statement with the preceding content about the suffering and martyrdom of Jesus and His disciples (Matt. 16:21, 24-26). This shows that the purpose for the Son of Man's glorious coming would be to vindicate His disciples by repaying each person "according to what he has done" (Matt. 16:27; cf. Isa. 40:1-5, 9-11; 62:10-11). The biblical writers reserved this language of rewards to describe the eschatological, postmortem day of judgment (e.g., Rom. 2:5-6; 14:10-12; 2 Cor. 5:10; 2 Tim. 4:1).[23] The language is most similar to John's apocalyptic vision of the general resurrection, in which the apostle saw God seated upon His throne to judge the dead "by the things which were written in the books, . . . each one according to his works" (Rev. 20:11-15). Those whose names are not found written in the Lamb's book of life will be thrown into the second death—hellfire (Rev. 20:15). As with Christ's prophecy to arrive in glory with His angels to dispense rewards and retribution (Matt. 16:27), these eternal rewards and punishments at the resurrection of the dead do not fit the historical events of the destruction of Jerusalem in AD 70.

Traditional commentators generally take one of several interpretive approaches to the second verse of Christ's prophecy ("there are some standing here who will not taste death until . . ." Matt. 16:28: Mark 9:1; Luke 9:27). One interpretation sees this statement as referring to the miraculous event that took place about a week later; upon the Mount of Transfiguration, the apostles Peter, James, and John became eyewitnesses of the glorified Jesus (Matt. 17:1-13; Mark 9:2-13; Luke 9:28-36).

---

22 Kik, 38, 167.

23 Contra Adams and Fisher, *The Time of the End*, 109, 111.

Proponents of this view point out that all three Synoptics locate the account of this event immediately after Christ's prophecy about "some standing here." One strength of this position is that Saint Peter later identified this event on the holy mountain as their "eyewitness" experience of seeing the glorified Jesus (2 Pet. 1:16-21). Peter contended that this experience is reason to believe that the apostles "did not follow cleverly devised myths when we made known to you the power and coming of our Lord Jesus Christ" (2 Pet. 1:16). By employing language similar to Jesus' statement (Matt. 16:28), the apostle linked his majestic eyewitness experience upon the Mount of Transfiguration with Christ's glorious return to bring rewards and recompense.

An alternative interpretation understands Jesus' prophecy about some of the first disciples seeing Him coming in His kingdom (Matt. 16:28) as referring to His post-resurrection appearances. The strength of this view is that eleven of the apostles saw and handled the glorified Jesus (1 John 1:1-2), which was a powerful and certain foretaste, and an "already and not yet" fulfillment, of His glorious return to consummate the kingdom in our future. The apostle Judas, of course, had died prior to Christ's resurrection. In addition, it should not escape our notice that Stephen saw a vision of the reigning Son of Man at His Father's right hand in the kingdom (Acts 7:56), and the apostle John, and possibly others, saw visions of Christ descending from heaven in kingdom glory with the holy angels (e.g., Rev. 19:11-16).

Another interpretation sees the fulfillment of Christ's prophecy as a series of prophetic events in which the first disciples saw the arrival of His kingdom. One strength of this position is that Mark and Luke substituted Matthew's phrase "see the Son of Man coming in his kingdom" with the statements "see the kingdom of God after it has come with power" and "see the kingdom of God," respectively (Mark 9:1; Luke 9:27). The living disciples saw the arrival of the kingdom in Christ's passion, post-resurrection appearances, and ascension into heaven, and by the gift and power of the Holy Spirit beginning at the day of Pentecost, enabling them to advance the gospel throughout the world. By seeing the arrival of Christ's inaugurated kingdom through the power and authority bestowed upon the apostolic Church, the disciples could already see the consummate return of Christ in His glorious kingdom.

DeMar provides the standard preterist critique of the futurist interpretations:

> Some claim that the 'coming' Jesus had in mind was the transfiguration. But the transfiguration cannot be its fulfillment since Jesus indicated that *some* who were standing with Him would still be alive when He came but *most* would be dead. If we adopt this view that the transfiguration is the fulfillment, we must conclude that most of the people with whom Jesus spoke were dead within a week of Jesus' prediction (Matt. 17:1)! . . . Others see Pentecost, with the coming of the Holy Spirit, as the fulfillment. But the same problem arises—nearly all the disciples would have had to die within a period of a few months after the events described by Jesus in Matthew 16:27-28.[24]

Contrary to DeMar's claims, the Lord's statement (Matt. 16:28) does not indicate that most of the original hearers would die prior to the His coming; it simply states that some would remain alive. The difference is subtle, yet of great importance, because it provides explanatory power for the various futurist interpretations.

The preterist interpretation is flawed for another reason. The apostle John explicitly denied that Christ had predicted that John would remain alive until His coming:

> "If it is my will that he [John] remain until I come, what is that to you [Peter]? You follow me!" So the saying spread abroad among the brothers that this disciple was not to die; yet Jesus did not say to him that he was not to die, but, "If it is my will that he remain until I come, what is that to you?" (John 21:22-23)

This parenthetical comment would have been unnecessary to include if Christ's coming in this passage does not refer to the Second Coming but to the divine judgment upon Jerusalem and its temple in AD 70, a

---

[24] DeMar, *Last Days' Madness*, 44; Similarly, Gentry, *The Olivet Discourse Made Easy*, loc. 1550; Sproul, 61-62.

judgment that the Holy Spirit knew would occur during the apostle's lifetime (cf. Matt. 16:28).

During Jesus' trial before the Sanhedrin, the high priest Caiaphas put Him under legal obligation to answer a question about His identity:

> But Jesus remained silent. And the high priest said to him, "I adjure you by the living God, tell us if you are the Christ, the Son of God." Jesus said to him, "You have said so. But I tell you, from now on you will see the Son of Man seated at the right hand of Power and coming on the clouds of heaven." (Matt. 26:63-64; cf. Mark 14:62; Luke 22:69).

France explains that preterist interpreters have recently challenged the traditional interpretation of this passage: "The 'coming on the clouds of heaven' cannot be read as a reference to the parousia, as has been the traditional exegesis until relatively recently."[25] He teaches that the elders of the Sanhedrin soon saw, in the destruction of Jerusalem in AD 70, the vindication of Christ after they had failed to suppress the movement of Christianity.[26] Many preterists correctly note that the phrase in the Lord's declaration before the Sanhedrin is often translated "hereafter" or "from now on," meaning from that point in time until the indefinite future.[27] However, this contradicts the preterist interpretation that members of the Sanhedrin did not "see" or recognize His coming until AD 70. Sproul admitted that Christ's words here "may refer to an indefinite future" and that "'seeing' the coming of Christ in the 'hereafter' does not demand a first-century fulfillment."[28]

---

[25] France, *The Gospel of Matthew*, 1027-28.

[26] France, *The Gospel of Matthew*, 1027-28. Similarly, DeMar, *Last Days' Madness*, 162-163; Gentry, *The Book of Revelation*, 36, 45; Hanegraaff, 27.

[27] The Greek is *ap artee* (ἀπ' ἄρτι) in Matt. 26:64; France, *The Gospel of Matthew*, 1027-28; Gentry, *The Olivet Discourse Made Easy*, loc. 598; Mathison, 183.

[28] Sproul, 100.

The traditional approach to this passage is to understand Jesus' response before the Sanhedrin, which is a combined allusion to two Old Testament prophecies (Ps. 110:1; Dan. 7:13), as describing the entirety of Christ's interadventual reign at God's right hand, which will be completed when He returns on clouds of glory (c.f. "to receive for himself a kingdom and then return" Luke 19:12). Blomberg explains, "Christ is first in God's presence and then coming on the clouds, presumably therefore coming from heaven to earth."[29] In other words, Jesus' statement encapsulates the mystery of His two advents, which correspond to the two stages of redemption that began with His earthly ministry, passion, resurrection, and ascension and will be completed at His glorious return. Christ was not claiming that Caiaphas and the Sanhedrin would conclude that He is the glorified Son of Man because of the events following His death and resurrection, or as preterists claim, because Jerusalem was destroyed in AD 70. The correct interpretation is that the larger Jewish nation, of which the Sanhedrin administered, began the historical process ("from now on") of recognizing and understanding that Jesus is the reigning Christ. This process will be completed when the surviving remnant of the nation is saved when they look upon the pierced and resurrected Lord returning from heaven. As an aside, this interpretation of Christ's declaration (Matt. 26:64) favors the last interpretation of His prophecy about "some standing here" (Matt. 16:28), as discussed above.

The examples of inaugurated eschatology discussed in this chapter provide a snapshot of how the biblical writers portrayed the eschaton. The faulty hermeneutics of preterism fail to leave room for the "already and not yet" principle of biblical prophecy. As we have seen throughout the previous chapters of this book, many of the faulty claims of preterism arise from a deficient understanding of this hermeneutical principle. As we will see, this deficiency, coupled with a noble desire to maintain a

---

[29] Blomberg in Beale and Carson, *Commentary on the New Testament Use*, 87-88.

consistent hermeneutic, leads many preterists to force many other future prophecies into a first-century mold.

Consistent with the traditional interpretation of the biblical texts, faithful Christians experience the power and glory of the resurrected Christ in this present age. Because of what Jesus has accomplished, we "already" experience the realities that will characterize the end of this age and the glories of the coming age. These include such realities as tribulation, Christ's heavenly kingdom, the eschatological Spirit, eternal life, and the other powers of the age to come. Although these eschatological events will take place in their proper time ("not yet"), we "already" see them in the present.

14

THE MILLENNIUM

MANY PRETERISTS EMBRACE the amillennial interpretation of Revelation 20 where the phrase "a thousand years" represents the entirety of the Christian era.[1] This historic interpretation maintains that the phrase must refer to a long period of time because the qualifier "thousand," when used elsewhere in Scripture, confers the sense of totality upon the noun it modifies. For example, God declared that He owns "the cattle on a thousand hills" (Ps. 50:10), which is a poetic manner of saying that He lays claim to every hill.

The prophetic vision of the thousand years begins with the binding of Satan:

---

[1] E.g., Kik, 41; cf. Gentry, *The Olivet Discourse*, loc. 1565.

THE MILLENNIUM

> Then I saw an angel coming down from heaven, holding in his hand the key to the bottomless pit and a great chain. And he seized the dragon, that ancient serpent, who is the devil and Satan, and bound him for a thousand years, and threw him into the pit, and shut it and sealed it over him, so that he might not deceive the nations any longer, until the thousand years were ended. After that he must be released for a little while. (Rev. 20:1-3)

Many preterists agree with the traditional amillennial interpretation that the binding of Satan is a symbol for the curtailing of his power to deceive the nations, beginning with the first advent of Christ, so that the gospel could "progress into all the world."[2] However, other preterists, such as Jordan, teach that Satan's binding and the millennial reign of the martyrs began in AD 70.[3] This interpretation is less than satisfying for a variety of reasons. First of all, the apostolic gospel had been successfully preached and accepted throughout the nations of the Roman Empire for many years prior to AD 70.

THE FIRST RESURRECTION

The apostle John continued his millennium passage with a description of the resurrection of the dead and the kingdom reign of Christ and the martyrs:

> Then I saw thrones, and seated on them were those to whom the authority to judge was committed. Also I saw the souls of those who had been beheaded for the testimony of Jesus and for the word of God, and those who had not worshiped the beast or its image and had not received its mark on their foreheads or their hands. They came to life and reigned with Christ for a thousand years. The rest of the dead did not come to life until the thousand years were ended. This is the first resurrection. Blessed and holy is the one who shares in the first resurrection! Over such the second death has no power,

---

[2] Gentry, *The Book of Revelation*, 105; Similarly, Kik, 41; Jordan, loc. 577.

[3] Jordan, loc. 577.

but they will be priests of God and of Christ, and they will reign with him for a thousand years. (Rev. 20:4-6)

The traditional amillennial interpretation is that the first resurrection is the Christian's union with Christ by participation in His death and resurrection; this takes place when a person receives the heavenly birth through the "washing of regeneration and renewing of the Holy Spirit" (John 5:24-26; Rom. 6:4; Eph. 2:6; Col. 2:12; 3:1; Titus 3:5).[4] In his Gospel, John recorded that the spiritually dead who hear Christ's voice and trust in Him in the present age have already "passed from death into life" (John 5:24-26). Furthermore, when others spoke about the resurrection on the last day, Jesus responded, "I am the resurrection and the life. Whoever believes in me, though he die, yet shall he live, and everyone who lives and believes in me shall never die" (John 11:24-25). Consequently, those who are crucified and raised with Christ will not experience the second death of hellfire (cf. Rev. 2:11; 20:6).

Chilton advocated this view of the first resurrection.[5] Gentry did also, and he made the following argument:

> Therefore, what John teaches through symbolic imagery is that the first resurrection refers to salvation and the second resurrection to a literal, bodily arising again from physical death. The first resurrection, then, occurs throughout Christian history (the 1000 years of Christ's reign); the second resurrection only at the end of history, on "the last day."[6]

Nevertheless, Gentry changed his view after interacting with other arguments:

> John could be symbolically presenting the new birth as the first resurrection and the bodily resurrection from death as the second resurrection. This is the Augustinian view—a view I myself held when

---

[4] E.g., Jordan, loc. 586; Kik, 43, 185, 188.

[5] Chilton, *Paradise Restored*, 197.

[6] Kenneth L. Gentry, *The Book of Revelation* (Powder Springs, GA: The American Vision, Inc., 2008), 112-13.

I wrote the first edition of this book. But since then, I have engaged in a deeper and more focused analysis of Revelation 20 and how it fits in John's larger narrative.[7]

Gentry explains that he changed his position after considering two pieces of biblical evidence. First, the passage depicts the first resurrection as including the martyrs who would be slain for refusing the mark of the Beast (Rev. 20:4), a mark that the wicked will receive during the forty-two months of unprecedented tribulation (Rev. 13:5-18). Gentry concluded that this evidence exposes his former interpretation to the charge of anachronism because it would require the martyrs of the great tribulation, which he equates with the Neronian persecution, as having been slain before their conversion to Christianity. Second, the Greek syntax of the passage shows that the first resurrection is the answer to the martyrs' prayers for vindication (Rev. 6:9-11).[8] Gentry explains that the apostle concluded that the martyrs' "coming to life" after being beheaded was "a fulfillment of the promise given to them after they are already in heaven."[9] For these reasons, Gentry later concluded that the first resurrection must be something experienced in a postmortem setting.[10]

Gentry's current interpretation is that this resurrection is a symbol for the vindication of the martyrs, which he believes took place in AD 70. He also teaches that God rewarded the martyrs at that time, enabling them to "arise to new life," although it is uncertain what he means by this phrase.[11] He also maintains the traditional view of the general resurrection occurring at the future return of Jesus. Gentry summarizes his new position as follows:

---

[7] Gentry, *The Book of Revelation*, 117.

[8] Gentry, *The Book of Revelation*, 119.

[9] Gentry, *The Book of Revelation*, 119, 121.

[10] Also Jordan, loc. 307.

[11] Gentry, *The Book of Revelation Made Easy*, 123.

John appears to be stating that by AD 70, the martyrs will be vindicated... Thus, their "coming to life," a fulfillment of the promise given to them *after they are already in heaven* (Rev. 6:11), appears to be an image of their vindication in the death of their opponents in AD 70, rather than at the very moment when the martyrs enter heaven... They are *deceased* Christians in *heaven*, who were *martyred* in the *first century*.[12]

Gentry's humility and willingness to change his interpretation when confronted with new evidence is commendable; however, his novel approach presents many formidable difficulties. One difficulty is that the Bible never presents vindication by itself as resurrection. Kik explains, "The fact that it [Rev. 20:4-6] is a resurrection knocks out the thought that it is descriptive of the life of the soul in the intermediate state... When the Christian soul leaves the body to dwell in heaven, it is not a *resurrection*."[13] In addition, preterists generally recognize that the New Testament "very seldom uses the Greek term 'psuche' [translated "souls"] to describe the disembodied spirit."[14] Consequently, Gentry is compelled by his particular preterist hermeneutic to invent a new type of "resurrection" that is foreign to Second Temple Judaism and Christianity.

Gentry recognizes the straightforward meaning of Saint John's teaching about "the rest of the dead," specifically, that those who do not receive the first resurrection must wait until the day of judgment, after the thousand years, to be resurrected (Rev. 20:5, 11-15). However, he erroneously concludes that this reading would exclude the martyrs of the Neronian persecution from the postmillennial resurrection—the general resurrection—because he thinks that they received "resurrection" or vivification in AD 70.[15] He attempts to avoid this difficulty by

---

12   Gentry, *The Book of Revelation Made Easy*, 120-21.

13   Kik, 42; cf. p. 180.

14   Kik, 226; cf. p. 228.

15   Cf. Gentry, *The Book of Revelation* (2008), 111-12.

arguing that "the rest of the dead" refers exclusively to the armies of the Beast and false prophet ("the rest") who are killed by the coming of Christ in the preceding vision (Rev. 19:21).[16] However, this expression is parenthetical, and it appears between two statements pertaining to the first resurrection ("came to life . . . for a thousand years" and "the first resurrection" Rev. 20:4-5). This grammatical structure demonstrates that the remainder of the dead are those who remain in the state of death while the righteous "come to life" in the first resurrection.

Gentry's interpretation posits at least three resurrections of the dead. First, he recognizes that Christians are resurrected with Christ through regeneration. Second, he invents a supposed "resurrection" of the faithful martyrs, including those killed by Emperor Nero, in AD 70. Third, he affirms the general resurrection at the glorious return of Jesus Christ. Clearly, then, Gentry fails to understand that the doctrine of resurrection is connected with the "already and not yet" mystery of Christ being raised as the firstfruits of those who will be resurrected on the last day (1 Cor. 15:12-26). This mystery was fully revealed to the apostolic Church.

DANIEL 12 AND THE RESURRECTION

The "man clothed in linen" gave the prophet Daniel a vision concerning the resurrection of the dead:

> At that time shall arise Michael, the great prince who has charge of your people. And there shall be a time of trouble, such as never has been since there was a nation till that time. But at that time your people shall be delivered, everyone whose name shall be found written in the book. And many of those who sleep in the dust of the earth shall awake, some to everlasting life, and some to shame and everlasting contempt. And those who are wise shall shine like the brightness of the sky above; and those who turn many to righteousness, like the stars forever and ever. But you, Daniel, shut up the

---

16 Gentry, *The Book of Revelation*, 121-23.

words and seal the book, until the time of the end. Many shall run to and fro, and knowledge shall increase. (Dan. 12:1-4)

This portion of Daniel's prophecy must be understood as a specific prediction about the resurrection of the dead, a point argued by traditional commentators.[17] The temporal indicator "at that time" appears twice in the first verse, and it functions to connect the deliverance of Daniel's people and the resurrection of the dead with the unprecedented "time of trouble" described in the immediately preceding verses (Dan. 11:31-45). These verses reveal that this tribulation will begin when the willful king forcefully removes the regular burnt offering and sets up his abomination of desolation in the Jerusalem temple sanctuary (Dan. 11:31-45; cf. Dan. 12:11; Matt. 24:15-29; 2 Thess. 2:3-12).

This resurrection theme continues in the angelic statement that the prophet "shall rest and shall stand in your allotted place at the end of the days" (Dan. 12:11-13). The idea is that Daniel would "rest" in the peace of sleep, a euphemism for death (e.g., Mark 5:39; John 11:11; 1 Thess. 5:6-10), but later "stand" through resurrection to receive his "allotted place," his apportioned inheritance in Christ's kingdom, at the end of the age (cf. Job 19:23-27). This prophecy undoubtedly gave rise to the Jewish doctrine that the resurrection of the dead would occur on the last day (John 6:44; 11:24; cf. John 6:39-40, 54).

Those who fail to recognize Daniel's prophecy as predicting the resurrection unwittingly compromise the central doctrine of Christianity—the resurrection of Jesus Christ—because this passage forms the theological foundation for the apostolic doctrine of the resurrection of the dead (Matt. 25:46; John 5:28-29; Acts 24:15; Rev. 20:4-6, 12-15). To demonstrate, I. Howard Marshall noted that the apostle Paul's defense of the resurrection uses the same vocabulary as this Old Testament

---

[17] E.g., Stephen R. Miller, *Daniel* (Nashville: Broadman & Holman. 1994); John Calvin, *Reformation Commentary on Scripture: Ezekiel, Daniel*, Edited by Carl L. Beckwith (Downer's Grove, IL: InterVarsity PressAcademic, 2012), 402-03.

prophecy (Dan. 12:1-4 in Acts 24:14-15).[18] In addition, although many ancient prophecies predicted the resurrection of the righteous (e.g., Isa. 25:9; 26:17-19, 21; Ezek. 37:4-14; Job 19:23-29), many scholars recognize the prophecy of Daniel 12 to be the most unambiguous prophecy about the resurrection in the Old Testament. Those who deny that this prophecy foretold the general resurrection implicitly agree with Christianity's critics who contend that Jesus and His apostles invented a doctrine not found in the teachings of Moses and the other prophets, a notion rejected by the apostles themselves (Acts 26:21-23). Consequently, Daniel's resurrection prophecy should not be regarded as a parenthetical statement about a temporally-disconnected hope or as a symbol for the vindication of the martyrs, as many partial preterists contend.

Gentry once argued correctly that Daniel's prophecy is about the resurrection of the dead that will take place at the end of the age.[19] He has since abandoned this position and now teaches that the passage was fulfilled in AD 70, but his interpretive shift illustrates another preterist dilemma.[20] Preterists who believe that the entirety of the prophecy was fulfilled in the first century must either deny that it predicts a literal, bodily resurrection or embrace the flagrant heresy of consistent preterism. This dilemma is evident in how partial preterists interpret the statement in the prophecy that the righteous "shall shine like the brightness of the sky . . . and like the stars" at the time of the end (Dan. 12:3). Jesus echoed this verse in a parable about the angels separating the wicked from the righteous in order to give them their respective, eternal destinies: "At the end of the age . . . the righteous will shine like the

---

[18] Marshall in Beale and Carson, *Commentary on the New Testament Use*, 598.

[19] Kenneth L. Gentry, *The Greatness of the Great Commission* (Tyler, TX: Institute for Christian Economics, 1990), 142; Similarly, Adams and Fisher, *The Time of the End*, 105.

[20] Kenneth L. Gentry, *He Shall Have Dominion: A Postmillennial Eschatology* (Draper, VA: Apologetics Group Media, 2009), 538; cf. Kenneth L. Gentry as quoted in Michael J. Sullivan, "A Full Preterist Response to Kenneth Gentry's Articles: Daniel 12, Tribulation, and Resurrection and Acts 24:15 and the Alleged Nearness of the Resurrection." As of October 24, 2012. *FullPreterism.com*. http://postmillennialism.com/2012/03/daniel-12-tribulation-and-resurrection/.

sun in the kingdom of their Father" (Matt. 13:39, 43). DeMar, Jordan, Leithart, McDurmon, and others consistently interpret both prophecies as having an AD 70 fulfillment. On the other hand, Gentry inconsistently sees the Danielic passage as having an AD 70 fulfillment, while Christ's statement in this harvest parable points to the end of the age in our future.

Preterist Sam Frost describes another method for interpreting Daniel's prophecy:

> Then we read, "And many of those who sleep in the dust of the earth shall awake, some to everlasting life, and some to shame and everlasting contempt." There is no "time" indicator here. If it read, "at that time many of those who sleep shall awake" we would have a different issue. But it doesn't. "And" (waw) can be seen as a simple connector. Those who suffered will be delivered, *and, by the way, they are also promised to awake unto eternal life*. A good number of scholars take this approach.[21]

A few observations demonstrate the fallacy of Frost's argument. The "man clothed in linen" swore to the prophet that "all these things [in the prophecy] would be finished" at the terminus of the period of "a time, times, and half a time, . . . when the shattering of the power of the holy people comes to an end" (Dan. 12:7). The context shows that this eschatological period would see the accomplishment of "all these things," that is, all the events mentioned in the preceding verses, including the resurrection of the dead (Dan. 12:1-4). Partial preterists correctly argue that the "all these things" in the Olivet Discourse (Matt. 24:34) must include the coming of the Son of Man in its preceding verses (Matt. 24:27-30); nevertheless, they deny the same logic as it pertains to the exact phrase and context in Daniel 12!

Frost then creatively argues that "the end" should not be equated with "the end of the days" later in the same verse (Dan. 12:13):

---

[21] Frost, Sam, [Article title unknown], As of November 8, 2012, *The Reign of Christ*, http://thereignofchrist.com/daniel-122/.

Daniel was told to "go your way till *the end*. And you shall rest and shall stand in your allotted place at *the end of the days*." The last phrase is an equivalent to "the last day" and resurrection is to occur on that day. *Bodily* resurrection. The first phrase, however, is the end of Daniel's life. Obviously, for the angel is not telling Daniel to "go your way" until "the time of the end"! (note the Septuagint *in loc*). Neither is the "end of the days" referring to the 1,290 or 1,335 days. The "end of the days" is in reference to *Dan* 12.2, the resurrection of the dead. Daniel, who will eventually die (reach his end) is promised participation in the resurrection. No notation of time is given for that time other than "the last day" or "end of the days" of history (which was thoroughly common in Second Temple Judaism).[22]

Frost's "piecemeal approach" to dividing Daniel's prophetic vision is forced and unconvincing. He wants to convince the reader that the unprecedented tribulation occurred in the First Jewish-Roman War but that the resurrection of the dead in the next verse will be fulfilled in our future (Dan. 12:1-2). He then completely divorces the period of 1,290 and 1,335 days from "the end of the days" appearing two verses later (Dan. 12:11, 13). Finally, he separates "the end," which he interprets as the prophet's death, from "the end of the days" within the same verse (Dan. 12:13). However, the phrase "the end" appears elsewhere in the prophecy, where it clearly means the end of the age (Dan. 11:27, 35, 40; 12:4).

The correct meaning of the prophecy is that the prophet Daniel would die ("you shall rest") and wait until his resurrection at "the end of the days" (Dan 12:13), the antecedent of which is the 1,290 days, the vast majority of which will comprise three and a half years of unprecedented tribulation (Dan. 12:11-12). This corresponds tightly with the arguments in previous chapters of this book that the return of Jesus and the resurrection of the dead will *immediately* follow the great tribulation.

---

[22] Frost, *The Reign of Christ*.

A NEW CREATION

The dogmatic teaching of the holy Church has always been that Christ will personally usher in His consummated kingdom of peace, tranquility, justice, and abundance upon the earth. This will begin when God's original creation ("the heavens and the earth" Gen. 1:1-2:1) is redeemed and gloriously transformed into a new heaven and new earth (Isa. 65:17-25; 66:22-23; 2 Pet. 3:12-13; Rev. 21:1-22:5).

By contrast, many preterists argue that the appearance of this new creation—"a new heaven and a new earth" (Rev. 21:1)—is a symbol for the new covenant's arrival in the first century AD. Most often, preterists see this arrival as having occurred during the so-called "transition period," the period between the crucifixion of Jesus and the destruction of Jerusalem in AD 70,[23] or less often, during one of these two prophetic events. They also teach that the dissolution of the old cosmos is a symbol for the "passing away" of the Mosaic covenant during this period. Most preterists interpret the fiery destruction of the harlot city Babylon as a fitting symbol for the Roman destruction of Jerusalem in AD 70, an event that supposedly enabled the heavenly descent of Christ's virgin bride—the new Jerusalem (Rev. 21:2). They also see this holy city as a symbol for the new covenant or the new covenant Church.

However, the preterist interpretation of the new creation reveals a glaring anachronism. The apostle John saw that the old creation must completely "pass away" before the new creation can arrive: "Then I saw a new heaven and a new earth, for the first heaven and the first earth had passed away. And I saw the holy city, new Jerusalem, coming down out of heaven from God" (Rev. 21:1-2; cf. Rev. 20:11-12). The causative participle "for" demonstrates that the new creation will appear *because* the old creation has been destroyed. Consequently, the preterist position necessitates the passing away of the Mosaic covenant and the destruc-

---

[23] Jordan, loc. 51, 75-84.

tion of the harlot city before the new covenant could arrive. This logically means that the new covenant did not arrive with the death, burial and resurrection of Jesus, but had to wait for the Roman destruction of Jerusalem in AD 70, an implication that contradicts His own teaching that the new covenant was given in His death (Luke 22:20).

Many preterists teach that the new Jerusalem descended from heaven in AD 70, despite the fact that most of these preterists adhere to the postmillennial doctrine of Dominion Theology, which teaches that the new creation symbolizes a Christianized planet in our future. These preterists want to "have their cake and eat it too" by interpreting the new creation as a symbol for the new covenant and as the literal earth, having been transformed under Christ's dominion. Gentry summarizes this position:

> John's picture of the new creation, however, *represents a present reality* which *the consummate order eventually fulfills, perfects, and replaces.* John's image is a picture of new covenant salvation *coming into the world in the first century.* . . . It seems *exegetically unlikely that we could surmise that the preceding* [vision] *actually applies to a reality thousands of years in the future.* . . . In other words, we expect the New Jerusalem order to immediately replace the Old Jerusalem, just as the new covenant immediately superseded the old covenant (Heb 8:13). *A gap seems unreasonable*—especially in light of the stated time frame [in Rev. 22:6].[24]
>
> The new creation begins flowing into and impacting history in the first century long before the consummate order. . . Like the mustard seed which grows to a great plant, so the first century church will work its message of peace into all the world. . . In the *consummate* New Creation, this will, of course, come to full and perfect fruition as we enter into eternal bliss in our resurrected bodies (Matt. 25:34). But in the present gospel-based new creation redemptive order, we experience this *in principle.*[25]

---

[24] Gentry, *The Book of Revelation* (2008), 114-15.

[25] Gentry, *The Book of Revelation*, 126, 129, 130.

DEBUNKING PRETERISM

The partial preterist view that the new creation is continually and progressively arriving during the present Church age creates significant difficulties. Most preterists teach that the new Jerusalem fully descended from heaven by AD 70, meaning that the new covenant descended to a new earth that only existed at that time "in principle," to borrow Gentry's expression. This interpretation is also hermeneutically inconsistent because it teaches that the passing away of the old creation is a metaphor for the dissolution of the Jewish kingdom and old covenant in AD 70, while maintaining that the appearance of the new creation describes a literal recreated universe in our future. In addition, Gentry backs himself into a corner by demanding that the arrival of the new creation be included in the events that "must soon take place" (Rev. 22:6). He wrote, "It seems exegetically unlikely that we could surmise that the preceding description actually applies to a reality thousands of years in the future."[26] This is an odd contention because Gentry agrees with the Christian claim that the new creation has not yet fully arrived, but by so agreeing, he nullifies his central argument that the qualifier "soon" cannot speak of an event two thousand years removed.

Partial preterists encounter another problem because the old creation was to disappear after the thousand years, but this is also when the resurrection and judgment of the dead were to occur: "Then I saw a great white throne and him who was seated on it. From his presence earth and sky fled away, and no place was found for them. And I saw the dead, great and small, standing before the throne, . . . and the dead were judged" (Rev. 20:11-12; cf. Rev. 21:1). As I demonstrated previously, partial preterists must conclude that the old creation passed away with the destruction of the Jewish kingdom in AD 70; otherwise, the new covenant has not yet arrived (cf. Rev. 21:1). Nevertheless, they cannot accept this conclusion without accepting the heretical notion that the general resurrection and judgment day also took place at that time, as full preterists argue.

---

26   Gentry, *The Book of Revelation*, 126.

Some partial preterists attempt to escape this conclusion by contending that the old creation passed away and the new creation consummately arrived in AD 70, while the resurrection will not take place until Christ's return in our future.[27] The tragic implication of this argument, also associated with full preterism, is that it compromises the foundational Christian doctrine that sin and death will be forever vanquished in the new creation. The apostle John described the conditions in the new Jerusalem: God "will wipe away every tear from their eyes, and death shall be no more, neither shall there be mourning, nor crying, nor pain anymore, for the former things have passed away" (Rev. 21:4). If this prophecy was fulfilled in AD 70, it must be dismissed as mere allegory by preterists who hold to this interpretation of the new creation. Furthermore, this interpretation leaves these preterists without any exegetical grounds to suggest that sin and death will be terminated at any point in the future.

---

[27] Some translate the verse "From his presence earth and sky had fled away" (Rev. 20:11), meaning that the old creation had previously disappeared.

15

THE COST OF CONSISTENCY

MANY PRETERISTS RECOGNIZE the artificiality of dividing the Olivet Discourse into preterist and futurist portions. For example, DeMar and Wright, argue that most eschatological prophecies were entirely fulfilled in the first century AD. However, this more consistent approach to preterism presents an entirely different set of difficulties, such as the fact that it leaves these interpreters without a single reference to the bodily return of Jesus Christ in the Synoptic Gospels! Suffice to say, it is unfathomable that Matthew, Mark, and Luke omitted an event of such theological magnitude. This chapter will explore many other tragic implications that arise from preterist hermeneutics.

THE REPRESENTATIVE YOU

The Lord Jesus taught, "When they persecute you in one town, flee to the next, for truly, I say to you, you will not have gone through all the towns of Israel before the Son of Man comes" (Matt. 10:23). The apostolic Church has understood this verse as referring to the Lord's Second Coming. The second-person plural pronoun ("you") in this passage and in the Olivet Discourse has a representative function and refers to the Lord's disciples more generally, that is, the Church, and not to the Twelve in a restricted sense. Sproul recognized that even the Protestant Reformer John Calvin interpreted the Olivet Discourse in this manner:

> Though Calvin acknowledged that the problem of false christs plagued the early church after the resurrection of Christ, he applied the warning to the church of all ages, not limiting it to the church of the first century. This application is quite legitimate, as the appearance of imposters is a perennial problem.[1]

Nevertheless, preterists vehemently disagree with this approach, arguing that the pronoun "you" in these passages must be understood as referring only to the original disciples.[2] They see the coming of the Son of Man as a metaphor for the ascension of Christ, as evidenced by the subsequent destruction of Jerusalem and the Second Temple (Matt. 10:23).[3] Gentry suggests that this verse means that the apostles would preach the gospel, and by so doing, guarantee judgment upon the Jewish kingdom: "As Israel sinfully continues to reject him, they [the apostles] will effectively secure and oversee Israel's judgment in AD 70."[4] Regarding Jesus' statement, Gentry quips, "Surely he is not referring to an event hundreds upon hundreds of years away."[5] DeMar explains that this argument also applies to the Olivet Discourse:

---

[1] Sproul, 41.

[2] DeMar, *Last Days' Madness*, 30, 573; Hanegraaff, 5-7, 72, 81, 87, 89, 94; Mathison, 175; Russell, 115; Sproul, 41, 55.

[3] Gentry, *The Olivet Discourse*, loc. 373; Hanegraaff, 18; Mathison, 175.

[4] Gentry, *The Olivet Discourse*, loc. 470.

[5] Gentry, *The Olivet Discourse*, loc. 1252, 1259.

Notice how many times Jesus used the plural *you* in Matthew 24 and in the parallel passages... Now if *you* heard Jesus say that all these things would happen to "this generation" while you were standing there listening to Him, and in every other instance of its use "this generation" meant the present generation, and you also heard Him say that when "you" would see these things, what would you conclude? The most natural (literal) interpretation is that it would happen to *your generation*, and maybe even to you personally.[6]

Ed Stevens, a full preterist, explains that such arguments are based on the premise of audience relevance: "The New Testament was not written to us originally. We are reading someone else's mail."[7] Likewise, Hanegraaff claims that in these passages Jesus was "directly and obviously addressing a first-century audience. When someone attempts to convince them otherwise, their baloney detectors should immediately register full."[8]

Preterists are unable to bear the burden of proving that Jesus restricted His intended audience to those first disciples who heard the sound of His voice. The textual evidence demonstrates that He often employed the second-person plural pronoun ("you") to collectively address His disciples—the holy Church. Matthew recorded many other teachings of Christ wherein He addressed us by using this pronoun: the moral imperatives in the Sermon on the Mount (Matt. 5:11-7:20), the requirement of absolute righteousness (Matt. 5:20), the knowledge of the secrets of the kingdom (Matt. 13:11-17), the imperative to become like little children (Matt. 18:3), instructions on Church discipline (Matt. 18:15-19), the command to be servants (Matt. 20:25-27; 23:11), the promise of answered prayer (Matt. 21:21-22), the command to observe the Eucharist (Matt. 26:27-29), and the command to fulfill the Great Commission (Matt. 28:16-20). A consistent application of the preterist

---

[6] DeMar, *Last Days' Madness*, 59.

[7] Edward Stevens as quoted in Russell, ix.

[8] Hanegraaff, 86.

argument regarding the second-person plural pronoun would mean that these teachings were only intended for the original hearers and not for the holy Church! In essence, the preterist's failure to recognize the fluidity of language unwittingly compromises any modern application of the gospel of Jesus.

The preterist argument about the second-person plural pronoun also requires Christ's original audience to have personally witnessed the events described in the Olivet Discourse. He prophesied, "So when you see the abomination of desolation . . . standing in the holy place" (Matt. 24:15). Preterists contend that the subject "you" in this verse refers only to the small number of original disciples or to the Twelve (cf. Matt. 24:3; Mark 13:3). This interpretation requires the original hearers to have seen the abomination of desolation. Nevertheless, nearly all the original hearers of the discourse had died before the First Jewish-Roman War. This conclusion is based upon two primary considerations: First, the sum of the range of the disciples' ages when the discourse was delivered and the nearly four decades that elapsed between the discourse and the destruction of the Second Temple in AD 70. Second, the historical records reveal that the martyrdoms of the apostles took place prior to Jerusalem's destruction. The few who were still alive, such as the apostle John, lived outside the vicinity of Jerusalem at the time of its destruction, so they could not have seen any event at the temple around AD 70.

The second-person plural pronoun argument is a double-edged sword for preterists because consistency demands that the argument would equally apply to the third-person plural pronoun ("we"). In other words, if Jesus and the apostles used the personal pronoun "you" to refer only to their immediate audiences, they must have necessarily included themselves, along with their immediate audience, whenever they employed the personal pronoun "we". An example of this is the apostle Paul's teaching to his Christian audience that "we who are alive, who are left until the coming of the Lord . . . will be caught up together with them in the clouds to meet the Lord in the air" (1 Thess. 4:15, 17) and "we shall not all sleep, but we shall all be changed" (1 Cor. 15:51).

Russell pointed this out, saying, "But the question for us is, to whom does the apostle refer when he says, 'We shall not all sleep,' etc.? Is it to some hypothetical persons living in some distant age of time, or is it of the Corinthians and himself that he is thinking?"[9] Thus preterists, on the basis of consistent logic, should extract the implication that Paul's original audience lived to see the return of Christ and that they were included in the rapture! Russell argued that this preterist argument, when consistently applied, leads the preterist into *full* preterism.

CONSISTENT PRETERISM

Many preterists adopt consistent preterism, known as full preterism, in order to maintain a consistent hermeneutic. Full preterism is the view that every prophecy of the Bible was fulfilled no later than the destruction of Jerusalem in AD 70. The most notable of these prophecies include those pertaining to the day of the Lord, the glorious return of Jesus, the resurrection of the dead, and the arrival of the new heaven and new earth. The strength of full preterism is that it agrees with the biblical testimony that the unprecedented tribulation would be immediately followed by Christ's return from heaven and the resurrection of the dead. Partial preterists agree with the Orthodox condemnation of full preterism as heresy, and they have given the label "hyper-preterism" to this eschatological position.

As I mentioned previously, this book critiques the foundations of preterism, and by doing so, largely dismantles full preterism by default. Notwithstanding, I will briefly examine the negative implications of consistent preterism in this chapter.

Most seriously, consistent preterism steals the blessed hope of a glorious resurrection from those who adopt its precepts. Sproul correctly noted, "The great weakness of full preterism—and what I regard to be

---

[9] Russell, 208.

its fatal flaw—is its treatment of the final resurrection."[10] Full preterism does this by rejecting the apostolic teachings about resurrection as the reconstitution, resuscitation, and glorification of human corpses with the properties of immortality. As Wright carefully demonstrated, this apostolic understanding of the nature of resurrection came over into Christianity from the prophetic tradition of ancient Judaism.[11]

Ed Stevens' individual body at death (IBD) position represents one example of how full preterism rejects the Orthodox doctrine of resurrection. This position is based on the premise that modern Christians will never be resurrected because the resurrection was a singular event that took place in AD 70. Stevens and his colleagues argue that the resurrection consisted only of disembodied souls being raised out of Sheol or Hades.[12] This view reduces resurrection to a mere transmigration of the soul, reminiscent of the afterlife concepts in Gnosticism, Manichaeism, and Neo-Platonism. Stevens teaches that the souls of the faithful departed, individual Christians who die after the AD 70 resurrection, immediately go to heaven upon their physical departure from earthly life.

However, the majority of full preterists embrace the collective body view (CBV) invented by Max King, a Christian universalist.[13] King contended that resurrection does not pertain to the resuscitation and glorification of human corpses nor does it describe the afterlife! He defined resurrection as the corporate or collective experience of the

---

[10] Sproul, 217

[11] Wright, *Jesus and the Victory of God*.

[12] Edward E. Stevens, *Expectations Demand a First Century Rapture* (Bradford, PA: International Preterist Association, 2003); Ian D. Harding, *Taken to Heaven by AD 70: A Preterist Study of the Eschatological Blessings Expected by the First Christians at the Parousia of Christ circa AD 70* (Bradford, PA: International Preterist Association, 2005).

[13] For example, Don K. Preston, *We Shall Meet Him in the Air: The Wedding of the King of Kings* (Ardmore, OK: JaDon Management, Inc. 2012); Similarly, Max R. King, *The Cross and the Parousia of Christ: The Two Dimensions of One Age-Changing Eschaton*. Reprint Edition (Warren, OH: Parkman Road Church of Christ, 1987).

nation of Israel wherein "the dead carcass of Judaism" transformed into the new covenant Church during the period leading up to the destruction of Jerusalem in AD 70. King's collective body view also rejects the Christian doctrine of resurrection as the rising of individual human bodies from the dead.

Contrary to the teachings of full preterism, Christianity affirms that resurrection is the miraculous raising of corpses from the tombs and graves to a glorified state of eternal existence. The prophet Isaiah foretold this event:

> Your dead shall live; their bodies shall rise. You who dwell in the dust, awake and sing for joy! . . . The earth will give birth to the dead. . . The Lord is coming out from his place. . . The earth will disclose the blood shed on it and will no more cover its slain. (Isa. 26:19, 21)

The book of Daniel, alluding to this prophecy, reads as follows: "And many of those who sleep in the dust of the earth shall awake, some to everlasting life, and some to shame and everlasting contempt" (Dan. 12:2). Other biblical texts also reveal that resurrection is concerned with the glorification of material bodies. For example, the resurrected body of our Lord Jesus consisted of "flesh and bones" (Luke 24:39), and the inhabitants of Jerusalem recognized the bodies of the righteous that emerged from the tombs (Matt. 27:51-53). In addition, the apostle Paul taught that God, who resurrected Christ from the dead, will also "give life to your mortal bodies through his Spirit who dwells in you" (Rom. 8:11; cf. Rom. 8:17-25, 30; 1 Cor. 6:14-15) and will "transform our lowly body to be like his glorious body" (Phil. 3:21; cf. 1 Cor. 15:43-44).

Consistent preterism is the modern expression of the ancient heresy of Hymenaeus, a teaching which arose during the apostolic period. As evidenced by the apostle Paul's warnings to Timothy, certain men taught the heresy that *the resurrection had already taken place*!

> But avoid irreverent babble, for it will lead people into more and more ungodliness, and their talk will spread like gangrene. Among them are Hymenaeus and Philetus, who have swerved from the

truth, saying that the resurrection has already happened. They are upsetting the faith of some. (2 Tim. 2:17-18)

While Hymenaeus and Philetus professed the Christian faith, they had not fully repented, and they led people into further ungodliness with their novel doctrine. Saint Paul considered the Hymenaean doctrine a form of blasphemy that caused Christians to reject "faith and a good conscience" and to make "shipwreck of their faith" (1 Tim. 1:18-20). Full preterists argue that this heresy cannot apply to anyone today because the resurrection took place in AD 70, decisively after the apostle wrote this letter. However, if the resurrection did not take place in the first century, full preterists are the textbook expression of the Hymenaean heresy.

Similarly, the apostle Paul warned the Christians in Thessalonica to avoid the false doctrine that the day of the Lord was imminent or had already arrived (lit. "was at hand"):

> Now concerning the coming of our Lord Jesus Christ and our being gathered together to him, we ask you, brothers, not to be quickly shaken in mind or alarmed, either by a spirit or a spoken word, or a letter seeming to be from us, to the effect that the day of the Lord has come. Let no one deceive you in any way. (2 Thess. 2:1-3).

Full preterists must deny that the Bible *explicitly* addresses the topic of the salvation of Christians who live beyond AD 70. Consequently, the implication for this view is that any Christian hope of a glorious afterlife, eternal reward, or kingdom inheritance is based on conjecture, inference, and deductive speculation, having no clear prophetic precedent in the Scriptures. Chilton explained, "According to this interpretation (which might be called post-everythingism), we are now living in a never-ending limbo era, with literally no prophecies left to be fulfilled. The world will just go on and on and on and on, until . . . ?"[14] The result is that full preterists often find themselves engaged in theological speculations, bizarre conundrums, and unnecessary doubts. According

---

14   Chilton, *Paradise Restored*, 138.

to full preterism, the answers to life's ultimate questions are based on a "theology of inference" instead of clear Scriptural reasoning. What follows are examples of the awkward questions that necessarily arise from the full preterist system:

- Since resurrection is not about glorified, physical bodies, did Jesus retain His body when He ascended into heaven?

- Since the Great Commission was fulfilled at "the end of the [Jewish] age," do modern Christians have a mandate to "make disciples of all nations"?

- Since Satan was thrown into the eternal lake of fire in AD 70, can he tempt or harm people today?

- Since we live in the new heaven and new earth where sin, death, and hell no longer exist, can modern Christians actually sin?

- Since the day of the Lord occurred in AD 70, can Christians live godly lives today when the apostles taught that the futurity of this day is the primary reason for godly living (Matt. 25:31-46; Col. 1:22-23; 1 Thess. 5:23-24; 2 Thess. 1:6-10, 12; 2 Pet. 3:11)?

- Since the Church has attained to "the knowledge of the Son of God, to mature manhood, to the measure of the stature of the fullness of Christ" (Eph. 4:13), do we need spiritual gifts, including bishops, presbyters, and deacons, any longer?

- Since the coming of Christ took place in AD 70, and Christians were to observe the Eucharist to proclaim His death "until he comes" (1 Cor. 11:26), should we continue to observe the sacrament?

- Since the holy Church—"the pillar and buttress of the truth" (1 Tim 3:15)—was glorified and gathered at the resurrection in AD 70, does the Church exist in a post-AD 70 setting?

Full preterism rejects the holy Church's consistent testimony that Jesus Christ will return in our future. It also dismisses the Nicene Creed and the other Orthodox theological dogmas accepted by Catholic Christianity and designed to protect Christians from heresy and schism. The Creed clearly communicates the future expectation that Jesus "will come to judge the living and the dead."

Not surprisingly, full preterists stumble over many other doctrines that are fundamental to Christianity. For example, Don Preston undermines the doctrine of the hypostatic union by teaching that Jesus of Nazareth no longer has a human body and is no longer a man. Other full preterists, such as Max King, have embraced universalism, the teaching that all people will be redeemed regardless of whether they believed in Jesus during their lifetimes. More recently, many full preterists have accepted the "Israel only" doctrine that the Scriptures only pertain to the salvation of the Jewish nation. Many others no longer profess the name of Jesus.

Even some partial preterists have rejected Orthodox teachings by claiming that the day of the Lord took place in the historical past (2 Thess. 2:1-3).[15] Most recently, several leading Protestant scholars and pastors have become "deeply concerned" that Gary DeMar may have become a full preterist. They posted a public plea for him to affirm whether he believes in the futurity of the bodily, glorious return of Christ, the general resurrection of the dead, and the final judgment of all men. Some of these men, including Dr. James White, Kenneth Gentry, and Jeff Durbin, are leading preterist teachers. Many people have since become convinced that DeMar is a full preterist, and they confess that his statements of refusal to answer these three pivotal questions is a tacit admission of guilt.[16]

---

15 E.g., Sproul, 108, 110-11, 115.

16 Kenneth L. Gentry, "Concerns Re: Gary DeMar," https://postmillennialworldview.com/2023/03/02/concerns-re-gary-demar/ accessed on 11 August 2023.

DEBUNKING PRETERISM

MELLO AS SOON OR CERTAIN?

Some full preterists contend that the Greek verb *mello* always or nearly always conveys a sense of imminence or immediacy, and that it should be translated "be on the point of, be about to."[17] They contend that the translational biases of Bible translators have led to this verb being translated in a manner that conveys certainty instead of immediacy. They also argue that the glorious return of Jesus, the resurrection of the dead, judgment day, and the arrival of the new Jerusalem must have occurred in the first century because the New Testament authors employed this verb with respect to these eschatological events (Acts 17:31; 24:15; Rom. 8:18; 2 Tim. 4:1; Heb. 13:14).

The consistent preterist argument regarding this Greek verb has created some difficulties for partial preterists. For example, Gentry made the grammatical argument that this verb conveys imminence about the future when used with the infinitive, whether in the aorist or present tense.[18] Apparently, he was unaware that one prophecy uses the present infinitive of this verb with reference to the general resurrection (Acts 24:15). Based on Gentry's argument, the grammar of this verse supports the full preterist teaching that the resurrection occurred in the first century. He later revised his position, and at first glance it appears that he merely qualified his original statement, but a closer examination reveals that he failed once again to mention that this verse uses the present infinitive:

> The supposed evidence for hyperpreterism lies in the phrase "there shall certainly be a resurrection." Here the Greek words behind "there shall certainly be" is *mellein esesthai*. Since the base word *mello* can mean "about to," this statement is thought to demonstrate

---

[17] The Greek verb *mello* (μέλλω) in Russell, 223, 262, 291, 304, 369, 386; cf. DeMar, *Last Days' Madness*, 430.

[18] Kenneth L. Gentry, *Before Jerusalem Fell: Dating the Book of Revelation* (Fountain Inn, SC: Victorious Hope, 2010), 141-42.

that Paul stated that the resurrection is "about to" happen. This is a misreading of Paul. . . . When *mello* is used with a future infinitive it "denotes certainty that an event will occur in the future." That, and nothing more. This is why *all* the standard translations of the Acts 24:15 do not translate *mello* as expressing nearness, but simply as a future fact.[19]

The correct translation of a New Testament word should primarily be based upon its common usage in first-century Greek literature, and such usage is reliably conveyed in virtually all lexicons; nevertheless, preterists will likely continue to debate the correct translation of the verb *mello*. The translation of this verb is a relative non-issue for non-preterist interpreters, who understand that the biblical authors always portrayed the day of the Lord as pressing into the present. Traditional interpreters understand that the imminence expressed in prophecy often reflects the prophetic perspective, and as such, this verb does not indicate an immediate, first-century fulfillment. Rather, Christ's judgment of the living and the dead is always impinging upon the present.

SQUARE PEG IN A ROUND HOLE

Those who adopt preterism must face the difficult challenge of preserving their eschatological model when it does not fit the biblical data. The temptation for the preterist is to see everything through the various lenses and presuppositions of preterism. Abraham Maslow once explained, "I suppose it is tempting, if the only tool you have is a hammer, to treat everything as if it were a nail."[20] The interpretive framework of preterism pushes advocates to search for first-century fulfillments of prophecy, often with ridiculous outcomes. While interpreting the Apoc-

---

[19] Sullivan, "A Full Preterist Response to Kenneth Gentry's Articles."

[20] Abraham H. Maslow, *The Psychology of Science: A Reconnaissance* (New York: Harper and Roe, 1966), 15.

alypse, for example, Gentry argues that the unprecedented earthquake that removes every mountain and island (Rev. 16:18-21; cf. Rev. 6:14) is a symbol for the demolition crews of Roman soldiers who "labored to overcome the mountainous defenses facing them."[21] In addition, he claims that the talent-sized hailstones that fall down upon people (Rev. 16:21) represent stone ballistics (not comprised of ice!) that the Roman armies catapulted towards Jerusalem to demolish it in AD 70.[22] He even suggests that the scarlet-colored Beast in Revelation 13 and 17 symbolizes Emperor Nero's red beard![23]

Some preterists argue that the parables of Jesus suggest that He promised to vindicate and reward first-century Christians within their lifetimes, which supposedly took place when God judged Jerusalem in AD 70. DeMar reasons that Christ promised to bring speedy justice to His elect during their lifetime because the widow in the parable of the unrighteous judge received justice *during her lifetime* (Luke 18:7-8).[24] Other preterists make the same argument with the parables in the Olivet Discourse, including the parable of the faithful servant (Matt. 24:42-51), the parable of the ten virgins (Matt. 25:1-13), and the parable of the talents (Matt. 25:14-30). Traditional commentators do not consider this manner of interpretation as valid because the parables were never intended to be forced into a theological straitjacket. Hanegraaff admits, "Some say that a parable is not designed to walk on all fours. In other words, every detail in the story doesn't have to have an analogy. That is probably true."[25]

---

[21] Gentry, *The Book of Revelation*, 94.

[22] Gentry, *The Book of Revelation*, 99.

[23] Gentry, *Before Jerusalem Fell*, 217.

[24] E.g., DeMar, *Last Days' Madness*, 382.

[25] Hampton IV Keathley, "Introduction to the Parables." As of August 8, 2017. *Bible.org*. https://bible.org/seriespage/introduction-parables.

THE COST OF CONSISTENCY

Preterists often force the historical evidence to fit biblical prophecies. For example, Jordan and DeMar postulate that Haman's attempted genocide of the Jews in the fifth century BC, as described in the book of Esther, fulfilled the ancient prophecy of Gog and Magog (Ezek. 38:1-39:24).[26] However, the prophetic details in Ezekiel's prophecy blatantly contradict the historical details recorded in Esther: First, Ezekiel prophesied that Gog's vast army would be utterly defeated in the mountains of Israel by a great earthquake, the sword, pestilence, and "torrential rains and hailstones, and fire and sulfur" (Ezek. 38:19-22; 39:2-6). To the contrary, Haman never took a vast army into Israel or Judah, and the Jews slaughtered their enemies with swords throughout the provinces of Persia without a single mention of an earthquake, rain, hailstones, or fire (Esther 9:2-10). Second, Ezekiel foretold that the Jews living in the land of Israel would take spoils from the defeated northern army (Ezek. 39:10), whereas the book of Esther specifies that the Jews *refused* to take plunder from their enemies (Esther 9:10-16). Third, Ezekiel predicted that the war of Gog and Magog would occur in "the latter years" and in "the latter days" (Ezek. 38:8, 16), but the setting of the book of Esther predates "the latter days" according to preterism (i.e., the first century) by nearly 540 years.[27] Fourth, two of the divine purposes for the war of Gog and Magog is to ensure that the nation of Israel trusts Him "from that day forward" and that the Gentiles never again profane His holy name (Ezek. 38:16, 23; 39:6-7, 22). The complete fulfillment of this prophecy requires Jacob's descendants to inherit the eternal blessings of the new covenant (Ezek. 39:25-29; cf. Deut. 30:1-10). Obviously, these events await a future fulfillment, as evidenced by the fact that the particular conditions have never been fully manifested to Israel or to the nations.

---

[26] DeMar, *Last Days' Madness*, 368; Gary Demar, "But Is It In The Bible?" As of October 24, 2012. *Grace Online Library*. http://www.graceonlinelibrary.org/eschatology/dispensationalism/but-is-it-in-the-bible-by-gary-demar.

[27] DeMar, *Last Days' Madness*, 366.

DEBUNKING PRETERISM

On the other hand, preterists generally interpret the Old Testament prophets in a highly allegorical manner, which, as DeMar admits, results in an interpretation which asserts that many prophecies had been fulfilled when the Jews returned from the Babylonian exile or when the first-century Judean Church was established.[28] The preterist interpretation of the following prophecy of Zechariah illustrates this allegorical method of interpretation:

> Behold, a day is coming for the LORD, when the spoil taken from you will be divided in your midst. For I will gather all the nations against Jerusalem to battle, and the city shall be taken and the houses plundered and the women raped. Half of the city shall go out into exile, but the rest of the people shall not be cut off from the city. Then the LORD will go out and fight against those nations as when he fights on a day of battle. On that day his feet shall stand on the Mount of Olives that lies before Jerusalem on the east, and the Mount of Olives shall be split in two from east to west by a very wide valley, so that one half of the Mount shall move northward, and the other half southward. And you shall flee to the valley of my mountains, for the valley of the mountains shall reach to Azal. And you shall flee as you fled from the earthquake in the days of Uzziah king of Judah. Then the LORD my God will come, and all the holy ones with him. On that day there shall be no light, cold, or frost. And there shall be a unique day, which is known to the LORD, neither day nor night, but at evening time there shall be light. On that day living waters shall flow out from Jerusalem, half of them to the eastern sea and half of them to the western sea. It shall continue in summer as in winter. And the LORD will be king over all the earth. On that day the LORD will be one and his name one. The whole land shall be turned into a plain from Geba to Rimmon south of Jerusalem. But Jerusalem shall remain aloft on its site from the Gate of Benjamin to the place of the former gate, to the Corner Gate, and from the Tower of Hananel to the king's winepresses. And it shall be inhabited, for there shall never again be a decree of utter destruction. Jerusalem shall dwell in security. (Zech. 14:1-11)

---

28 DeMar, *Last Days' Madness*, 408.

This prophecy predicts the return of Christ Jesus and the deliverance of the Jewish remnant from the forces of the invading forces at the end of the age (Zech. 14:1-5; cf. Ezek. 38-39; Zech. 12:9-10; 14:12-21). Zechariah prophesied that a massive earthquake will create a new valley through which those in the vicinity of Jerusalem can flee (Zech. 14:4-5); this will dramatically change the topography of the land of Israel (Zech. 14:8, 10). Then the Lord God will go forth "with all the holy ones" to fight the international forces that had gathered against Jerusalem, and once again, "His feet shall stand on the Mount of Olives" (Zech. 14:2-5; cf. Zech. 12:9-10; Matt. 25:31; Acts 1:9-11). God alone knows the exact day of His return (Zech. 14:6-7; cf. Matt. 24:36; Mark 13:32). Afterwards, He will be "king over all the earth," and Jerusalem will "dwell in security" (Zech. 14:9, 11). Nothing in this passage indicates that it should be interpreted metaphorically.

Wright admits that Jesus delivered His Olivet Prophecy on the Mount of Olives because it served as a reminder of the eschatological prophecy of Zechariah 14:

> The context is the coming of the divine kingdom (Zechariah 14.9) and the coming great battle of the nations against Jerusalem (14.1-3). Zechariah 14.4-5 speaks of Israel's god standing on the Mount of Olives, and of a great earthquake, after which "YHWH your god will come, and all the holy ones with him."[29]

The Mount of Olives described in Zechariah's prophecy is also reminiscent of the angelic promise, given in that very location, prophesying that the same Jesus who visibly ascended "will come in the same way as you saw him go into heaven" (Acts 1:11). This promise, coupled with Zechariah's prophecy, strongly suggests that Christ will visibly descend from heaven and stand upon the Mount of Olives to make war against His enemies.

Many preterists equate the eschatological battle of Zechariah 12 and 14 with the Roman destruction of Jerusalem in AD 70. The greatest

---

[29] Wright, 344.

difficulty with this interpretation is that the prophecy predicts that the Lord would arrive with His holy ones to deliver the Jewish people and to fight against those who had invaded Jerusalem (Zech. 14:3-5; cf. Zech. 12:7-9). Aware of this difficulty, DeMar argues that this prophecy was fulfilled when God turned His wrath against Rome after using the empire to judge Jerusalem. However, the Roman Empire prospered for several centuries beyond Jerusalem's fall in AD 70, but this fact does not deter DeMar. He continues his allegorical interpretation by arguing that the Mount of Olives (Zech. 14:4-5) does not refer to an actual mountain or hill but is a symbol representing a kingdom.[30] He also claims that the earthquake that will split the Mount of Olives (Zech. 14:4) is a metaphor for the "breaking down of the Jewish/Gentile division" (cf. Eph. 2:14).[31] DeMar simply cannot allow for a literal fulfillment of the prophecy because it supports the traditional, futurist interpretation.

As an aside, most preterists insist upon the early date for the writing of the book of Revelation (c. AD 67-68).[32] This position rests upon several considerations which were discussed in previous chapters. Certain scholars of the late-date persuasion have adequately addressed these considerations, and therefore, they will not be detailed in this book.

Preterist conclusions drive many of its proponents to innovate novel interpretations, most of which are based on sloppy exegesis. Worse yet, many of these innovations are examples of the extreme "newspaper exegesis" of which they accuse dispensationalists; in fact, they make Hal Lindsey's "Cobra helicopters" seem comparatively mild. Proper exegesis would lead preterists to the literal interpretations found in respected conservative commentaries. But as I have demonstrated, preterists would rather completely rework the eschatological passages than embrace the

---

30 DeMar, *Last Days' Madness*, 437, 439.

31 Gary DeMar, "Zechariah 14 and the Coming of Christ." As of August 8, 2017. *Preterist Archive*. http://www.preteristarchive.com/Modern/2001_demar_zechariah-14.html.

32 See Gentry, *Before Jerusalem Fell*, 115.

traditional, futurist position. Those who stop short of embracing consistent preterism are still compelled, by the magnetism of their presuppositions, to conform the data accordingly, thus running roughshod over many exegetical considerations. Consequently, they are driven by constraint to maintain extreme interpretations that strain credulity.

16

THE END ACCORDING TO PRETERISM

ACCORDING TO PRETERISM, the destruction of the Jewish kingdom and its temple in AD 70 demonstrates that God has divorced the Jews for disobeying and rejecting His Son. Gentry claims that the theme of the book of Revelation is the divorce of old covenant Israel "as God's people" so that he may "take a new wife," that is, the new covenant Church. Chilton emphasized the apparent irreversibility of this action by adding that Jerusalem has been "divorced and executed."[1] Russell agreed that the Jews "ceased to be the covenant nation" when the theocratic nation of Jews was dissolved in AD 70."[2] Chilton emphasized the apparent irreversibility of this

---

[1] Chilton, *Paradise Restored*, 191.

[2] Hanegraaff, 49.

action by adding that Jerusalem has been "divorced and executed."[3] Russell agreed that Israel "ceased to be the covenant nation" when the theocratic nation of Jews was dissolved in AD 70.[4]

Preterist Jordan details how many preterists understand the implications of AD 70 for the identity of God's chosen people:

> The Church is the new chosen people, the new priestly nation. With the elimination of the old chosen people in AD 70, the designation of everyone else as "Gentiles" ceased to have any meaning. While people who are racially and culturally Jewish and Greek and Roman continued to exist after AD 70, these people no longer had the particular callings they had in the Old Creation. The Roman Empire was no longer a special Guardian Beast, and the Jews were no longer a special priestly nation. After AD 70, all that remain are believers and unbelievers.[5]

TO A NATION PRODUCING ITS FRUIT

Preterists tout many of the Bible passages that they believe teach that the Gentiles completely replaced the Jews. One such passage is Jesus' parable of the wicked husbandmen (Matt. 21:33-46; Mark 12:1-12; Luke 20:9-19). The parable is a retelling of Isaiah's song about God's vineyard where the symbolic vineyard is identified as "the house of Israel" (Isa. 5:1-7). Christ's parable describes a master who plants a vineyard, leaves for another country, and sends his servants to gather his fruit from the master's tenants. In a shocking act of defiance, the tenants beat and murder the servants and the master's son-heir. The parable describes the consequences for such insolence:

> "When therefore the owner of the vineyard comes, what will he do to those tenants?" They [the chief priests and elders] said to

---

[3] Chilton, *Paradise Restored*, 191.

[4] Russell, 204, 546.

[5] Jordan, loc. 482.

him, "He will put those wretches to a miserable death and let out the vineyard to other tenants who will give him the fruits in their seasons." . . . "Therefore I [Jesus] tell you, the kingdom of God will be taken away from you and given to a people producing its fruits." (Matt. 21:40-41, 43)

Preterists subtly neglect the fact that the apostolic Church is comprised of believing Gentiles and Jews. Gentry correctly observes that the kingdom of God was effectively taken away from national Israel and given to Christianity, the new holy nation (cf. 1 Pet. 2:9), in the first century AD.[6] However, Chilton took this a step further by claiming that this parable refers to a Gentile nation replacing the Jewish nation.[7] Similarly, Kik also affirmed the notion that the Gentiles took the place of the Jews.[8]

The careful reader will not miss the subtle, but significant, difference between this preterist proposition and the teaching of the Scriptures. Christ's pronouncement, "The kingdom of God will be taken away from you and given to a people producing its fruits" (Matt. 21:43; cf. Deut. 32:21), refers to Him stripping the kingdom from the largely unrepentant nation and giving it to His own disciples, specifically, to the Jewish apostles and to the Jewish (and later, Gentile) converts who received their gospel (cf. Matt. 21:45). This interpretation is further supported by the Master's statement in the preceding context that the Jewish tax collectors and prostitutes would enter God's kingdom (Matt. 21:31), the very ones that people normally presume would be the last to enter. Furthermore, this stripping of the kingdom from the Jewish nation began shortly after Pentecost and did not wait for the destruction of Jerusalem in AD 70. Finally, it may be preferable to interpret the arrival of the vineyard owner as the return of Christ at the end of the

---

[6] Gentry, *The Olivet Discourse*, loc. 527, 557, 1902; Gentry, *The Book of Revelation*, 37, 55.

[7] Chilton, *Paradise Restored*, 78.

[8] Kik, 78.

age to destroy the ungodly and to reward his saints (cf. 2 Thess. 1:7-10; 2 Pet. 3:4-7).

Preterists also advance their interpretation by appealing to the narrative of Jesus cursing the barren fig tree (Matt. 21:18-22; Mark 11:12-14, 20-25; cf. Luke 13:6-9):

> In the morning, as he [Jesus] was returning to the city, he became hungry. And seeing a fig tree by the wayside, he went to it and found nothing on it but only leaves. And he said to it, "May no fruit ever come from you again!" And the fig tree withered at once. (Matt. 21:18-19)

Many preterists teach that the barren fig tree in this prophetic drama is a metaphor for the Jewish kingdom.[9] Gentry suggests that the cursing of the tree signifies the destruction of Jerusalem that would take place in AD 70. In his view, the curse functioned as a warning that the Jewish kingdom had "reached a point of no return."[10]

Nevertheless, the text itself identifies the primary purpose of the narrative, which is to demonstrate the efficacy of the prayer of faith, not to depict the cursing of the Jewish nation in perpetuity (Matt. 21:21-22; Mark 11:21-25). In addition, although the barren fig tree likely functions as a metaphor for the Jewish kingdom (cf. Mic. 7:1; Hosea 9:10), the context appears to limit the symbol to the *contemporary* kingdom and its leaders—the chief priests, scribes, and Pharisees (Matt. 21:15, 23, 45). To further emphasize this distinction, Matthew highlighted the fact that the Jewish disciples of Jesus, unlike these leaders, produced good fruit (Matt. 3:10; 7:17-19; 13:23; John 15:2-8, 16), and Matthew communicated that Christ ordained the Jewish apostles to be the administrators of this new nation—the holy Church (Matt. 19:28; Eph. 2:20; Rev. 21:10-14).

---

9 Chilton, *Paradise Restored*, 80; DeMar, *Last Days' Madness*, 400; Gentry, *The Book of Revelation*, 142.

10 Gentry, *The Olivet Discourse*, loc. 303, 519.

The cumulative evidence shows that the prophetic message of Christ's cursing of the barren fig tree includes the concept that He was removing the contemporary, wicked shepherds from reigning over the kingdom of God. These rejected leaders were eventually removed, and their kingdom and temple destroyed, because they did not recognize the time of the Lord's visitation (Luke 19:41-44; Matt. 23:37-39). However, contrary to preterist claims, Jesus clearly anticipated that the Jewish nation would eventually receive Him as the returning King (Matt. 23:39; cf. Luke 21:24).

A NEW TEMPLE

Preterists have developed several theological principles related to the destruction of the Jerusalem temple in AD 70. Gentry explains,

> [This prophecy is about] the removing of the old covenant temple system so that the new covenant kingdom may remain in its place (Heb 12:27-28). In fact, the New Testament looks with holy anticipation to the final change from the old order to the new order, as the Temple system approaches its dramatic disestablishment in AD 70. This transition leads to "the restoration of all things" (Matt 17:11), "the regeneration" (Matt 19:28), the "times of refreshing" (Acts 3:20), the "times of the restitution of all things" (Acts 3:21), the "time of reformation" (Heb 9:10), a "new heavens and a new earth" (Rev 21:1; cf. 2 Cor 5:17; Gal 6:15), "all things new" (Rev 21:5 [cf. 22:6, 10]; cf. 2 Cor 5:17; Gal 6:15).[11]

Gentry incorrectly asserts that all the above eschatological events occurred with the destruction of the Second Temple. However, the prophecy in the book of Hebrews describes the day of Christ (Heb. 12:27-28), not the termination of the Mosaic "temple system" in the first century. Ironically, in the above quote, Gentry alludes to several events and "times" that only refer to the consummated kingdom of Christ, with

---

11 Gentry, *The Olivet Discourse*, loc. 1555.

the likely exception of "the time of reformation" (Heb. 9:10). Although many of these eschatological events have "already and not yet" aspects pertaining to the new covenant, none of them deal with the events surrounding the destruction of the temple in AD 70. The most revealing of these biblical references is about the "times of refreshing" and "the time for restoring all the things," which the apostle Peter equated with God "sending the Christ appointed for you, Jesus, whom heaven must receive until" that time (Acts 3:20-21). In other words, the New Testament teaches that these times of restoration will take place when Jesus returns from heaven! Presumably, Gentry does not realize that his quote could be used to support the full preterist argument that the Second Coming took place in AD 70.

THE END OF WHAT?

As mentioned in previous chapters, the Scriptures describe a future period known as "the latter days" or "the last days." A sparse number of Old Testament verses contain the specific phrase "the latter days," but these passages provide the reader with a unique opportunity to identity this period and its features. These passages convey that this period will include the great tribulation; this will result in Israel's national repentance and acceptance of Christ (Deut. 4:30-31; Dan. 10:14; 12:1-2; Hosea 3:5; cf. Jer. 23:20; 30:24). During the latter days, the war of Gog and Magog will ensue (Ezek. 38:8, 16), but Christ will destroy Israel's enemies (Num. 24:14, 17-19). The unprecedented tribulation will be completed when God resurrects the dead "on the last day" (Dan. 12:1-2; John 6:39-54; 11:24; 12:48; cf. Dan. 10:14). Cosmic darkness will herald the arrival of the day of Christ, and He will pour out His Spirit on all peoples (Joel 2:28-32; cf. Acts 2:16-17). Then the holy temple in Jerusalem will be exalted above the mountains, and the nations will make pilgrimage to find God there (Mic. 4:1-4; Isa. 2:1-5; cf. Zech. 14:9-11, 16-19).

DEBUNKING PRETERISM

The New Testament authors clearly taught that "the last days" and "the last hour" had arrived during the apostolic period (Acts 2:16-17; Heb. 1:1-2; 1 Pet. 1:20; 1 John 2:18). Many futurist commentators define the last days as the interval between the first and second advents of Christ, in other words, the Christian era. Interestingly, Gentry agrees with this approach: "The last days begin in earnest in the transitional era between Christ's death and the temple's destruction; they stretch from the first coming to his second coming, ending with the 'last day' at the resurrection (John 6:39-44; 11:24)."[12] One strength of this position is that the holy prophets and apostles sometimes juxtaposed "the latter days" with "the former days" (Ezek. 38:16-17; Zech. 8:11; Mal. 3:4; Rom. 15:4; Heb. 10:32).

However, it is preferable to understand "the last days" and "the end of the ages" as having arrived, in one sense, with the first advent of Christ to inaugurate the new covenant. Traditional interpreters recognize the last days as referring to the final years of eschatological events leading up to the consummate return of Jesus (the "not yet"). Those who hold this view contend that the last days arrived in an "already and not yet" sense with the first coming of Christ (1 Pet. 1:20; Heb. 1:1-2), the arrival of the eschatological Spirit (Acts 2:16-17), the conversion of the Gentiles (Acts 15:16), the appearance of false prophets and antichrists (1 John 2:18-19), the manifestation of increasing lawlessness (2 Tim. 3:1-9; 2 Pet. 3:3), the outbreak of tribulation (Rev. 1:9), the arrival of the new creation (2 Cor. 5:17), and the like.

Another opinion is the preterist view that "the last days" refers to the final period of the old covenant that supposedly ended with Jerusalem's destruction in AD 70.[13] Many of these preterists consider the end of the age to refer to the end of Jewish polity in AD 70. For example, Russell considered the end of the age to be the "extinction" of "the Jewish age or

---

[12] Gentry, *The Olivet Discourse*, loc. 1565.

[13] Chilton, *Paradise Restored*, 119; DeMar, *Last Days' Madness*, 36, 38, 292; Mathison, 189; Sproul, 97.

dispensation" and the time for the "passing away" of the Mosaic economy.[14] He summarized, "It was the winding up of the Mosaic dispensation; the end of the long probation of the Theocratic nation; when the whole frame and fabric of the Jewish polity were to be swept away, and 'the kingdom of God to come with power.'"[15] France describes it as the period for transferring Israel's kingdom to God's international people.[16] Gentry concurs with this assessment and adds that the destruction of Jerusalem in AD 70 terminated the old covenant age and economy.[17] He states, "This horrible judgment of God punctuates the end of the old covenant era and the beginning of Christ's kingdom on earth."[18] DeMar considers Jerusalem's fall to be the end of "the Old Covenant order" and the consummation and full realization of the new covenant.[19] He explains, "This fullness [of the gospel] was accomplished with the obliteration of the symbols of the Old Covenant: the temple, priesthood, and sacrificial system."[20] The age to come, in DeMar's view, designates the Christian era.[21] Chilton stated, "We must remember that 'the end' . . . is *not* the end of the world, but rather *the end of the age*, the end of the temple, the sacrificial system, the covenant nation of Israel, and the last remnants of the pre-Christian era."[22] Hank Hanegraaff considers AD 70 to be "the end of the old covenant age," an age characterized by temple

---

[14] Russell, 242, 59, 25, 37, 204.

[15] Russell, 121.

[16] R. T. France, *The Gospel According to Matthew: An Introduction and Commentary*, Tyndale New Testament Commentaries (Leicester, UK: InterVarsityPress, 1985), 5, 337; Similarly, DeMar, *Last Days' Madness*, 189.

[17] Gentry, *The Book of Revelation*, 91, 166.

[18] Gentry, *The Olivet Discourse*, loc. 1839.

[19] DeMar, *Last Days' Madness*, 37, 55, 173.

[20] DeMar, *Last Days' Madness*, 226.

[21] DeMar, *Last Days' Madness*, 191.

[22] Chilton, *Paradise Restored*, 89, 97.

and sacrifices.²³ Sproul called this the end of the "age of the Jews" and "the Jewish dispensation."²⁴

Preterists often point out that "the ends of the ages" (1 Cor. 10:11), "the end of the ages" (Heb. 9:26), "the last times" (1 Pet. 1:20), "the end of all things" (1 Pet. 4:7), and "the last hour" (1 John 2:18) had arrived during the apostolic period.²⁵ Sproul asked, "What does Jesus [in the Olivet Discourse] mean by the end? The end of what? Is Jesus speaking of the end of the temple? The end of the world? The end of the age?"²⁶ Sproul answered, "Fundamental to preterism is the contention that the phrase 'end of the age' refers specifically to the end of the Jewish age and the beginning of the age of the Gentiles, or the church age."²⁷ As expected, DeMar interprets these expressions as meaning that Jerusalem and the temple would soon be destroyed in AD 70.²⁸ He declares, "The end of what? Jesus [in the Olivet Discourse] is answering questions about the destruction of the temple and the 'end of the age,' the end of the Jewish dispensation, the Old Covenant order."²⁹ DeMar reasons that the destruction of Jerusalem in AD 70 must have been "the end" because it was "the only proximate eschatological event" on the horizon.³⁰ DeMar's statement betrays the faulty premise that the destruction of Jerusalem was the only proximate event. As demonstrated in a previous chapter of this book, the day of Christ is near, soon, and at hand.

---

23   Hanegraaff, 84-85.

24   Sproul, 56.

25   Russell, 197; Sproul, 96-97.

26   Sproul, 43; cf. p. 96

27   Sproul, 79-80, cf. pp. 100, 115.

28   DeMar, *Last Days' Madness,* 70, 87; cf. Russell, 272.

29   DeMar, *Last Days' Madness,* 86.

30   DeMar, *Last Days' Madness,* 190.

However, Gentry breaks rank with other preterists and agrees with the traditional interpretation that the end of the age will be completed when Jesus returns in glory: "As noted, sunteleia ["end"] appears first in Matthew 24:3 and points to the end of history."[31] One difficulty with Gentry's position, not shared by the futurist view, is that it requires a distinction between the end of the so-called Jewish age in AD 70 and the end of the age at Christ's return. Gentry also agrees with futurism's assessment that the angelic separation of the righteous from the wicked and the subsequent fiery destruction of the wicked will occur at the end of the age in our future (Matt. 13:39-40, 49).[32] His agreement contrasts sharply with other preterists, such as DeMar and Sproul, who consistently saw the end of the age as referring to the fiery destruction of the kingdom of Israel in AD 70.[33]

Russell erroneously accused futurists of teaching that the end of the age refers to "the close of human history, the end of time, and the destruction of the earth."[34] Preterists commonly present this straw man argument against futurism. Contrary to this argument, futurists do not teach that the end of the age is the end of the planet per se. Rather, the planet will be destroyed only in a limited sense, and human history will continue forever beyond the return of the Lord. By definition, the holy Church understands that the consummated kingdom of God will arrive "on earth as it is in heaven" (Matt. 6:10).

Mathison makes the excellent point that the reader should not "automatically assume that a reference to 'the end' means 'the end of the *Jewish* age.'"[35] Sproul admitted, "There are four references in Matthew's Gospel to 'the end of the age.' None explicitly specifies the *Jewish* age.

---

[31] Gentry, *The Olivet Discourse*, loc. 1037.

[32] Gentry, *The Olivet Discourse*, loc. 1032-37.

[33] E.g., Sproul, 108.

[34] Russell, 121.

[35] Mathison, 166.

This must be supplied on the assumption that the phrase is elliptical and the term Jewish is tacitly understood."[36] Nevertheless, the careful reader who examines the pertinent passages recognizes that the end of the age is *not* the termination of the Mosaic covenant or the destruction of the Jewish kingdom in AD 70.

Instead, the end of the age will be concurrent with the return of Christ (Matt. 24:3, 6, 14, 30). This is when God will separate the wicked from the righteous and will subsequently burn the wicked with fire (Matt. 13:39-40, 49). He will resurrect the dead and reward the faithful with eternal life (Mark 10:30; Luke 18:30; 20:34-35). Such descriptions demonstrate that this end is the completion of "the present evil age" (Gal. 1:4), the age characterized by sin and death (cf. 1 Cor. 15:24). Yet once preterists decide that these end-time prophecies are *only* concerned with the events of the First Jewish-Roman War, they necessarily redefine what "end" the apostles had in mind.

The writer of the book of Hebrews explained that Christians "have tasted the heavenly gift, have shared in the Holy Spirit, and have tasted the goodness of the word of God and the powers of the age to come" (Heb. 6:4-5). In one sense, these believers had approached the heavenly Jerusalem:

> But you have come to Mount Zion and to the city of the living God, the heavenly Jerusalem, and to innumerable angels in festal gathering, and to the assembly of the firstborn who are enrolled in heaven, and to God, the judge of all, and to the spirits of the righteous made perfect, and to Jesus, the mediator of the new covenant. (Heb. 12:22-24)

These Hebrew Christians had approached the heavenly city *in the same manner* as they had approached the heavenly beings enumerated in the passage. These beings include myriads of angels, assembled Christians "enrolled in heaven," God the Father, the perfected spirits of the righteous, and the resurrected Jesus. Elsewhere, the writer of Hebrews

---

[36] Sproul, 94-95.

communicates that Christ is in heaven (Heb. 1:3-4, 13; 4:14; 9). Therefore, we can surmise that these enumerated *heavenly* persons belong to the *heavenly* Jerusalem. In a literal sense, the Church militant has "not yet" entered the heavenly city or joined these persons in heaven; however, we have "already" approached them in a certain spiritual and proleptic manner. This passage represents another example of how believers have received the eternal promises in an "already and not yet" manner. The present accessibility of this heavenly city does not negate the doctrine that the righteous will be glorified and gathered together to meet the returning Christ, who will abide with us in the new Jerusalem in the new heavens and new earth.

It is preferable to understand the biblical texts regarding the arrival of the last days, the last hour, and the end of the age as representing the "already and not yet" principle of prophecy. Solid exegesis does not lend credence to the preterist teaching that these phrases refer to the supposed end of the Mosaic age or to the destruction of the Second Temple. In addition, the apostolic Church has always understood that the age to come awaits a future fulfillment at the return of Jesus. This is evidenced by a line of the Nicene Creed: "We look for the resurrection of the dead and the life of the world [literally 'age'] to come."[37] However, if "the age to come" is redefined to mean the so-called, present "Christian age," as preterism insists, it is easy to see how this could threaten the future Christian hope of eternal life.

The preterist reinterpretation of phrases, such as "the end of the age," is a derived necessity to support preterist claims. Tragically, these renderings also support their faulty premise that the passion, resurrection, and ascension of Christ, and the subsequent baptism of the Spirit, did not sufficiently inaugurate the new covenant, but that this inauguration awaited the decimation of the Jewish kingdom in AD 70. One

---

37   "Nicene Creed," *Wikipedia*, On August 18, 2017. https://en.wikipedia.org/wiki/Nicene_Creed; The Greek phrase ζωὴν τοῦ μέλλοντος αἰῶνος is translated here as "life in the age to come."

unfortunate result of this interpretation is that the prophetic future for the Jewish nation is rejected as theologically "out of bounds."

A NEW CREATION

Russell summarized the common preterist sentiments regarding the dissolution of the Mosaic covenant and its relationship to the dissolution of the old cosmos:

> What, then, is the great catastrophe symbolically represented as the shaking of the earth and heavens? No doubt it is the overthrow and abolition of the Mosaic dispensation, or old covenant; the destruction of the Jewish church and state, together with all the institutions and ordinances connected therewith. There were 'heavenly things' belonging to that dispensation: the laws, and statutes, and ordinances, which were divine in their origin, and might be properly called the *'spiritualia'* of Judaism—these were the *heavens*, which were to be shaken and removed. There were also 'earthly things:' the literal Jerusalem, the material temple, the land of Canaan—these were the earth, which was in like manner to be shaken and removed. The symbols are, in fact equivalent to those employed by our Lord when predicting the doom of Israel, . . . that is to say, the reference can only be the judgment of the Jewish nation and the abrogation of the Mosaic economy at the Parousia.[38]

As I explained previously, many preterists interpret the replacement of the old heavens and earth with the new heavens and earth as a metaphor for the destruction of Jerusalem in AD 70 and the transition from the old to the new covenant, which they believe was completed at that time.[39]

Preterists often quote a particular verse from the book of Hebrews to support their contention that the old covenant passed away in AD

---

[38] Russell, 289-90.

[39] DeMar, *Last Days' Madness*, 192; Gentry, *The Olivet Discourse*, loc. 1555; Kik, 32; Russell, 121.

70.⁴⁰ The verse reads as follows: "In speaking of a new covenant, he [God] makes the first one obsolete. And what is becoming obsolete and growing old is ready to vanish away" (Heb. 8:13). DeMar summarizes the preterist interpretation: "With the destruction of Jerusalem in A.D. 70 the Old Covenant that had faded in glory was obliterated."⁴¹ DeMar correctly interprets the first sentence of this passage as referring to the fact that the new covenant rendered the Mosaic covenant obsolete in Christ; however, he reads his foregone conclusion into the text, specifically, that the "vanishing away" and supposed "obliteration" of the old covenant refers to the destruction of Jerusalem in AD 70.

Because of improper hermeneutics and faulty presuppositions, most preterists have concluded that the crowning event of the new covenant was God's permanent rejection of the Jewish nation in AD 70. At very least, this theological conclusion has created a wide berth for antisemitic and anti-Zionist attitudes to prosper. Suffice it to say that the evidence presented in this chapter shows that preterism supports the theology of Israel's permanent rejection.

---

40   DeMar, *Last Days' Madness*, 37-38; Gentry, *The Olivet Discourse*, loc. 132, 1550-55; 2192; Gentry, *The Book of Revelation*, 47; Hanegraaff, 19.

41   DeMar, *Last Days' Madness*, 225.

17

ALL ISRAEL WILL BE SAVED

IF THE OLIVET PROPHECY IS ABOUT the permanent desolation of the Jewish kingdom in AD 70, the reader must wonder why Jesus' disciples later asked Him if He was going to immediately "restore the kingdom to Israel" (Acts 1:6). Preterists would have us believe that the disciples misunderstood the very foundation of the Lord's teaching about the kingdom of God after they had spent more than three years learning about it from His own lips, proclaiming its message, and hearing Him teach about it for an additional forty days after His resurrection (Acts 1:3)! Hanegraaff teaches, "Jesus reoriented their thinking [in Acts 1:6] from a restored Jewish state to a kingdom that knows no borders or boundaries,"[1] but this conclusion is somewhat misguided. The apostles were not confused about the Master's teaching regarding the *nature* of God's kingdom, and they correctly understood the Old Testament

---

[1] Hanegraaff, 182.

prophecies concerning the final restoration of Israel's kingdom. Their question ("Lord, will you at this time restore the kingdom to Israel?") indicates that they were ignorant of the *timing* of the kingdom being restored to Israel (cf. Luke 19:11).

In addition, Christ's answer did not deny the future restoration of the nation, but it showed the disciples that they had not yet been given the knowledge of the divinely-ordained "times or seasons" (Acts 1:7). His answer began to prepare them to consider the purposes for this mysterious, interadventual delay. One primary purpose has been for the apostolic Church to present the testimony of the gospel before all the nations ("you will be my witnesses" Acts 1:8; cf. Isa. 43:10-12; 44:8; Matt. 28:19; Luke 24:47). The disciples had not yet understood the apostolic mystery, namely, that the Gentiles would be grafted into Israel as coheirs of her promises prior to the day of Christ (Rom. 11:25-26; Eph. 3:6; Col. 1:27).

Chilton summarized the "serious problem" that preterists face regarding the divine election of the Jews:

> Old Israel has been excommunicated, cut off from the covenant by the righteous judgment of God. On the surface, this presents a serious problem: What about God's promises to Abraham, Isaac, and Jacob? God had sworn that He would be the God of Abraham's seed, that the covenant would be established with Abraham's seed "throughout their generations, for an everlasting covenant" (Gen. 17:7). If salvation has gone from the Jews to the Gentiles, what does that say about God's faithfulness to His word? Is there a place for ethnic Israel in prophecy? These questions are answered most directly in Scripture by the Apostle Paul in Romans 11. God never totally rejected ethnic Israel.[2]

Some preterists teach, based largely on Romans 11, that the Jewish nation will one day receive the gospel.[3] Chilton continued, "The people

---

[2] Chilton, *Paradise Restored*, 125.

[3] Chilton, *Paradise Restored*, 126; Gentry, *The Olivet Discourse*, loc. 826; Gentry, *The Book of Revelation*, 89; Kik, 81.

of Israel, as a whole, will turn back to the faith of their fathers and will acknowledge Jesus Christ as Lord and Savior. Their fall into apostasy is not permanent, says Paul."[4] Even DeMar admits, "Israel may yet have a role to play in prophecy."[5]

However, preterists often stipulate certain caveats to this promise. For example, Gentry claims, "[Israel's] special place of prominence in God's plan has been removed, however. Her geopolitical distinctiveness has ended; she will not be exalted above or distinguished from the other nations."[6] In the same vein, J. Marcellus Kik provides the following explanation:

> Even in the present time there are some within the Church who simply cannot believe that the old dispensation has been terminated. They still look for a temporal Jewish kingdom whose capital, Jerusalem, will hold sway over all the earth. This was the carnal conception of his kingdom which Christ fought and the apostles opposed, and against which his Church must still fight. It is true that we look forward to the conversion of the Jewish nation, and that the whole world will be blessed by this conversion. But this is something entirely different from the idea of a temporal Jewish kingdom holding sway over all the nations of the world.[7]

The apostle Paul desired and earnestly prayed for the salvation of the Jewish nation: "Brothers, my heart's desire and prayer to God for them is that they may be saved" (Rom. 10:1). While Paul expressed tremendous grief regarding their recalcitrance to God, he expressed the intercessory heart of Christ, so that he would have, if possible, suffered God's curse in order for them to attain salvation:

> I am speaking the truth in Christ—I am not lying; my conscience bears me witness in the Holy Spirit— that I have great sorrow and

---

[4] Chilton, *Paradise Restored*, 126.

[5] DeMar, *Last Days' Madness*, 344.

[6] Gentry, *The Book of Revelation*, 89.

[7] Kik, 75-76.

unceasing anguish in my heart. For I could wish that I myself were accursed and cut off from Christ for the sake of my brothers,1 my kinsmen according to the flesh. They are Israelites, and to them belong the adoption, the glory, the covenants, the giving of the law, the worship, and the promises. (Rom. 9:1-4)

The above passage is found in a section of the epistle (Rom. 9-11) wherein Paul often employed the term "Israel" to denote the ethnic descendants of Jacob who largely continued in an obstinate, disobedient, reprobate condition (Rom. 9:6, 27, 31; 10:19, 21; 11:2, 7, 11, 25-26). He variously called them "my brothers, my kinsmen according to the flesh," "Israelites," and "my flesh" (Rom. 9:3; 11:1, 14). Furthermore, the apostle taught that God's covenants and promises continued to belong to these ethnic Israelites (Rom. 9:4), and he called them "his [God's] people" (Rom. 11:1). Throughout Romans 11 he contrasted these unbelieving Israelites (they/them) with the Gentiles and remnant of Jews who had trusted in Christ.[8]

In this passage, Saint Paul taught the future certainty of Israel's national redemption. The Jewish nation had rejected the Lord and His prophets, had failed to obtain salvation because they pursued it on the basis of obedience to the law of Moses, and had rejected the gospel due to their hardened hearts (Rom. 11:3-10). On the other hand, many of the Gentiles had accepted the gospel of salvation, after Israel rejected it, in order that the Gentiles might make Israel jealous unto salvation (Rom. 11:11-14, 31; cf. Deut. 32:21). The apostle contrasted the nation's ongoing failure to obtain the promises, a rejection that had resulted in reconciliation for the nations (Rom. 11:15), to its future acceptance and full inclusion into those promises: "Now if their [Israel's] trespass means riches for the world, and if their failure means riches for the Gentiles, how much more will their full inclusion [lit. "fullness"] mean!" (Rom. 11:12). This acceptance always results in resurrection life ("what will

---

[8] The apostle Paul consistently employed the pronouns they, them, their, and those, to describe the unbelieving Jewish nation.

their acceptance mean but life from the dead?" Rom. 11:15; cf. Rom. 11:2).

Paul continued to contrast unbelieving Israel with the largely Gentile Church by using the analogy of the olive tree (Rom. 11:16-24). Gentile Christians were being grafted into the tree, a symbol for the nation of Israel, whereas many of the "natural branches" (i.e., ethnic Jews) had been broken off because of their unbelief (Rom. 11:16-24). The apostle warned these Gentiles not to be arrogant toward ethnic Israel because they were being grafted into their promises because the unbelieving Jews had been broken off (Rom. 11:18-20), and in like manner, the Gentiles could be broken off through unbelief (Rom. 11:22). The apostle then discussed the concept of the Lord grafting ethnic Jews back into the promises through faith in Jesus Christ (Rom. 11:23-24). He concluded with the following synopsis of Israel's future, national redemption:

> Lest you be wise in your own sight, I do not want you to be unaware of this mystery, brothers: a partial hardening has come upon Israel, until the fullness of the Gentiles has come in. And in this way all Israel will be saved, as it is written, "The Deliverer will come from Zion, he will banish ungodliness from Jacob"; "and this will be my covenant with them when I take away their sins." As regards the gospel, they are enemies for your sake. But as regards election, they are beloved for the sake of their forefathers. For the gifts and the calling of God are irrevocable. (Rom. 11:25-29)

In this passage, the apostle Paul taught the mystery of the national restoration of Israel ("all Israel will be saved" Rom. 11:25-26). The "partial hardening" of the Jewish nation will continue "until the fullness of the Gentiles has come" (Rom. 11:25). The larger context indicates that this "fullness" will include the believing Gentiles' provocation of Israel so that the surviving remnant of the nation finds salvation when Jesus returns from heaven ("The Deliverer will come from Zion" Rom. 11:26 from Isa. 59:20-21; cf. Deut. 32:21, 43) and eradicates sin and ungodliness from the descendants of Jacob (Rom. 11:26-27; cf. Isa. 27:9). This restoration of Israel is intrinsically bound up with the consummation of the new covenant ("my covenant with them when I take away their sins" Rom. 11:27; cf. Isa. 27:9) and the irrevocable gifts and election of the nation that God promised to the patriarchs ("But as regards election, they are beloved for the sake of their forefathers. For the gifts and the calling of God are irrevocable" Rom. 11:28-29).

By saving the entire remnant of surviving Jews, Christ will once again demonstrate that He "will have mercy on whom I have mercy, and I will have compassion on whom I have compassion" (Rom. 9:15). In summary fashion, the apostle declared the following doxology: "Oh, the depth of the riches and wisdom and knowledge of God! How unsearchable are his judgments and how inscrutable his ways!" (Rom. 11:33). What a sobering assessment about the unsearchable riches of God's kindnesses toward the Jewish nation and toward all the nations.

Chilton correctly saw the sequence of Israel's restoration in the prophecy of Romans 11:

> 1. The Jewish apostasy resulted in the salvation of the Gentiles; 2. The salvation of the Gentiles will someday bring about the restoration of ethnic Israel; and, finally, 3. The restoration of Israel will cause an even greater revival among the Gentiles, which (compared to everything earlier) will be much greater "riches" (v. 12), like "life from the dead" (v. 15)."[9]

Most preterists reject the notions that the Lord will return in glory to restore the kingdom to Israel and that He will bring the light of His glory to all the nations through their priestly stewardship. Nevertheless, the Lord recognized that the children of Jerusalem were not yet able to be gathered "under her wings" (Matt. 23:37; Luke 13:34), but He explained that they would yet praise Him with the words "Blessed is he who comes in the name of the Lord" (Matt. 23:39).

Preterists regards modern Jews as vestigial organs of the ancient covenant nation. According to preterism, the Jewish nation will never obtain the full measure of salvation in Jesus Christ. This is tantamount to God having brought the Jewish nation to the point of labor pains

---

[9] Chilton, *Paradise Restored*, 126.

without deliverance—a "giving birth to wind" (Isa. 26:18). Nevertheless, the biblical evidence and the testimony of the apostolic Church is that the Lord Jesus has faithfully preserved the nation (Deut. 32:10; cf. Exod. 4:22).

My distant uncle, Mark Twain, outlined the miracle of Israel's preservation:

> If the statistics are right, the Jews constitute but one quarter of one percent of the human race. It suggests a nebulous puff of star dust lost in the blaze of the Milky Way. Properly, the Jew ought hardly to be heard of, but he is heard of, has always been heard of. He is as prominent on the planet as any other people, and his importance is extravagantly out of proportion to the smallness of his bulk. His contributions to the world's list of great names in literature, science, art, music, finance, medicine and abstruse learning are also very out of proportion to the weakness of his numbers. He has made a marvelous fight in this world in all ages; and has done it with his hands tied behind him. He could be vain of himself and be excused for it. The Egyptians, the Babylonians and the Persians rose, filled the planet with sound and splendor, then faded to dream-stuff and passed away; the Greeks and Romans followed and made a vast noise, and they were gone; other people have sprung up and held their torch high for a time but it burned out, and they sit in twilight now, and have vanished. The Jew saw them all, survived them all, and is now what he always was, exhibiting no decadence, no infirmities, of age, no weakening of his parts, no slowing of his energies, no dulling of his alert but aggressive mind. All things are mortal but the Jews; all other forces pass, but he remains. What is the secret of his immortality?[10]

---

10   Samuel Clemens (Mark Twain), Quote from September 1897 as published in *The National Jewish Post & Observer* for June 6, 1984.

18

RESTORING THE KINGDOM TO ISRAEL

THE LORD MADE AN EVERLASTING COVENANT with the patriarch Abraham and his posterity which includes giving them "all the land of Canaan, as an everlasting possession" (Gen. 17:8; cf. Gen. 12:1-3, 12; 13:14-17; 15:18-21; 17:1-14; 26:3-4; 28:4). The land of the Canaanites has always belonged to Abraham and his offspring (Gen. 13:15; cf. Gen. 17:7-8), and this covenant will continue as long as the nation exists "throughout their generations" (Gen. 17:9). Moses utilized the strongest Hebrew words available to communicate the eternal perpetuity of these land promises.[1] In addition, the Lord promised to remember this covenant for a thousand generations:

> He remembers his covenant forever, the word that he commanded,
> for a thousand generations, the covenant that he made with

---

[1] This same language is used for God's everlasting covenant with Noah, which specifies that He would never again ("for perpetual generations") destroy the earth with a flood (Gen. 9:12-16).

Abraham, his sworn promise to Isaac, which he confirmed to Jacob as a statute, to Israel as an everlasting covenant, saying, "To you I will give the land of Canaan as your portion for an inheritance." (Ps. 105:8-9, 10-11; cf. 1 Chron. 16:15-22).

Clearly then, the Old Testament anticipates a literal fulfillment of the very land which God had promised to the patriarchs. Nevertheless, preterists typically deny that the land of Israel has any future prophetic significance. Hanegraaff asserts, "For Palestine was but a preliminary phase in the patriarchal promise... The climax of the promise would not be Palestine regained but Paradise restored."[2]

Hanegraaff also rehearses a common misperception about typology, claiming that the land of Israel and Jerusalem are typological for Jesus Himself.[3] Preterists are unable to offer any solid exegesis in support of this interpretation. However, if the land promises had found their fulfillment in Christ or in His apostolic Church, we would expect the New Testament to provide abundant evidence of how these promises have been modified, reinterpreted, or superseded; nevertheless, it does not communicate any supposed fulfillment. Neither the prophets, apostles, or Christ Himself taught an allegorical fulfillment of the land promises. Rather, it appears that they assumed the correctness of the traditional Jewish interpretation of those promises.

Preterism allegorizes many prophecies regarding the final return of the surviving Jews to the Promised Land. Preterists treat the prophecies about the conditions of the consummated kingdom and the detailed geographical boundaries of the glorified Jerusalem in the same way. David Baron, a nineteenth-century Jewish believer in Jesus, wrote in detail about this interpretive blunder:

> There is, first of all, the old-fashioned way of so-called spiritualizing the prophecies—making Israel and Zion to mean the Church, and The Land to signify heaven; but I confess this system of interpreta-

---

[2] Hanegraaff, 53.

[3] Hanegraaff, 170.

tion has no consistency about it, and makes the Word of God the most meaningless and unintelligible book in the world. For instance, we read here "I will bring again the captivity of My people Israel and Judah . . . and I will cause them to return to the land that I gave to their fathers." (KJV) If Israel be the Church, who is Judah? If Judah be the Church, who is Israel? What is the "captivity" the Church has endured? And where is "the land" from which the Church has been driven out, and to which it will return? . . . In what particular locality in heaven are the tower of Hananel and the corner gate? And what will our allegorical interpretations make of the hill Gareb, and Goah, and the brook Kidron? All these are known to me in the environs of the literal Jerusalem in Canaan; but I confess some difficulty in locating them in heavenly places. If Israel does not mean Israel, and "the land God gave to the fathers" does not mean Palestine, then I do not know what is meant. The announcement is: "He that scatters Israel will gather him." (Jer. 31:10) Now, when it comes to scattering—of course, this is allowed to refer to literal Israel, to the Jews, "scattered and peeled"; but when, in the same sentence, a gathering of the same people is mentioned—oh, this is the gathering of the spiritual Israel. What consistency or honesty, I pray, is there in such interpretations![4]

As I will demonstrate, the fulfillment of the everlasting covenant requires the *entirety* of the Jewish nation receive eternal righteousness through Jesus Christ; only then will the *entire* territory of the Promised Land be possessed as a *permanent* inheritance. DeMar scoffs at the traditional futurist position that "the land promises were never completely fulfilled."[5] Admittedly, during a few brief periods, the nation of Israel possessed almost all the land that had been sworn to the patriarchs (Gen. 15:18-21; cf. Gen. 13:14-18). Nevertheless, they never completely drove out the foreign nations, despite the fact that their territory extended to most of these boundaries after the conquest under the prophet Joshua and during the reign of King Solomon (Josh. 21:43; 23:4-13; 1 Kings

---

[4] David Baron, *The Jewish Problem, Its Solution; or, Israel's Present and Future . . . Introduction by Rev. A. T. Pierson* (London: Morgan & Scott, 1894), 12-14.

[5] DeMar, *Last Days' Madness*, 398.

4:21). The nation has never been able to retain the land due to national disobedience; consequently, they have been exiled multiple times. More recently, the Jews of the diaspora have suffered pogroms, the Inquisition, blood libels, the Holocaust, and Islamic jihad.

Against all odds, the Jews have miraculously survived and maintained their unique ethnic identity. Even more astonishingly, they have again returned to their ancient homeland, largely after the 1947-48 creation of the modern State of Israel. And despite being vastly outnumbered and surrounded by hostile Arab forces, the Israel Defense Forces has miraculously won several decisive wars, including the War of Independence, Sinai War, Six-Day War, and Yom Kippur War. The modern world is faced with the question of the secret to Jewish survival and the reason for their most recent return to the land and to Jerusalem. Sproul asked, "What is the significance of modern Israel and Jerusalem to biblical prophecy?"[6]

Preterists cannot adequately account for the modern State of Israel. This is especially true for preterists who entirely disconnect the nation from the new and everlasting covenant and see its existence as historical happenstance. Furthermore, the preterist claim that the nation is the result of a self-fulfilling prophecy of Christian Zionism betrays an ignorance of God's preservation of a unique Jewish identity throughout history. No other people have endured as much long-standing persecution as the Jews, and no other nation has been exiled three separate times over three millennia, only to later return to its homeland. These historical circumstances defy human logic and demonstrate the Lord's providence regarding His ancient nation.

THE NEW COVENANT

Current estimates reveal that 16 million Jews live throughout the world, 7 million of whom reside in the State of Israel. However, the

---

[6] Sproul, 30.

Jewish State, and the relatively recent regathering to the land that made it possible, must be understood as preliminary and provisional because the entire nation has not yet received regeneration and the eternal kingdom of Christ, as the ancient prophets foretold. Modern Israel is largely secular and falls far short of the gloriously-transformed remnant of surviving Jews who will have looked upon the returning Christ.

The enduring dilemma is that the vast majority of the nation has always had uncircumcised hearts and has refused to love the God of Israel with all their heart, soul, and mind (Deut. 6:5-6; cf. Lev. 26:41-42; Deut. 10:12-13; 26:16; 31:26-29). While God has not yet given the nation "a heart" to perceive the truth (Deut. 29:4), He promised to circumcise their heart:

> And when all these things come upon you [Israel], the blessing and the curse, which I have set before you, and you call them to mind among all the nations where the Lord your God has driven you, and return to the Lord your God, you and your children, and obey his voice in all that I command you today, with all your heart and with all your soul, then the Lord your God will restore your fortunes and have mercy on you, and he will gather you again from all the peoples where the Lord your God has scattered you. If your outcasts are in the uttermost parts of heaven, from there the Lord your God will gather you, and from there he will take you. And the Lord your God will bring you into the land that your fathers possessed, that you may possess it. And he will make you more prosperous and numerous than your fathers. And the Lord your God will circumcise your heart and the heart of your offspring, so that you will love the Lord your God with all your heart and with all your soul, that you may live. (Deut. 30:1-6)

In this prophecy, Moses outlined the promises that later prophets and the holy apostles called the new covenant. These promises include the Lord having compassion on the nation and gathering the people from the lands of their captivity, that is, all the nations where He had scattered them (Deut. 30:3; cf. Deut. 32:36). In addition, He pledged to give them the Promised Land (Deut. 30:5). He will regather the nation, even if the people will have been scattered to "the farthest parts under heaven" (Deut. 30:4). This demonstrates that no obstacle, not even nearly two thousand years of exile, will prevent God from bringing His people back to the land. He will also make them more prosperous and numerous than their fathers, and most importantly, He will "circumcise" the nation's heart so that they thoroughly and completely love Him (Deut. 30:5). These new covenant blessings will fulfill the expectations of the Abrahamic covenant (cf. Deut. 4:31; 30:6; Ezek. 16:60).

The apostle Paul taught that those baptized into Jesus Christ, whether Jews or Gentiles, have already received this inward circumcision: "You were also circumcised with the circumcision made without hands, by putting off the body of the sins of the flesh, by the circumcision of Christ, buried with Him in baptism, in which you also were raised with Him through faith in the working of God" (Col. 2:11-12; cf. Rom. 6:3-9).[7] However, the miraculous circumcision of the nation of Israel, promised in Deuteronomy, will include national repentance ("and you return to the Lord your God and obey His voice . . . with all your heart and with all your soul" Deut. 30:2; "when you turn to the Lord" Deut. 4:29-30).

> But from there [throughout all the nations] you will seek the Lord your God, and you will find Him if you seek Him with all your heart and with all your soul. When you are in distress, and all these things come upon you in the latter days, when you turn to the Lord your God and obey His voice (for the Lord your God is a merciful God), He will not forsake you nor destroy you, nor forget the covenant of your fathers which He swore to them. (Deut. 4:29-31)

This national repentance and the subsequent regathering of the Jewish people to the Promised Land will take place "in the latter days" (Deut. 4:30), more specifically, when the nation has experienced intense tribulation ("when you are in distress, and all these things come upon you" Deut. 4:30; "when all these things come upon you" Deut. 30:1; Jer.

---

[7] The remainder of this chapter uses the NKJV of the Bible for the Scripture references.

30:6-7). Consequently, any setting prior to the great tribulation does not fulfill the primary scope of this prophecy.

The prophet Jeremiah referred to God making a "new covenant" with the houses of Israel and Judah:

> Behold, the days are coming, says the Lord, when I will make a new covenant with the house of Israel and with the house of Judah . . . But this is the covenant that I will make with the house of Israel after those days, says the Lord: I will put My law in their minds, and write it on their hearts; and I will be their God, and they shall be My people. No more shall every man teach his neighbor, and every man his brother, saying, "Know the Lord," for they all shall know Me, from the least of them to the greatest of them, says the Lord. For I will forgive their iniquity, and their sin I will remember no more. (Jer. 31:31, 33-34; cf. Heb. 8:8-12)

As the Lord previously wrote His commandments upon stone tablets at Mount Sinai (Exod. 34:1-4; Deut. 10:1-4), His new covenant consists of Him writing His law on the tablet of the hearts of the people ("I will put My law in their minds, and write it on their hearts" Jer. 31:33; cf. Ezek. 37:24). This heart transplant will involve God removing their stony heart and replacing it with a compliant heart of flesh so that they wholeheartedly trust in Him (Ezek. 11:19; 36:26-27; cf. Jer. 24:7).[8] Those belonging to the holy apostolic Church have already received the gift of the Holy Spirit: "You are an epistle of Christ . . . written not with ink but by the Spirit of the living God, not on tablets of stone but on tablets of flesh, that is, of the heart . . . the new covenant" (2 Cor. 3:3, 6-11). When the Jewish nation receives the new covenant, they will be included among the holy Church, and the Lord will become their God (Jer. 24:7; 30:22; 31:33; 32:38; Ezek. 11:20; 34:30-31; 36:28; 37:27; Zech. 8:8; Heb. 8:13).

One purpose of Jesus Christ coming to redeem His people was to fulfill the covenantal promises given to the patriarchs (Luke 1:68-75).

---

[8] The *stone* tablets of the law and the *flesh* of Jesus Christ are fitting corollaries to these two conditions of the heart.

More to the point, He inaugurated the new covenant with His sacrificial death on the cross. He testified to this after He blessed the cup of wine at the Last Supper (Matt. 26:27; Mark 14:23; Luke 22:20), declaring, "For this is My blood of the new covenant, which is shed for many for the remission of sins" (Matt. 26:28). This covenant will be consummated when the nation receives Christ's sacrificial blood: "I will remember My covenant with you in the days of your youth, and I will establish an everlasting covenant with you . . . when I provide you an atonement for all you have done" (Ezek. 16:60, 63; cf. Deut. 32:43; Dan. 9:24). Furthermore, the Father sent His Suffering Servant, whom He raised up through resurrection, to be an everlasting covenant for Israel and to restore and "raise up" the tribes of Jacob (Isa. 42:6 with 49:6).

The Almighty pledged the Promised Land to the nation of Israel as an everlasting possession, but only when all the people receive His everlasting righteousness: "Your people shall all be righteous; they shall inherit the land forever . . . that I may be glorified" (Isa. 60:21; cf. Dan. 9:24). The Lord will forgive the sins of all Israel's people:

> I will bring back Israel to his home, and he shall feed on Carmel and Bashan; his soul shall be satisfied on Mount Ephraim and Gilead. . . . The iniquity of Israel shall be sought, but there shall be none; and the sins of Judah, but they shall not be found; for I will pardon those whom I preserve. (Jer. 50:19, 20; cf. "I will forgive their iniquity, and their sin I will remember no more" Jer. 31:34; cf. Ezek. 11:18; 36:25, 29; 37:23)

No longer will anyone need to evangelize the people of Israel ("no more shall every man teach his neighbor . . . saying, 'Know the Lord,'" because they will all know the Lord "from the least of them to the greatest of them" Jer. 31:34; cf. Jer. 32:37; Ezek. 39:22). The nation will be committed to righteousness and all its children "shall be taught by the Lord" (Isa. 54:13-17), and the Holy Spirit will speak behind them so to speak, saying, "This is the way, walk in it" (Isa. 30:21). They will never depart from Him because of their fear of the Lord (Jer. 32:40); there will be no defectors! The remnant will be completely righteous, honest, and without deceit (Zeph. 3:13). These prophecies were not fulfilled in the nation's history but await a future fulfillment.

Because of their righteousness, the descendants of Israel will never again be "cast off" for their iniquities (Jer. 31:37). The nation is permanent, like the fixed orders of the solar system and oceanic currents: "If those ordinances depart from before Me, says the Lord, then the seed of Israel shall also cease from being a nation before Me forever" (Jer. 31:36; cf. Isa. 66:22; Jer. 31:35; 33:23-26). As God promised to never again cover the Earth with a flood, He promised an everlasting "covenant of peace" to mercifully preserve the nation (Isa. 54:9-10).

The prophet Ezekiel also wrote about the new covenant and connected the nation's acceptance of it with their final ingathering to the land of Israel:

> I will gather you from the peoples, assemble you from the countries where you have been scattered, and I will give you the land of Israel. And they will go there, and they will take away all its detestable things and all its abominations from there. Then I will give them one heart, and I will put a new spirit within them, and take the stony heart out of their flesh, and give them a heart of flesh, that they may walk in My statutes and keep My judgments and do them; and they shall be My people, and I will be their God. (Ezek. 11:17-20; cf. Jer. 32:37-41; Ezek. 36:24-27)

As this passage demonstrates, the national reception of the everlasting covenant cannot be divorced from the reception of the Promised Land (cf. Isa. 60:21; Jer. 50:19-20). This land is the same which the Canaanites once possessed and which God promised to the patriarchs (Ezek. 36:28; cf. Ps. 105:8-11). Furthermore, the Promised Land cannot be allegorized to refer to a non-earthly place in heaven without causing violence to the sacred text. The following passage illustrates the importance of a literal interpretation:

> On the day that I cleanse you from all your iniquities, I will also enable you to dwell in the cities, and the ruins shall be rebuilt. The desolate land shall be tilled instead of lying desolate in the sight of all who pass by. So they will say, "This land that was desolate

has become like the garden of Eden; and the wasted, desolate, and ruined cities are now fortified and inhabited." Then the nations which are left all around you shall know that I, the Lord, have rebuilt the ruined places and planted what was desolate. I, the Lord, have spoken it, and I will do it. (Ezek. 36:33-36)

The immediate context reveals that the new covenant will take place when God has completely purified the nation of Israel ("on the day that I cleanse you from all your iniquities" Ezek. 36:33; cf. Ezek. 36:24-27). The following chapter reveals that the everlasting covenant will consist of the Israelites returning to their ancestral homeland and fully accepting their Messiah:

> Surely I will take the children of Israel from among the nations, wherever they have gone, and will gather them from every side and bring them into their own land; and I will make them one nation in the land, on the mountains of Israel; and one king shall be king over them all . . . I will deliver them from all their dwelling places in which they have sinned and will cleanse them. Then they shall be My people, and I will be their God. David My servant shall be king over them, and they shall all have one shepherd; they shall also walk in My judgments and observe My statutes and do them. Then they shall dwell in the land that I have given to Jacob My servant, where your fathers dwelt; and they shall dwell there, they, their children, and their children's children, forever; and My servant David shall be their prince forever. Moreover I will make a covenant of peace with them, and it shall be an everlasting covenant with them; I will establish them and multiply them. (Ezek. 37:21-26; cf. Ezek. 37:15-21)

This new and everlasting covenant of peace will include the eternal reign of Jesus Christ over the nation of Israel ("David My Servant shall be King over them, and they shall all have one Shepherd" Ezek. 37:24-25; cf. Isa. 55:3-4; Jer. 32:37; Ezek. 34:23-25; 37:24-26; Hosea 1:11). This reign will occur in the land of Israel after Israel has regathered from their dispersion throughout the nations (Ezek. 37:21-22, 25; cf. Jer. 32:37; Ezek. 11:17; 34:23-25, 31). In addition, they will live there in eternal perpetuity ("they shall dwell there, they, their children, and their children's children, forever" Ezek. 37:25).[9] This prophecy emphasizes that the Promised Land is the same geographical region where the patriarchs once lived ("in the land that I have given to Jacob My servant, where your fathers dwelt" Ezek. 37:25).

The Lord promised to assemble the entire nation of Israel back to their land (Jer. 23:3; Ezek. 28:25; Mic. 2:12; Zech. 10:9). Isaiah taught, "The Lord will have mercy on Jacob, and will still choose Israel, and settle them in their own land" (Isa. 14:1; cf. Jer. 24:6). The people will be firmly "planted" in the land and will never again be "plucked up" or oppressed by their enemies (2 Sam. 7:10; Jer. 24:6; Amos 9:15; cf. Jer. 24:6; 32:41). The Lord has spoken, "For a mere moment I have forsaken you, but with great mercies I will gather you. With a little wrath I hid My face from you for a moment; but with everlasting kindness I will have mercy on you" (Isa. 54:7-8).

As we have seen, the Jews will be removed and dispersed throughout the nations by one final, short captivity, which will begin with the Antichrist's invasion of the Promised Land (Zech. 14:2; Luke 21:24). Nevertheless, the Lord will not allow all the descendants of Jacob and Judah to be destroyed by their enemies, but He will save a remnant to inherit the land (Isa. 65:8-9; Jer. 31:7; cf. Isa. 49:19).

This gathering will take place at the sounding of the last trumpet that also signals Christ's return and the resurrection. Isaiah declared, "You will be gathered one by one, O you children of Israel. So it shall be in that day: The great trumpet will be blown; they will come, who are about to perish in the land of Assyria and they who are outcasts in the land of Egypt, and shall worship the Lord in the holy mount at Jerusalem" (Isa. 27:12-13; cf. Isa. 19:23-25; Jer. 31:7-9).

God will save the remnant of Jews by bringing them out from all the nations of their captivity. They will travel back to the land with weeping and supplications because He will pour out "the Spirit of grace and supplication" upon them so that they mourn when they look

---

[9] cf. Jer. 32:37, 41; Ezek. 11:17; 34:25-29; 36:24, 28; 37:25-26; 39:26-28.

upon the pierced and returning Christ (Jer. 31:9; Zech. 12:10; cf. Matt. 24:30). He will no longer hide His face when He pours His Spirit upon them (Ezek. 39:29; cf. Isa. 32:15; 59:21). Once Jerusalem experiences the tribulation ("for as soon as Zion was in labor"), the entire nation will be born from heaven "in one day"—the day of Christ (Isa. 66:7-8; cf. Mic. 4:9-10; 5:3).

> Peoples shall yet come, inhabitants of many cities; the inhabitants of one city shall go to another, saying, "Let us continue to go and pray before the Lord, and seek the Lord of hosts. I myself will go also." Yes, many peoples and strong nations shall come to seek the Lord of hosts in Jerusalem, and to pray before the Lord. . . In those days ten men from every language of the nations shall grasp the sleeve of a Jewish man, saying, "Let us go with you, for we have heard that God is with you." (Zech. 8:20-22, 23)

Every nation will send a delegation of men to accompany each Jewish man as he journeys to the Holy City (Zech. 8:23; cf. Isa. 45:14, 24; 60:14). These representatives will entreat favor from the Lord and pray to Him in Jerusalem on behalf of their nations ("to pray before the Lord" Zech. 8:22). The imagery is that Gentiles will cling to the corners of Jewish men's sleeves in order to accompany them to the Holy City (Zech. 8:23; cf. Matt. 14:35-36; Mark 5:27-28; 6:56). These representatives of the nations will speak to Jews, "We have heard that God is with you" (Zech. 8:23; cf. Isa. 7:14).

The everlasting covenant includes the nations knowing the descendants of Jacob as "the posterity whom the Lord has blessed" (Isa. 61:8-9). As the Jews brought the gospel to the nations, the Gentiles will assist in bringing their newly converted Jewish brethren back to their ancestral land by ships and by flight (Isa. 60:8-9). Others will transport the people upon "horses and in chariots and in litters, on mules and on camels, to My holy mountain Jerusalem" (Isa. 66:20). Some Gentiles will even carry Jews in their arms and upon their shoulders (Isa. 49:22; cf. Isa. 14:1-2). Leaders of nations ("kings shall be your foster fathers, and their queens your nursing mothers" Isa. 49:23) will even bow down to them in veneration and honor ("they shall bow down to you with their faces to the earth, and lick up the dust of your feet" Isa. 49:23; cf. Rev. 3:9).

After Israel returns to the land, their "wasted, desolate, and ruined cities" will be rebuilt so they look like the garden of Eden (Ezek. 36:35; cf. Jer. 31:4; Amos 9:14). The Lord declares, "And they will dwell safely there, build houses, and plant vineyards; yes, they will dwell securely," which will occur when judgments fall on those who despise them (Ezek. 28:26). Rebuilding desolate cities, constructing houses, and planting vineyards demonstrate beyond all reasonable doubt that the land of Israel, and not heaven per se, is in view. The people will dwell safely in the land with no fear (Jer. 30:10; 46:27; Ezek. 39:26).

As we have seen, Christ inaugurated the new and everlasting covenant by His death (Luke 22:20; 1 Cor. 11:25), and the Holy Spirit seals the holy Church, whether Jews or Gentiles, into the covenant (2 Cor. 3:1-6). When this covenant is consummated, all Jacob's descendants will have permanent holiness and security in the Promised Land. The ultimate seed of the patriarchs—Jesus Christ—is the nation's hope for receiving the Abrahamic promises (Gal. 3:16, 19, 29), and by His grace, all the surviving Jews will receive His everlasting righteousness and become joint heirs of these eternal promises (cf. Rom. 4:16-17).[10] Nothing will fulfill the expectations of the covenant except a permanent and complete salvation of Israel's surviving children under the headship of Christ.

THE EVERLASTING CITY

The prophets taught that Jerusalem will serve as the eternal capital of Christ's throne and kingdom (Mic. 4:7) and the quintessential glory of Israel and the world. The Lord promised to make the city the eternal

---

[10] The Gentiles who trust in Christ are also heirs of the everlasting covenant. Together, the two groups comprise the one holy Church.

place of His rest (Ps. 132:13-14), and the place where His name would remain forever (1 Kings 9:3; 2 Kings 21:7; 2 Chron. 7:16; 33:7). When He returns, He will inherit Judah and "will again choose Jerusalem" (Zech. 2:12; cf. Obad. 1:17; Zech. 8:2). The Lord asked, "Can a woman forget her nursing child and not have compassion on the son of her womb? Surely they may forget, yet I will not forget you [Zion]. See, I have inscribed you on the palms of My hands; your walls are continually before Me" (Isa. 49:15-16).

Mount Zion will be the epicenter for the gathering of Israel's descendants (Jer. 3:14, 18; Zech. 8:8, 22). God will gather together Jerusalem's children, and the armies of the nations will no longer bring desolation and destruction upon the land (Isa. 49:17-19; cf. Isa. 60:4, 17-18). In those days

> the children of Israel shall come, they and the children of Judah together; with continual weeping they shall come and seek the Lord their God. They shall ask the way to Zion, with their faces toward it, saying, "Come and let us join ourselves to the Lord in a perpetual covenant that will not be forgotten." (Jer. 50:4-5)

The prophet Zechariah expounded that the topography of Jerusalem and its surrounding region will be transformed. The unprecedented earthquake on the day of Christ will significantly elevate the Holy City (Zech. 14:4-11; cf. Isa. 40:3-4). The new Jerusalem will be built "upon its own mound" to provide a perpetual location for the royal palace (Jer. 30:18; cf. Ps. 48:3; Isa. 2:1-5). It will be elevated to become part of a mountain plain which will include Geba to the north and Rimmon to the south:

> All the land shall be turned into a plain from Geba to Rimmon south of Jerusalem. Jerusalem shall be raised up and inhabited in her place from Benjamin's Gate to the place of the First Gate and the Corner Gate, and from the Tower of Hananel to the king's winepresses. The people shall dwell in it; and no longer shall there be utter destruction, but Jerusalem shall be safely inhabited. (Zech. 14:10-11)

The city shall be built for the Lord from the Tower of Hananel to the Corner Gate. The surveyor's line shall again extend straight forward over the hill Gareb; then it shall turn toward Goath. And the whole valley of the dead bodies and of the ashes, and all the fields as far as the Brook Kidron, to the corner of the Horse Gate toward the east, shall be holy to the Lord. It shall not be plucked up or thrown down anymore forever. (Jer. 31:38-40)

Micah also prophesied the great elevation of the Holy City:

Now it shall come to pass in the latter days that the mountain of the Lord's house shall be established on the top of the mountains and shall be exalted above the hills; and peoples shall flow to it. Many nations shall come and say, "Come, and let us go up to the mountain of the Lord, to the house of the God of Jacob; He will teach us His ways, and we shall walk in His paths." For out of Zion the law shall go forth and the word of the Lord from Jerusalem. (Mic. 4:1-2; cf. Isa. 2:2-3)

Based on the other prophetic witnesses of Scripture, we understand that the glorified Jerusalem ("the mountain of the Lord's house" Mic. 4:1) will be elevated above all mountains ("the top of the mountains and shall be exalted above the hills" Mic. 4:1; cf. Isa. 2:2-3; 40:9; Rev. 21). Everyone will see its glory, and many Gentiles will ascend the mountain and will flow there to learn Christ's ways, while His teachings will proceed from this place to the nations (Mic. 4:2; cf. Acts 1:8). The Holy City "shall be inhabited *again* in her own place" (Zech. 12:6).

Jesus taught that His kingdom is heavenly and "not of this world" (John 18:36; 2 Tim. 4:18). Such statements must be understood as describing the origin or source of the kingdom because the domain of Christ's reign will include heaven and earth. To demonstrate, the Scriptures express that the humble will inherit the earth when He consummates His kingdom (Matt. 5:5; cf. Eccles. 1:4; Matt. 6:10). This is why the apostle Paul taught that God will give His saints "all things," including the world (Rom. 8:32; 1 Cor. 3:21-22).

After He returns in glory, Jesus will be King over the entire Earth (Zech. 14:9). King Solomon summarized, "He shall have dominion also from sea to sea, and from the River to the ends of the earth" (Ps. 72:8). At that time, everyone on the planet will fear His holy name (Isa. 59:19). The only begotten Son will acquire the nations, even "the ends of the earth," as an eternal inheritance (Ps. 1:6-8; cf. Ps. 67:7). Consequently, "the earth shall be full of the knowledge of the Lord as the waters cover the sea" (Isa. 11:9; cf. Hab. 2:14).

This does not imply that the God-Man will begin to reign from David's throne only at His return (cf. Matt. 19:28; Matt. 25:31-32). Rather, His heavenly reign began when He ascended to sit at God's right hand (Acts 2:29-36; cf. Matt. 28:18), and He will continue to reign until His enemies become His footstool (Ps. 110:1-2; 1 Cor. 15:24-26; Heb. 10:12-13). In the meantime, He mysteriously reigns "in the midst" of His enemies in an "already and not yet" manner (Ps. 110:2).

The returning Lord will also bring abundant rainfall, "the former rain and the latter rain in the first month," to Jerusalem (Joel 2:23; cf. Ps. 72:6; Ezek. 34:26; Hosea 6:3; Zech. 10:1). As a result, the brooks of Judah will flood (Joel 3:18), while rivers and streams will flow on every high mountain and hill (Isa. 30:25; cf. Isa. 41:18). The deserts will produce springs, streams, and pools, sustaining new grasses, reeds, and rushes (Isa. 35:6-7; 41:18; cf. Zech. 10:1), so they abundantly "blossom as the rose" and praise the Lord "with joy and singing" so to speak (Isa. 35:1-2; cf. 1 Chron. 16:31-32).

At this time, the Holy Spirit will be poured out from heaven so that Israel's "wilderness becomes a fruitful field, and the fruitful field is counted as a forest" (Isa. 32:15). Instead of the curse of thorns and briers (cf. Gen. 3:18), the Earth will produce cypress and myrtle trees forever (Isa. 55:13). Cedar, acacia, myrtle, cypress, olive, pine, and box trees will also flourish (Isa. 41:19; 60:13).

Plants will produce buds and blossoms throughout Israel, and the world will be filled with its fruit (Isa. 27:6). No one will experience hunger because the "garden of renown"—the garden of Eden—will nourish them (Ezek. 34:29). The land will produce abundant grain in open pastures, lush vineyards, fruit-bearing trees, and olive oil (Hosea

2:15, 21-22; Joel 2:18-19, 22; cf. Ps. 67:6; 72:16; Isa. 30:23; Jer. 31:12; Ezek. 34:27; 36:29-30; Amos 9:13-14; Zech. 8:12; 9:17). The abundant rain will lead to threshing floors being filled with wheat and vats overflowing with wine and oil (Joel 2:24; cf. Ezek. 34:27). He also prophesied, "And it will come to pass in that day that the mountains shall drip with new wine, the hills shall flow with milk" (Joel 3:18).

The land of Israel will also be filled with flocks and herds (Isa. 65:10; Jer. 31:12, 24-25, 27). The oxen will feed in large pastures (Isa. 30:23-24), and Gentiles will participate in feeding animals, plowing fields, and dressing vineyards (Isa. 61:5-7). The Lord's people, like stall-fed calves, will eat plentifully (Mal. 4:2; cf. Joel 2:26).

Meanwhile, the forsaken land of Israel will become "an eternal excellence, a joy of many generations" (Isa. 60:15). Her people will rebuild and repair the ruined, desolate cities "of many generations" (Isa. 61:4; cf. Jer. 31:28; Ezek. 38:8), and Gentiles will help with the construction (Isa. 60:10). In the new Jerusalem, people will continue to toil with their hands to construct houses, engage in agricultural endeavors, and eat:

> Behold, I create new heavens and a new earth. . . . They shall build houses and inhabit them; they shall plant vineyards and eat their fruit. They shall not build and another inhabit; they shall not plant and another eat . . . and My elect shall long enjoy the work of their hands. They shall not labor in vain (Isa. 65:17, 21–23; cf. Jer. 31:28).

These blessed conditions of the future consummated kingdom have not yet been fulfilled. They also describe conditions on earth, which can either be understood literally within the framework of futurism or explained away by the allegorizing hermeneutic of preterism.

19

REPENTING OF PRETERISM

MY JOURNEY INTO PRETERISM began in earnest during my first master's degree training at Midwestern Baptist Theological Seminary in 2000. Like many of my colleagues, I struggled to find biblical support for the pretribulational dispensationalist perspective, which proliferated on the Protestant theological landscape. Although my Hebrew and Greek professors held to other futurist eschatological positions, including historic premillennialism and amillennialism, they provided me with little exegesis of the pertinent eschatological scriptures.

During my seminary training, I became increasingly confused by the time statements in the New Testament that indicate a "near," "soon," and "at hand" coming of the Son of Man. I became persuaded that preterism interpreted these statements coherently and consistently. My position was reinforced once I became familiar with preterist works, especially those of R. C. Sproul, Hank Hanegraaff, N. T. Wright, Gary DeMar, Kenneth Gentry, David Chilton, and R. T. France. My conviction was further strengthened after Hanegraaff announced that he had become convinced of preterism and began promulgating these views on his *Bible Answer Man* radio program.

Initially, I spent several years as a partial preterist, but then began to seriously consider full preterism. I had always considered full preterism to be a blatant heresy, largely due to its rejection of the Nicene Creed and repudiation of the doctrine of the individual, bodily resurrection of the dead. Nevertheless, once I was introduced to full preterist arguments, beginning with those in the works of James Stuart Russell, Don K. Preston, and Edward Stevens, I began the arduous process of embracing the position. This noble process derived from my commitment to maintain a consistent hermeneutic, but it ultimately proved to be a misguided gambit. In time, I discovered how full preterism differs dramatically from Orthodox Christianity in every area of theology, including Christology, soteriology, ecclesiology, pneumatology, angelology, and of course, eschatology.

Later, I became a teacher for a preterist Bible study for a few years. I also presented and defended preterist eschatology as the host of *Fulfilled Life*, an online radio program on Covenant Key FM. During this time, like many full preterists, I engaged in sharp disputes over trivialities and arrogant controversies about the foundational doctrines of Christianity. In retrospect, it is apparent to me that my striving against the apostolic Christian faith and its ecclesiastical authority prevented me from experiencing much joy and peace.

By 2013, I had written and published a booklet, *Let No Man Separate*, in defense of consistent preterism, and Don Preston invited me to be a conference speaker at his Preterist Pilgrim Weekend, a full preterist prophecy conference held in Ardmore, Oklahoma. But God, who is gracious and full of compassion, had different plans for my life. On the very night that I received the first box of booklets from my publisher, I sensed a burden to reexamine the biblical doctrine of resurrection; this examination led me to repent of my involvement with full preterism and to discard these newly-published materials. Over the next several months, I engaged in the process of abandoning preterism altogether, and the spiritual rewards have been immeasurable.

Four years later, the fresh burden upon my heart was to author a book that provided readers with a road map for refuting preterism and a brief framework for discovering the eschatology of Christ and His apostles. I completed the first edition of *Debunking Preterism* in only three months, pushed forward in the writing by a sense of urgency that preterism needed to be confronted, largely because of its rapid growth and inherent dangers, especially in light of the nearness of the Lord's return. The book advances sound biblical exegesis to demonstrate the truthfulness of the traditional, post-tribulational eschatology of the holy apostolic Church and to expose the faulty premises and conclusions of preterist eschatology.

THE IMPLICATIONS OF PRETERISM

As demonstrated throughout this book, preterism reinterprets many passages that are concerned with the future unprecedented tribulation, the glorious return of Jesus, and the consummated kingdom of God. Consequently, those who have embraced preterism will undoubtedly be caught off guard by the construction of the Third Temple in Jerusalem; as a result, they may experience theological confusion and disbelief in the fulfillment of many prophecies. Succinctly put, preterists will be unprepared for the unprecedented tribulation that will come upon "the whole world, to try those who dwell on the earth" (Rev. 3:10). They may fall victim to the prophesied "strong delusion" when the Antichrist sets up the abomination of desolation and begins his worldwide assault on Jews and Christians (2 Thess. 2:8-12); then for forty-two months, he will force "all who dwell on earth," those from "every tribe and people and language and nation," to worship him (Rev. 13:5-8).

In addition, preterists have created theological disunity and other unnecessary divisions among those who profess Christ, because preterism undermines a proper understanding of many prophecies that describe our blessed hope at the appearance of Christ. Many preterists have descended into further theological confusion, and some have unwittingly accepted the ancient heresy that the day of the Lord is "at hand" or has already arrived (2 Thess. 2:1-3). Others have stopped short of embracing full preterism, not because of a proper understanding of biblical eschatology, but because of their purported commitment to Orthodoxy as defined by the Ecumenical Councils and the early creeds of the Church.

My prayer and purpose for writing this book is that many people will repent of the false doctrines of preterism. As demonstrated herein, the subtle allure of preterism lies in its primary claim, specifically, that its interpretation of the time statements of Scripture is based on clear, logical argumentation. However, the entire preterist hermeneutic is built upon an inadequate understanding of these statements, of the prophetic perspective, and of the "already and not yet" principle of eschatology. My desire is that Christians who read this book will become more informed about preterism and better equipped to challenge its arguments, in order to warn others of its dangers.

SOURCES

Adams, Jay E., and Milton C. Fisher. *The Time of the End*. Hackettstown, NJ: Timeless Texts, 2000.

Baron, David. *The Jewish Problem, Its Solution; or, Israel's Present and Future ... Introduction by Rev. A. T. Pierson*. London: Morgan & Scott, 1894.

Beale, G. K. *The New International Greek Testament Commentary*. Carlisle: Paternoster Press, 1999.

----------. *1-2 Thessalonians*. The IVP New Testament Commentary Series. Downers Grove, IL: Inter Varsity Press, 2003.

Beale, G. K., and D. A. Carson. *Commentary on the New Testament Use of the Old Testament*. Grand Rapids: Baker Academic, 2007.

Bell, William E., Jr. "A Critical Evaluation of the Pretribulational Rapture Doctrine in Christian Eschatology," (Th.D. dissertation, New York University, April 1967): 249-50.

Bercot, David W. *A Dictionary of Early Christian Beliefs: A Reference Guide to More Than 700 Topics Discussed by the Early Church Fathers*. Peabody, MA: Hendrickson Publishers, Inc, 1998.

Bruce, F. F. *The Epistles to the Colossians, Philemon and to the Ephesians*. Grand Rapids: Eerdmans, 1984.

Caird, G. B. *Jesus and the Jewish Nation*. London: University of London, the Athlone Press, 1965.

Caird, G. B., and L. D. Hurst. *New Testament Theology*. Oxford: Clarendon Press, 1994.

Calvin, John. *Commentary on a Harmony of the Evangelists, Matthew, Mark, and Luke*. Trans. William Pringle, vol. 3. Grand Rapids: Baker, 1984.

SOURCES

----------. *Reformation Commentary on Scripture: Ezekiel, Daniel.* Edited by Carl L. Beckwith. Downer's Grove, IL: InterVarsity PressAcademic, 2012

Carson, D. A., "Matthew," in Frank E. Gaebelein, ed., *The Expositor's Bible Commentary*, vol. 8. Grand Rapids: Zondervan, 1984.

Chilton, David. *The Days of Vengeance: An Exposition of the Book of Revelation.* Horn Lake, MS: Dominion Press, 2006.

Chilton, David. *Paradise Restored: A Biblical Theology of Dominion.* Horn Lake, MS: Dominion Press, 2007.

Danker, Frederick W., Walter Bauer, and William F. Arndt. *A Greek-English Lexicon of the New Testament and Other Early Christian literature.* 3rd ed. Chicago: University of Chicago Press, 2000.

DeMar, Gary, *Last Days' Madness: Obsession of the Modern Church.* Atlanta: American Vision, 1999.

----------. "But Is It In The Bible?" As of October 24, 2012. *Grace Online Library.* http://www.graceonlinelibrary.org/eschatology/dispensationalism/but-is-it-in-the-bible-by-gary-demar

----------. "Zechariah 14 and the Coming of Christ." As of August 8, 2017. *Preterist Archive.* http://www.preteristarchive.com/Modern/2001_demar_zechariah-14.html

Fee, Gordon D. *The First and Second Letters to the Thessalonians.* Grand Rapids: William B. Eerdmans Publishing, 2009.

France, R. T. *The Gospel According to Matthew: An Introduction and Commentary.* Tyndale New Testament Commentaries. Leicester, UK: InterVarsityPress, 1985.

----------. *The Gospel of Mark: a Commentary on the Greek Text.* Grand Rapids: W.B. Eerdmans, 2002.

----------. *The Gospel of Matthew. The New International Commentary on the New Testament.* Grand Rapids: William B. Eerdman's Publishing, 2007.

Frost, Sam. [Article title unknown]. As of November 8, 2012. *The Reign of Christ.* http://thereignofchrist.com/daniel-122/.

Gaebelein, Frank E., et. al. *The Expositor's Bible commentary With the New International Version of the Holy Bible.* Grand Rapids: Zondervan Publishing House, 1981.

Gentry, Kenneth L. *The Greatness of the Great Commission*. Tyler, TX: Institute for Christian Economics, 1990.

----------. *Before Jerusalem Fell: Dating the book of Revelation: An Exegetical and Historical Argument for a Pre-A.D. 70 Composition*. Revised ed. Powder Springs, GA: American Vision, 1998.

----------. *The Book of Revelation Made Easy*. Powder Springs, GA: The American Vision, Inc., 2008.

----------. *He Shall Have Dominion: A Postmillennial Eschatology*. Draper, VA: Apologetics Group Media, 2009.

----------. *Before Jerusalem Fell: Dating the Book of Revelation*. Fountain Inn, SC: Victorious Hope, 2010.

----------. *The Book of Revelation Made Easy: You Can Understand Bible Prophecy*. Powder Springs, GA: American Vision Press, 2010.

----------. *The Olivet Discourse Made Easy: You Can Understand Jesus' Great Prophetic Discourse*. Draper, VA: Apologetics Groucom, 2010. Kindle Edition.

Hanegraaff, Hank. *The Apocalypse Code: Find Out What the Bible Really Says About the End Times and Why It Matters Today*. Nashville: Thomas Nelson, 2007.

Harding, Ian D. *Taken to Heaven by AD 70: A Preterist Study of the Eschatological Blessings Expected by the First Christians at the Parousia of Christ circa AD 70*. Bradford, PA: International Preterist Association, 2005.

Hartman, Lars. *Prophecy Interpreted: The Formation of Some Jewish Apocalyptic Texts and of the Eschatological Discourse Mark 13 Par*. Lund: Gleerup (1966), 187-90.

Howard, T. L. "*The Literary Unity of 1 Thessalonians 4:13-5:11*," GTJ 9 (1988): 163-90.

Hughes, Philip Edgcumbe. *The Book of the Revelation: A Commentary*. Grand Rapids: Eerdmann, 1990.

Hyldahl, Niels. "Auferstehung Christi – Auferstehung der Toten (1 Thess. 4:4, 13-18)," In: *S. Pedersen [Hrsg.]. Die Paulinische Literatur und Theologie* (TeolSt 7) (1980), 130.

Ice, Thomas, and Kenneth L. Gentry. *The Great Tribulation, Past or Future?: Two Evangelicals Debate the Question*. Grand Rapids, MI: Kregel Publications, 1999.

SOURCES

Jordan, James B. *The Vindication of Jesus Christ: a Brief Reader's Guide to Revelation*. Monroe, LA: Athanasius Press, 2008. Kindle Edition.

Keathley, Hampton, IV. "Introduction to the Parables." As of August 8, 2017. *Bible.org*. https://bible.org/seriespage/introduction-parables.

Kik, J. Marcellus. *An Eschatology of Victory*. Phillipsburg, NJ: Presbyterian and Reformed Publishing Company, 1971.

King, Max R. *The Cross and the Parousia of Christ: The Two Dimensions of One Age-Changing Eschaton*. Reprint Edition. Warren, OH: Parkman Road Church of Christ, 1987.

Ladd, George Eldon. *A Commentary on the Revelation of John*. Grand Rapids: Eerdmans, 1972.

----------. *The Presence of the Future*. Grand Rapids: Eerdmans, 1974.

Leithart, Peter J. *The Promise of His Appearing: An Exposition of Second Peter*. Moscow, ID: Canon Press, 2004.

Lövestam, O. Evald. *Jesus and 'this Generation': A New Testament Study*. Coniectanea Biblica. New Testament Series 25. Stockholm: Lund, 1995.

Marshall, I. Howard. *1 and 2 Thessalonians*. Grand Rapids: Eerdmans, 1983.

Maslow, Abraham H. *The Psychology of Science: A Reconnaissance*. New York: Harper and Roe, 1966.

Mathison, Keith A. *When Shall These Things Be?: A Reformed Response to Hyper-preterism*. Phillipsburg, NJ: P & R Publishing, 2004.

Miller, Stephen R. *Daniel*. Nashville: Broadman & Holman. 1994.

Mounce, Robert H. *The Book of Revelation*. The New International Commentary of the New Testament. Grand Rapids, MI: W. B. Eerdmans, 1998.

Newman, Carey C. "In Grateful Dialogue." Jesus & the Restoration of Israel: a Critical Assessment of N.T. Wright's Jesus and the Victory of God. Downers Grove, IL: InterVarsityPress, 1999.

Nisbett, Nehemiah. *An Attempt to Illustrate Various Important Passages in the Epistles, &c. of the New Testament: From Our Lord's Prophecies of the Destruction of Jerusalem, and from Some Prophecies of the Old Testament*. London, 1787.

Orchard, J. Bernard. *"Thessalonians and the Synoptic Gospel,"* Biblica 19 (1938): 19-42.

Osborne, Grant R. *Revelation*. Baker Exegetical Commentary on the New Testament. Grand Rapids: Baker Academic, 2002.

Owen, John. *The Works of John Owen*. 16 volumes. London: Banner of Truth, 1965-68.

Piper, John. "Has the Gospel Been Preached to the Whole Creation Already?" On March 14, 2017. *Desiring God*. http://www.desiringgod.org/articles/has-the-gospel-been-preached-to-the-whole-creation-already.

Preston, Don K. *We Shall Meet Him in the Air: The Wedding of the King of Kings*. Ardmore, OK: JaDon Management, Inc. 2012.

──────. *Who is This Babylon?* Ardmore, OK: JaDon Management Inc., 2011.

Rigaux, Béda. *The Letters of St. Paul, Modern Studies*. Chicago: Franciscan Herald (1968), 539.

Russell, J. Stuart. *The Parousia: the New Testament Doctrine of Christ's Second Coming*. Edited by Edward E. Stevens. Bradford, PA: International Preterist Association, 2003.

Seyoon, Kim. *"The Jesus Tradition in 1 Thess 4.13-5.11,"* New Testament Studies 48 (2002): 231-42.

Sproul, R. C. *The Last Days According to Jesus: When Did Jesus Say He Would Return?* Grand Rapids: Baker, 2015.

Stevens, Edward E. *Expectations Demand a First Century Rapture*. Bradford, PA: International Preterist Association, 2003.

Sullivan, Michael J. "A Full Preterist Response to Kenneth Gentry's Articles: Daniel 12, Tribulation, and Resurrection and Acts 24:15 and the Alleged Nearness of the Resurrection." As of October 24, 2012. *FullPreterism.com*. http://postmillennialism.com/2012/03/daniel-12-tribulation-and-resurrection/.

Twain, Mark. Quote from September 1897 as published in *The National Jewish Post & Observer* for June 6, 1984.

Wanamaker, Charles A. *The Epistles to the Thessalonians: A Commentary on the Greek Text*. Grand Rapids: W. B. Eerdmans, 1990.

SOURCES

Waterman, G. Henry. *"The Sources of Paul's Teaching on the 2nd Coming of Jesus in 1 and 2 Thessalonians,"* JETS 18 (1975): 105-13.

Wright, N. T. *Jesus and the Victory of God.* Minneapolis: Fortress Press, 1996.

ANCIENT SOURCES

The Babylonian Talmud. *Talmud Bavli: Tractate Sanhedrin 98a4.* The Schottenstein ed. Vol. III. Brooklyn, NY: Mesorah, 2014.

Eusebius, *Ecclesiastical History* 3.5.3.

Philo of Alexandria. *Flaccus.* Vol. 25. 3.8; 4.21.

----------. *On the Embassy to Gaius.* 31.213.

Josephus. *Jewish Antiquities* 10.11.7; 18.6.10; 20.8.5; 20.97-98.

----------. *The Wars of the Jews* 2.14.5; 4.9.2; 6.2.1; 6.5.3. 6.94.

Tacitus. *The Annals of Imperial Rome.* Trans. Michael Grant. London: Penguin Books, 1989

SCRIPTURE INDEX

1 Chron. 16:15-22 244
1 Chron. 16:31-32 258
1 Cor. 2:12-16 125
1 Cor. 3:21-22 257
1 Cor. 6:14-15 210
1 Cor. 7:1, 25 147
1 Cor. 7:10-11, 25 125
1 Cor. 7:29, 31 16
1 Cor. 7:40 125
1 Cor. 8:1 147
1 Cor. 9:14 125
1 Cor. 10:11 15, 230
1 Cor. 11:23-25 125
1 Cor. 11:25 255
1 Cor. 11:26 212
1 Cor. 12:1 147
1 Cor. 15 122
1 Cor. 15:12-26 195
1 Cor. 15:20-23 15
1 Cor. 15:20-23, 50-54 120
1 Cor. 15:23 97, 114
1 Cor. 15:23-26, 50-55 131

1 Cor. 15:24 232
1 Cor. 15:24-26 258
1 Cor. 15:43-44 210
1 Cor. 15:50-57 130
1 Cor. 15:51 129, 130, 207
1 Cor. 15:54 121
1 Cor. 16:1, 12 147
1 John 1:1 26
1 John 1:1-2 185
1 John 1:2 152
1 John 2:18 16, 228, 230
1 John 2:18-19 228
1 John 2:18, 22 152
1 John 2:18-27 152
1 John 2:28 152
1 John 3:2 152, 153
1 John 3:5, 8 153
1 John 4:3 146, 152
1 John 4:3-5 152
1 John 4:9 153
1 John 4:17 152
1 John 5:11, 13 171
1 Kings 4:21 245

1 Kings 8:11-13 115
1 Kings 9:3 256
1 Pet. 1:8, 13 95
1 Pet. 1:20 15, 228, 230
1 Pet. 2:9 224
1 Pet. 4:7 16, 230
1 Thess. 2:13 125
1 Thess. 2:14-15 35
1 Thess. 2:16 36
1 Thess. 4 122, 146
1 Thess. 4-5 123, 125, 126, 129
1 Thess. 4:13-5:11 124, 125, 126
1 Thess. 4:13-18 125, 130, 178
1 Thess. 4:15 124, 125
1 Thess. 4:15-17 124, 125
1 Thess. 4:15, 17 207
1 Thess. 4:15-18 126
1 Thess. 4:16 129, 131
1 Thess. 4:16-5:9 126
1 Thess. 4:16-17 110, 114, 116, 120, 128,

SCRIPTURE INDEX

129
1 Thess. 5:1-8 20
1 Thess. 5:1-11 125, 126
1 Thess. 5:3 79
1 Thess. 5:6-10 196
1 Thess. 5:10-11 125
1 Thess. 5:23-24 212
1 Tim. 1:18-20 211
1 Tim 3:15 212
1 Tim. 3:16 146
2 Chron. 7:16 256
2 Chron. 33:7 256
2 Cor. 3:1-6 255
2 Cor. 3:3, 6-11 249
2 Cor. 4:4 39
2 Cor. 4:16-18 17
2 Cor. 5:4 130
2 Cor. 5:10 184
2 Cor 5:17 226
2 Cor. 5:17 97, 172, 228
2 Cor. 13:3 125
2 John 1:7 152
2 John 7 152
2 Kings 2:1, 11 180
2 Kings 2:9, 15 181
2 Kings 21:7 256
2 Pet. 1:16 185
2 Pet. 1:16-21 185
2 Pet. 3 16, 20, 21, 94, 96
2 Pet. 3:1-13 19
2 Pet. 3:3 228
2 Pet. 3:3-12 19
2 Pet. 3:4 19, 95
2 Pet. 3:4-5 23
2 Pet. 3:4-7 225
2 Pet. 3:4-13 94, 95
2 Pet. 3:5-7 95
2 Pet. 3:5-7, 10-13 89
2 Pet. 3:7 23
2 Pet. 3:7, 10, 12 95
2 Pet. 3:7, 10, 12-13 160
2 Pet. 3:8 21

2 Pet. 3:9 19, 21, 82
2 Pet 3:10 93
2 Pet. 3:10 19
2 Pet. 3:10-12 23
2 Pet. 3:10-13 93
2 Pet. 3:11 212
2 Pet. 3:12-13 200
2 Pet. 3:13 96
2 Sam. 7:10 253
2 Sam. 15:30-31 42
2 Sam. 22:10 115
2 Thess. 1-2 145
2 Thess. 1:5-10 147
2 Thess. 1:6-10, 12 212
2 Thess. 1:7-10 110, 225
2 Thess. 1:8 120, 129
2 Thess. 2:1 129, 145, 146, 147
2 Thess. 2:1-3 211, 213, 263
2 Thess. 2:1-8 97, 178
2 Thess. 2:1, 8 162
2 Thess. 2:1-10 140, 141
2 Thess. 2:1-12 145
2 Thess. 2:2 146
2 Thess. 2:3 140
2 Thess. 2:3-4 68, 153
2 Thess. 2:3-12 196
2 Thess. 2:4 79, 148, 154
2 Thess. 2:6 146
2 Thess. 2:6-7 146, 151
2 Thess. 2:8 138, 149
2 Thess. 2:8-12 262
2 Thess. 2:9-10 146
2 Thess. 2:11-12 151
2 Thess. 2:13 26
2 Tim. 2:17-18 97, 211
2 Tim. 3:1-9 228
2 Tim. 4:1 184, 214
2 Tim. 4:18 257

A

Acts 1:3 236
Acts 1:6 236
Acts 1:7 237
Acts 1:8 237, 257
Acts 1:9-11 102, 110, 114, 116, 219
Acts 1:11 219
Acts 2:5 54
Acts 2:16-17 15, 227, 228
Acts 2:19 89
Acts 2:20-21 85
Acts 2:23 35
Acts 2:23-39 15
Acts 2:29-36 258
Acts 2:40 31, 33, 34, 35
Acts 3:17 36
Acts 3:20 226
Acts 3:20-21 15, 227
Acts 3:21 226
Acts 5:30 35
Acts 7:51-52 36
Acts 7:56 185
Acts 11:27-29 50
Acts 11:28 55
Acts 15:16 228
Acts 17:6 55
Acts 17:30-31 26
Acts 17:31 214
Acts 19:27 55
Acts 24:5 55
Acts 24:14-15 197
Acts 24:15 196, 214, 215
Acts 26:21-23 197
Amos 5:19-20 86
Amos 8:8 87
Amos 8:9 86
Amos 9:13-14 259
Amos 9:14 175, 255
Amos 9:15 253

C

Col. 1:5-6 55
Col. 1:5-6, 23 54
Col. 1:13 26
Col. 1:22-23 212
Col. 1:23 56
Col 1:27 46
Col. 1:27 237
Col. 2:11-12 248
Col. 2:12 192
Col. 3:1 26, 192

D

Dan. 6-12 44
Dan. 7 103, 107, 109, 114
Dan. 7:2, 6-7, 9 107
Dan. 7:8, 20, 24 143
Dan. 7:9-10, 22, 26 104
Dan. 7:9-12 104
Dan 7:9, 26 162
Dan. 7:9-27 44
Dan. 7:10-14 162
Dan 7:11 162
Dan. 7:11 108, 141
Dan. 7:11, 24-26 104
Dan. 7:13 99, 104, 108, 109, 116, 188
Dan. 7:13-14 101, 104, 129, 157
Dan. 7:14 104
Dan. 7:14, 22, 27 162
Dan. 7:18, 22, 27 104
Dan. 7:25 138
Dan. 8 62, 74
Dan. 8:9-11 140
Dan. 8:9-12 69
Dan. 8:10 89
Dan. 8:11 140
Dan. 8:11-12 81
Dan. 8:11-13 61, 62
Dan. 8:11-14 148, 149

Dan. 8:12-14 65
Dan. 8:14 139
Dan. 8:15 116
Dan. 8:17 62
Dan. 8:17-19 131
Dan. 8:19 62
Dan. 8:25 79
Dan. 8:26 25, 26
Dan. 9 44, 62, 63, 74
Dan. 9:1-19 62, 77, 82
Dan. 9:2 78
Dan. 9:16-18 77
Dan. 9:24 62, 78, 83, 250
Dan. 9:24-27 77, 78, 79, 83
Dan. 9:26 62, 78, 140
Dan. 9:26-27 61, 62, 82
Dan. 9:27 62, 63, 64, 65, 69, 79, 81, 139, 140, 148, 149, 153, 179
Dan. 10:6 LXX 104
Dan. 10-12 175, 176
Dan. 10:14 227
Dan. 11 175
Dan. 11:2-3 175
Dan. 11:4-35 175
Dan. 11-12 74
Dan. 11:13 63
Dan. 11:21 175, 178
Dan. 11:21-24 79
Dan. 11:21-35 176, 178
Dan. 11:27 62, 131
Dan. 11:27-28 79
Dan. 11:27, 35, 40 199
Dan. 11:30 176
Dan. 11:30-36 176
Dan. 11:31 61, 62, 63, 65, 69, 79, 140, 148, 149, 154, 176, 179
Dan. 11:31-32 81
Dan. 11:31-45 196

Dan. 11:31, 45 44
Dan. 11:33-35 176
Dan. 11:35 131
Dan. 11:36 140, 141, 175, 178
Dan. 11:36-12:3 175
Dan. 11:36-37 140
Dan. 11:36-45 175
Dan. 11:40 63, 131
Dan. 11:45 81, 179
Dan. 12 198
Dan. 12:1 26, 60, 64, 69
Dan. 12:1-2 53, 70, 199, 227
Dan. 12:1-3 129, 171
Dan. 12:1-3, 11 179
Dan. 12:1-4 44, 60, 196, 197, 198
Dan. 12:1- 9 131
Dan. 12:1-13 LXX 159
Dan. 12:2 210
Dan. 12:3 121, 197
Dan. 12:4 25, 26, 46, 63, 199
Dan. 12:7 37, 69, 83, 138, 198
Dan. 12:8-10 46
Dan. 12:9 63
Dan. 12:9-10 26
Dan. 12:10 26, 176
Dan. 12:11 61, 62, 63, 64, 65, 69, 79, 81, 140, 148, 149, 176, 179, 196, 199
Dan. 12:11-12 139, 199
Dan. 12:11-13 62, 196
Dan. 12:11 LXX 63
Dan 12:13 199
Dan. 12:13 46, 63, 198, 199
Deut. 1:34-39 31
Deut. 1:35 30, 31

SCRIPTURE INDEX

Deut. 4:25-31 32
Deut. 4:29-30 248
Deut. 4:29-31 248
Deut. 4:30 37, 248
Deut. 4:30-31 37, 227
Deut. 4:31 248
Deut. 6:5-6 247
Deut. 10:1-4 249
Deut. 10:12-13 247
Deut. 26:16 247
Deut. 29:4 247
Deut. 30:1 37, 248
Deut. 30:1-6 247
Deut. 30:1-10 37, 217
Deut. 30:2 248
Deut. 30:3 247
Deut. 30:4 248
Deut. 30:5 247, 248
Deut. 30:6 248
Deut. 31:16-29 32
Deut. 31:17 31
Deut. 31:17-18 37
Deut. 31:21, 27 31
Deut. 31:26-29 247
Deut. 31:29 37
Deut. 32:5 31, 32
Deut. 32:5, 20 30, 34
Deut. 32:10 242
Deut. 32:20 31, 34, 37
Deut. 32:21 224, 239
Deut. 32:21-30 37
Deut. 32:21, 43 240
Deut. 32:29 37
Deut. 32:33 36
Deut. 32:36 247
Deut. 32:43 250
Deut. 33:2 115

E

Eccles. 1:4 257
Eccles. 3:11 17

Eph. 2:6 26, 192
Eph. 2:14 220
Eph. 2:20 225
Eph. 3:6 46, 237
Eph. 4:13 212
Esther 9:2-10 217
Esther 9:10-16 217
Exod. 3:2-16 116
Exod. 4:22 242
Exod. 13:21-22 115
Exod. 14:19-20 116
Exod. 14:19-20, 24 115
Exod. 14:21-22 117
Exod. 19:9-11 115
Exod. 20:5 117
Exod. 20:21 115
Exod. 24:10-11 116
Exod. 24:15-18 115
Exod. 33:2, 9-10 115
Exod. 34:1-4 249
Exod. 34:5 115
Exod. 34:6-7 117
Ezek. 1:26-28 116
Ezek. 10:1 116
Ezek. 11:17 252
Ezek. 11:17-20 251
Ezek. 11:18 250
Ezek. 11:19 249
Ezek. 11:20 249
Ezek. 12:23 24
Ezek. 16:60 248
Ezek. 16:60, 63 250
Ezek. 28:25 253
Ezek. 28:26 255
Ezek. 30:3 22, 86, 117
Ezek. 32:7 85
Ezek. 32:7-8 86
Ezek. 34:17, 20 162
Ezek. 34:23-25, 31 252
Ezek. 34:26 258
Ezek. 34:27 259
Ezek. 34:29 258

Ezek. 34:30-31 249
Ezek. 36:24-27 251, 252
Ezek. 36:25, 29 250
Ezek. 36:26-27 249
Ezek. 36:28 249, 251
Ezek. 36:29-30 259
Ezek. 36:33 252
Ezek. 36:33-36 252
Ezek. 36:35 255
Ezek. 37:4-14 197
Ezek. 37:15-21 252
Ezek. 37:21-22, 25 252
Ezek. 37:21-26 252
Ezek. 37:21-28 37
Ezek. 37:23 250
Ezek. 37:24 249
Ezek. 37:24-26 252
Ezek. 37:25 253
Ezek. 37:27 249
Ezek. 38:1-39:24 92, 217
Ezek. 38:8 70, 259
Ezek. 38:8, 11, 14 79
Ezek. 38:8, 16 217, 227
Ezek. 38:16-17 228
Ezek. 38:16, 23 217
Ezek. 38:18-20 87
Ezek. 38:19-22 217
Ezek. 38:21-23 92
Ezek. 38-39 219
Ezek. 39:2-6 217
Ezek. 39:3-20 92
Ezek. 39:6-7, 22 217
Ezek. 39:10 217
Ezek. 39:17-20 73
Ezek. 39:22 250
Ezek. 39:25-29 217
Ezek. 39:26 255
Ezek. 39:29 254
Ezra 1:3, 5 47
Ezra 5:2, 11, 15, 17 47
Ezra 6:3, 7-8 47

SCRIPTURE INDEX

G

Gal. 1:4 39, 170, 232
Gal. 3:16, 19, 29 255
Gal. 4:12 125
Gal. 6:15 226
Gen. 1:1-2:1 200
Gen. 1-2 95
Gen. 1:28 (LXX) 55
Gen. 3:15 36, 39, 146
Gen. 3:18 258
Gen. 4:8-11 35
Gen. 6-9 95
Gen. 9:12-16 243
Gen. 12:1-3, 12 243
Gen. 12:3 111
Gen. 13:14-17 243
Gen. 13:14-18 245
Gen. 13:15 243
Gen. 15:18-21 243, 245
Gen. 17:1-14 243
Gen. 17:5 113
Gen. 17:7 237
Gen. 17:7-8 243
Gen. 17:8 243
Gen. 17:9 243
Gen. 26:3-4 243
Gen. 28:4 243
Gen. 28:14 111
Gen. 29:27-28 78

H

Hab. 2:3-4 24
Hab. 2:14 258
Hag. 1:2 47
Hag. 2:6 22
Hag. 2:6-7 24
Heb. 1:1-2 228
Heb. 1:2 15
Heb. 1:3-4, 13 233
Heb. 3:7-4:11 34
Heb. 3:7-19 31
Heb. 3:10 39
Heb. 4:14 233
Heb. 6:4-5 232
Heb. 8:8-12 249
Heb 8:13 201
Heb. 8:13 235, 249
Heb. 9 233
Heb 9:10 226
Heb. 9:10 227
Heb. 9:26 15, 230
Heb. 10:12-13 258
Heb. 10:24-27 18
Heb. 10:25 16
Heb. 10:32 228
Heb. 10:37 16
Heb. 11 90
Heb. 11:10, 16 97
Heb. 12:9 25
Heb. 12:22 97
Heb. 12:22-23 97
Heb. 12:22-24 232
Heb. 12:26-28 24
Heb 12:27-28 226
Heb. 12:27-28 226
Heb. 13:14 214
Hosea 1:11 252
Hosea 2:2-5 31
Hosea 2:15, 21-22 258
Hosea 3:5 227
Hosea 6:3 258
Hosea 9:10 225

I

Isa. 1:2-4 32
Isa. 2:1-5 227, 256
Isa. 2:2-3 257
Isa. 2:13-16 87
Isa. 5:1-7 223
Isa. 6:1-5, 8 116
Isa. 6:9-10 26
Isa. 6:9-13 26
Isa. 7:14 254
Isa. 7:14-16 172
Isa. 7:15-16 172
Isa. 8:16 26
Isa. 9:1-7 172
Isa. 11:4 LXX 141
Isa. 11:9 258
Isa. 11:12 99
Isa. 13 91
Isa. 13:4-6 92
Isa. 13:6 22
Isa. 13:9 22
Isa. 13:10 85, 86
Isa. 13:14-16 92
Isa. 13:22 22, 24
Isa. 14:1 253
Isa. 14:1-2 254
Isa. 14:20 32
Isa. 19:1 117
Isa. 19:1-4 117
Isa. 19:23-25 118, 253
Isa. 24 95, 121
Isa. 24:19-23 121
Isa. 24:23 86
Isa. 24-27 121
Isa. 25:6-9 121
Isa. 25:9 197
Isa. 26:17-19, 21 197
Isa. 26:17-27:1 121
Isa. 26:18 242
Isa. 26:19, 21 210
Isa. 26:21 121
Isa. 27:6 258
Isa. 27:9 240, 241
Isa. 27:12-13 121, 253
Isa. 28:14-16, 18 79
Isa. 29:9-14 26
Isa. 30:21 250
Isa. 30:23 259
Isa. 30:23-24 259
Isa. 30:25 87, 258

Isa. 32:15 254, 258
Isa. 34:4 85, 86, 87
Isa. 34:8 174
Isa. 35:1-2 258
Isa. 35:6-7 258
Isa. 40:1-5, 9-11 184
Isa. 40:3-4 256
Isa. 40:4 87
Isa. 40:9 257
Isa. 41:18 258
Isa. 41:19 258
Isa. 42:6 250
Isa. 43:10-12 237
Isa. 44:8 237
Isa. 45:14, 24 254
Isa. 49:6 250
Isa. 49:15-16 256
Isa. 49:17-19 256
Isa. 49:19 253
Isa. 49:22 254
Isa. 49:23 254, 255
Isa. 50:3 86, 87
Isa. 53:8 78
Isa. 54:7-8 253
Isa. 54:9 159
Isa. 54:9-10 251
Isa. 54:13-17 250
Isa. 55:3-4 252
Isa. 55:13 258
Isa. 56:1 24
Isa. 58:12 175
Isa. 59:9-10 86
Isa. 59:19 258
Isa. 59:20-21 240
Isa. 59:21 254
Isa. 60:4, 17-18 256
Isa. 60:8-9 254
Isa. 60:10 259
Isa. 60:13 258
Isa. 60:14 254
Isa. 60:15 259
Isa. 60:21 175, 250, 251

Isa. 61:1-2 174
Isa. 61:2 69
Isa. 61:2-4 174, 175
Isa. 61:4 259
Isa. 61:5-7 259
Isa. 61:8-9 254
Isa. 62:10-11 184
Isa. 63:4 69
Isa. 63:18 70
Isa. 64:10-11 70
Isa. 65:8-9 253
Isa. 65:10 259
Isa. 65:17, 21–23 259
Isa. 65:17-25 96, 200
Isa. 66:7-8 254
Isa. 66:20 254
Isa. 66:22 96, 251
Isa. 66:22-23 200

J

James 1:18 26
James 5:7-8 162
James 5:7-9 16
Jer. 2:30-31 35
Jer. 3:14, 18 256
Jer. 5:18-19 37
Jer. 23:3 253
Jer. 23:20 227
Jer. 24:6 253
Jer. 24:7 249
Jer. 25:11-12 78, 83
Jer. 29:10 78, 83
Jer. 30:3, 10 71
Jer. 30:6 71
Jer. 30:6-7 71, 248
Jer. 30:7-9, 11, 16 71
Jer. 30:9 71
Jer. 30:10 255
Jer. 30:18 256
Jer. 30:22 249
Jer. 30:24 227

Jer. 31:4 255
Jer. 31:7 253
Jer. 31:7-9 253
Jer. 31:9 114, 254
Jer. 31:10 245
Jer. 31:12 259
Jer. 31:12, 24-25, 27 259
Jer. 31:28 259
Jer. 31:31, 33-34 249
Jer. 31:33 249
Jer. 31:33-40 37
Jer. 31:34 250
Jer. 31:35 251
Jer. 31:36 251
Jer. 31:37 251
Jer. 31:38-40 257
Jer. 32:37 250, 252
Jer. 32:37-41 251
Jer. 32:38 249
Jer. 32:40 250
Jer. 32:41 253
Jer. 33:23-26 251
Jer. 46:27 255
Jer. 50:4 114
Jer. 50:4-5 256
Jer. 50:19-20 251
Job 19:23-27 196
Job 19:23-29 197
Job 27:8, 17-22 23
Joel 1:15 22
Joel 2:1 22
Joel 2:1-2 117
Joel 2:2-3 86
Joel 2:10, 31 86
Joel 2:18-19, 22 259
Joel 2:23 258
Joel 2:24 259
Joel 2:26 259
Joel 2:28-32 227
Joel 2:30 87, 89
Joel 2:30-31 85, 87
Joel 3:1-16 92

SCRIPTURE INDEX

Joel 3:14 22
Joel 3:15 86
Joel 3:18 258, 259
John 1:21 180
John 3:36 171
John 4:23 171
John 5:24 171
John 5:24-26 172, 192
John 5:25 171
John 5:25, 28 171
John 5:28-29 196
John 6:39-40, 44, 54 131
John 6:39-40, 54 196
John 6:39-44 228
John 6:39-44, 54 171
John 6:39-54 227
John 6:40, 47, 54 171
John 6:44 196
John 8:44 36
John 11:11 196
John 11:24 131, 196, 227, 228
John 11:24-25 192
John 11:52 118
John 12:31 39, 171, 172
John 12:48 131, 227
John 14:2-3, 12 171
John 14:18-20, 23, 28-29 171
John 14:30 39
John 15:2-8, 16 225
John 16:5, 7, 10, 28 171
John 16:11 39, 171
John 16:16-19 171
John 16:16-19, 20-24 171
John 16:20-24 171
John 16:32 171
John 18:36 170, 257
John 19:37 111, 172
John 20:25-29 111
John 21:22-23 186
Josh. 21:43 245

Josh. 23:4-13 245

L

Lev. 26 83
Lev. 26:41-42 247
Luke 1:17, 76 181
Luke 1:68-75 249
Luke 2:1 55, 142
Luke 3:7-8 32
Luke 4:18-21 174
Luke 7:24 118
Luke 7:27 180
Luke 7:31 30
Luke 7:31-35 33, 35
Luke 8:8 26
Luke 8:10 26
Luke 9:26-27 182
Luke 9:27 184, 185
Luke 9:28-36 184
Luke 9:37-43 33
Luke 9:41 30
Luke 9:52 118
Luke 10:18 171
Luke 10:23 26
Luke 11:16, 29-32 33
Luke 11:29 31
Luke 11:30-32, 50-51 30
Luke 11:47-51 35
Luke 11:49-51 34
Luke 11:52 170
Luke 12 167
Luke 12:19-20 23
Luke 12:31 170
Luke 12:45-46 20
Luke 13:6-9 225
Luke 13:28 164, 171
Luke 13:34 241
Luke 13:34-36 35
Luke 14:16-24 164
Luke 14:35 26
Luke 16:8-9 36

Luke 16:16 170
Luke 17 41, 167
Luke 17:21 170
Luke 17:22-37 34
Luke 17:24, 29 160
Luke 17:25 30, 35
Luke 17:26 159
Luke 17:26-27 160
Luke 17:26-30 166
Luke 17:26-37 164, 165, 166
Luke 17:28 160
Luke 17:28-32 160
Luke 17:31 165
Luke 17:34 39
Luke 17:35-37 166
Luke 17:37 73, 165
Luke 18:7 20
Luke 18:7-8 216
Luke 18:30 232
Luke 19:11 237
Luke 19:12 109, 188
Luke 19:12, 15 170
Luke 19:27 165
Luke 19:41-44 42, 226
Luke 20:9-19 223
Luke 20:34-35 232
Luke 21 34, 41, 167
Luke 21:6 45
Luke 21:7 43
Luke 21:8-11 50, 52
Luke 21:9 53
Luke 21:12 52
Luke 21:12-19 53
Luke 21:20 68
Luke 21:20-21 40, 66
Luke 21:20-24 67, 69, 148
Luke 21:22 68, 175
Luke 21:22-23 53
Luke 21:24 69, 70, 226, 253

SCRIPTURE INDEX

Luke 21:25 88
Luke 21:25-26 85
Luke 21:25-33 164
Luke 21:26 54
Luke 21:26-27 145
Luke 21:27 101, 115, 116, 127
Luke 21:31-32 130, 131
Luke 21:32 27, 30, 37
Luke 21:34-36 20
Luke 22:20 201, 250, 255
Luke 22:69 109, 187
Luke 23:7 38
Luke 23:42 170
Luke 24:39 210
Luke 24:47 237

M

Mal. 3:1-2 180
Mal. 3:1, 3 180
Mal. 3:4 228
Mal. 4:1 22
Mal. 4:1-3 180
Mal. 4:2 259
Mal. 4:5-6 180
Mark 1:2 180
Mark 4:9, 23 26
Mark 5:27-28 254
Mark 5:39 196
Mark 6:56 254
Mark 8:11-13 33
Mark 8:12 30
Mark 8:38 31, 34
Mark 8:38-9:1 182
Mark 9:1 184, 185
Mark 9:2-13 184
Mark 9:12-13 180
Mark 9:14-29 33
Mark 9:19 30
Mark 9:47 171
Mark 10:15 170

Mark 10:23-25 171
Mark 10:30 232
Mark 11:12-14, 20-25 225
Mark 11:21-25 225
Mark 12:1-12 223
Mark 12:24-25 158
Mark 12:26 158
Mark 13 34, 41
Mark 13:3 207
Mark 13:4 43, 163
Mark 13:9-13 53
Mark 13:10 119
Mark 13:14 65, 68, 179
Mark 13:14-19 69, 148
Mark 13:14-20 67
Mark 13:14-24 53
Mark 13:20 67
Mark 13:24-25 85, 88
Mark 13:24-27 129, 145
Mark 13:26 101, 103, 115, 116, 132
Mark 13:26-27 127
Mark 13:27 118, 129
Mark 13:30 27, 30, 37, 38, 39
Mark 13:32 156, 160, 219
Mark 13:36 162
Mark 14:23 250
Mark 14:25 171
Mark 14:62 109, 187
Mark 16:15-18 57
Matt. 3:7 36
Matt. 3:7-9 32
Matt. 3:10 225
Matt. 5:4 175
Matt. 5:5 257
Matt. 5:11-7:20 206
Matt. 5:12 35
Matt. 5:20 206
Matt. 6:10 231, 257

Matt. 6:33 170
Matt. 7:17-19 225
Matt. 8:11 171
Matt 8:12 173
Matt. 8:12 164, 165
Matt. 10:17-22, 34-39 52
Matt. 10:23 205
Matt. 11:9-10 180
Matt. 11:11 170
Matt. 11:14-15 180
Matt. 11:15 26
Matt. 11:16 30
Matt. 11:16-19 33, 35
Matt. 12:28 170
Matt. 12:34 32, 36
Matt. 12:38-42 33
Matt. 12:39 31
Matt. 12:41-42 30
Matt. 12:45 31
Matt. 13:11 26
Matt. 13:11-17 206
Matt. 13:23 225
Matt. 13:30 120
Matt. 13:38 39
Matt. 13:39-40, 49 231, 232
Matt. 13:39-43 120
Matt. 13:39, 43 198
Matt. 13:39-43, 49-50 165
Matt. 13:41 120
Matt. 13:42, 50 164
Matt. 14:35-36 254
Matt. 16:1-4 33
Matt. 16:4 31
Matt. 16:16-17 26
Matt. 16:21, 24-26 184
Matt. 16:27 120, 184
Matt. 16:27-28 182, 183, 186
Matt. 16:28 183, 184, 185, 186, 187, 188

277

SCRIPTURE INDEX

Matt. 17:1-13 184
Matt 17:11 226
Matt. 17:14-20 33
Matt. 17:17 30
Matt. 18:3 206
Matt. 18:15-19 206
Matt 19:28 226
Matt. 19:28 225, 258
Matt. 20:1-16 158
Matt. 20:2-6 158
Matt. 20:6, 12 158
Matt. 20:25-27 206
Matt. 21:15, 23, 45 225
Matt. 21:18-19 225
Matt. 21:18-22 225
Matt. 21:21-22 206, 225
Matt. 21:31 170, 224
Matt. 21:33-41 35
Matt. 21:33-43 164
Matt. 21:33-46 223
Matt. 21:40-41, 43 224
Matt. 21:43 224
Matt. 21:45 224
Matt. 22:1-14 164
Matt. 22:3-6 165
Matt. 22:7 165
Matt. 22:13 164
Matt. 22:29-30 158
Matt. 22:30 158
Matt. 22:31 157
Matt. 22:31-32 158
Matt. 23:1 38
Matt. 23:11 206
Matt. 23:12 173
Matt. 23:13 170
Matt. 23:15, 31, 33 36
Matt. 23:29 35
Matt. 23:29-31 35
Matt. 23:29-36 35, 36
Matt. 23:32 36
Matt. 23:33 32, 36
Matt. 23:34-35 35

Matt. 23:34-36 34
Matt. 23:35 35
Matt. 23:36 30, 34, 37
Matt. 23:37 38, 241
Matt. 23:37-39 226
Matt. 23:38 35
Matt. 23:38-39 37, 43
Matt. 23:39 226, 241
Matt. 24 34, 41, 126, 167
Matt. 24:1-3 42
Matt. 24:3 43, 159, 162, 207, 231
Matt. 24:3, 6, 14, 30 232
Matt. 24:4-8 50, 52
Matt. 24:4-14 161
Matt. 24:4-31 163
Matt. 24:4-33 40
Matt. 24:6 51, 130
Matt. 24:8 51
Matt. 24:9-13 52, 53
Matt. 24:13-14 130
Matt. 24:14 53, 54, 55, 56, 57, 119
Matt. 24:15 59, 60, 63, 65, 67, 68, 79, 140, 149, 157, 207
Matt. 24:15-16 179
Matt. 24:15-19 67
Matt. 24:15-20 66
Matt. 24:15-21 69, 148
Matt. 24:15-22 58
Matt. 24:15-28 27
Matt. 24:15-29 53, 161, 196
Matt. 24:15-35 165
Matt. 24:16 45, 68
Matt. 24:17-18 165
Matt. 24:17-20 68
Matt. 24:19 157
Matt. 24:21 60, 154
Matt. 24:21-22 70
Matt. 24:21-29 53

Matt. 24:22 67, 157
Matt. 24:23-28 72
Matt. 24:24-26 152
Matt. 24:26 72
Matt. 24:27 72, 162
Matt. 24:27-30 163, 164, 198
Matt. 24:27, 30 102
Matt. 24:27-35 159
Matt. 24:28 73, 165
Matt. 24:29 84, 85, 86, 87, 88, 127, 157
Matt. 24:29-30 160
Matt. 24:29-31 129, 145
Matt. 24:29-33 27
Matt. 24:29-35 161
Matt. 24:30 44, 99, 101, 103, 108, 110, 111, 112, 113, 115, 116, 132, 162, 172, 254
Matt. 24:30-31 127, 128, 129
Matt. 24:31 118, 119, 120, 129, 130, 146
Matt. 24:33 161
Matt. 24:33-34 37
Matt. 24:34 27, 28, 30, 34, 37, 38, 39, 40, 46, 130, 157, 163, 198
Matt. 24:34-35 161
Matt. 24:36 126, 156, 157, 158, 160, 161, 163, 169, 219
Matt 24:36-25:46 164
Matt. 24:36-41 166
Matt. 24:36, 44 16
Matt. 24:36-46 163
Matt. 24:37 157, 159
Matt. 24:37-39 159, 166
Matt. 24:37-41 166
Matt. 24:38 159

SCRIPTURE INDEX

Matt. 24:39 20, 157
Matt. 24:40-42 166
Matt. 24:42 16, 157
Matt. 24:42-44 162
Matt. 24:42-51 216
Matt. 24:43-44 19
Matt. 24:44 157
Matt. 24:48-50 20
Matt. 24:48-51 20
Matt. 24:50 157
Matt. 24:51 164, 165
Matt. 25:1-13 216
Matt. 25:5 20
Matt. 25:6, 19, 31 162
Matt. 25:11-13 20
Matt. 25:13 16, 157
Matt. 25:14-30 216
Matt. 25:19 20
Matt. 25:30 20, 164, 165
Matt. 25:31 162, 219
Matt. 25:31-32 258
Matt. 25:31-46 212
Matt. 25:32 56, 113
Matt. 25:32, 34, 46 162
Matt. 25:34 201
Matt. 25:41-46 162
Matt. 25:41, 46 165
Matt. 25:46 196
Matt. 26:27 250
Matt. 26:27-29 206
Matt. 26:28 79, 250
Matt. 26:61 47
Matt. 26:63-64 187
Matt. 26:64 109, 112, 188
Matt. 27:45-46 158
Matt. 27:46 158
Matt. 27:51-53 210
Matt. 28:16-20 206
Matt. 28:18 258
Matt. 28:18-20 57, 104, 119
Matt. 28:19 57, 237

Matt. 28:20 57
Mic. 1:3-4 117
Mic. 1:3-5 117
Mic. 2:12 253
Mic. 4:1 257
Mic. 4:1-2 257
Mic. 4:1-4 227
Mic. 4:2 257
Mic. 4:7 255
Mic. 4:9-10 254
Mic. 5:3 254
Mic. 7:1 225

N

Nah. 1:2 117
Nah. 1:3 117
Nah. 1:3-4 117
Num. 11:25 115
Num. 24:14, 17-19 227
Num. 24:14, 23-24 176
Num. 32:14 32

O

Obad. 1:15 22
Obad. 1:17 256

P

Phil. 2:12-16 34
Phil. 2:14-16 32
Phil. 2:15 31
Phil. 3:21 210
Phil. 4:5 16
Ps. 1:6-8 258
Ps. 12:7 30, 34, 35
Ps. 14:2-5 32
Ps. 14:5 30
Ps. 18:6-17 117
Ps. 19:4 (LXX) 55
Ps. 48:3 256
Ps. 49:19 30

Ps. 50:10 190
Ps. 67:6 259
Ps. 67:7 258
Ps. 71:17 111
Ps. 71:18 30
Ps. 72:6 258
Ps. 72:8 258
Ps. 72:16 259
Ps. 73:15 30
Ps. 90:4 19
Ps. 97:1-6 117
Ps. 105:8-9, 10-11 244
Ps. 105:8-11 251
Ps. 110:1 188
Ps. 110:1-2 258
Ps. 110:2 258
Ps. 112:2 30
Ps. 118:26 38
Ps. 132:13-14 256

R

Rev. 1:1, 3 10
Rev. 1:6 104
Rev. 1:7 108, 109, 110, 111, 112, 172
Rev. 1:8 108
Rev. 1:9 17, 53, 228
Rev. 1:13 104
Rev. 1:14 104
Rev. 1:20 89
Rev. 2:2-3:21 17
Rev. 2-3 17
Rev. 2:5 108
Rev. 2:7, 11, 17, 29 26
Rev. 2:9-10 53
Rev. 2:11 192
Rev. 2:16 108
Rev. 2:22 53
Rev. 2:25 108
Rev. 2:26-27 105
Rev. 2:28 89

SCRIPTURE INDEX

Rev. 3:3 19, 108
Rev. 3:6, 13, 22 26
Rev. 3:9 255
Rev. 3:10 17, 262
Rev. 3:11 10, 108
Rev. 3:21 105
Rev. 4:1-3, 5 107
Rev. 4-5 107
Rev. 5:6-9 108
Rev. 5:9-10 104
Rev. 6 87
Rev. 6:3-15 113
Rev. 6:9-11 53, 147, 193
Rev. 6:11 17
Rev. 6:12 87
Rev. 6:12-14 86, 87
Rev. 6:12-17 52
Rev. 6:13 89
Rev. 6:13-14 87
Rev. 6:14 216
Rev. 6-19 7
Rev. 7:14 17, 53
Rev. 7:17 121
Rev. 8:1-2 108
Rev. 8:7 113
Rev. 8:7-12 52
Rev. 8:10-12 89
Rev. 9:1-2 52
Rev. 10:7 130
Rev. 11:2 139, 140
Rev. 11:2-3 64, 69
Rev. 11:3 139
Rev. 11:3-13 181
Rev. 11:13 87
Rev. 11:13, 19 52
Rev. 11:15 130, 131
Rev. 11:15-18 108, 120
Rev. 11:17-18 130
Rev. 12:1 89
Rev. 12:4 89
Rev. 12:4-17 171
Rev. 12:6 139

Rev. 12:6, 9-17 146
Rev. 12:6, 14-17 64
Rev. 12:7-17 53
Rev. 12:9 146
Rev. 12:11 171
Rev. 12:14 139
Rev. 13 216
Rev. 13:3 146
Rev. 13:3, 12-15 142
Rev. 13:4-10 64
Rev. 13:5 139
Rev. 13:5-6 178
Rev. 13:5-8 53, 262
Rev. 13:5-10 137
Rev. 13:5-18 193
Rev. 13:18 134
Rev. 14:4 26
Rev. 14:6 57
Rev. 14:12 17
Rev. 14:13 147
Rev. 14:14 108
Rev. 14:14-16 108
Rev. 16:12-16 92
Rev. 16:14 23
Rev. 16:15 19, 108
Rev. 16:18-21 52, 87, 216
Rev. 16:21 216
Rev. 17 216
Rev. 17:7-11 141
Rev. 17:8 142
Rev. 17:10 143
Rev. 17:10-11 143
Rev. 17:11 142, 143
Rev. 17:12 144
Rev. 17:12-14 144
Rev. 18:8-10 160
Rev. 19:7 121
Rev. 19:11-16 108, 185
Rev. 19:11-21 104, 108
Rev. 19:17-18, 21 73
Rev. 19:17-20 149
Rev. 19:19-21 138

Rev. 19:20-21 141
Rev. 19:21 195
Rev. 20 190, 193
Rev. 20:1-3 191
Rev. 20:4 53, 193
Rev. 20:4-5 195
Rev. 20:4-6 192, 194
Rev. 20:4-6, 12-15 196
Rev. 20:5, 11-15 194
Rev. 20:6 192
Rev. 20:11-12 200, 202
Rev. 20:11-15 104, 184
Rev. 20:15 184
Rev. 21 257
Rev 21:1 226
Rev. 21:1 96, 200, 202
Rev. 21:1-2 200
Rev. 21:1-4 3
Rev. 21:1-22:5 96, 97, 200
Rev. 21:2 200
Rev. 21:4 97, 121, 203
Rev 21:5 226
Rev. 21:10-14 225
Rev. 22:6 201, 202
Rev. 22:6-7 10
Rev. 22:6, 10 226
Rev. 22:10 25
Rev. 22:10, 12 10
Rev. 22:12 17
Rev. 22:16 89
Rev. 22:20 10
Rom. 1:8 54
Rom. 2:5-6 184
Rom. 3:9 32
Rom. 4:16-17 255
Rom. 6:3-9 248
Rom. 6:4 26, 192
Rom. 8:11 210
Rom. 8:17-25, 30 210
Rom. 8:18 214
Rom. 8:18-25 96

SCRIPTURE INDEX

Rom. 8:23 26, 97
Rom. 8:32 257
Rom. 9:1-4 239
Rom. 9:3 239
Rom. 9:4 239
Rom. 9:6, 27, 31 239
Rom. 9-11 239
Rom. 9:15 241
Rom. 10:1 238
Rom. 10:18 54, 55, 56
Rom. 10:19, 21 239
Rom. 11 237, 241
Rom. 11:1 239
Rom. 11:1, 14 239
Rom. 11:2 240
Rom. 11:2, 7, 11, 25, 26 239
Rom. 11:3-10 239
Rom. 11:7-8 26
Rom. 11:11-14, 31 239
Rom. 11:12 239, 241
Rom. 11:15 239, 240, 241
Rom. 11:16-24 240
Rom. 11:18-20 240
Rom. 11:22 240
Rom. 11:23-24 240
Rom. 11:25 240
Rom. 11:25-26 46, 237, 240
Rom. 11:25-27 83
Rom. 11:25-29 240
Rom. 11:26 240
Rom. 11:26-27 240
Rom. 11:27 241
Rom. 11:28-29 241
Rom. 11:33 241
Rom. 13:12 16
Rom. 14:10-12 184
Rom. 15:4 228
Rom. 16:19, 26 54
Rom. 16:20 16
Rom. 16:26 55

T

Titus 3:5 192

Z

Zech. 2:12 256
Zech. 8:2 256
Zech. 8:8 249
Zech. 8:8, 22 256
Zech. 8:11 228
Zech. 8:12 259
Zech. 8:20-22, 23 254
Zech. 8:22 254
Zech. 8:23 254
Zech. 9:17 259
Zech. 10:1 258
Zech. 10:9 253
Zech. 12 112, 219
Zech. 12:2-6, 11 113
Zech. 12:3-9 113
Zech. 12:6 257
Zech. 12:7-9 220
Zech. 12:9-10 219
Zech. 12:10 83, 108, 111, 113, 172, 254
Zech. 12:10-14 175
Zech. 12:10 LXX 99
Zech. 14 219
Zech. 14:1-3 69
Zech. 14.1-3 219
Zech. 14:1-5 92, 219
Zech. 14:1-11 218
Zech. 14:2 253
Zech. 14:2-5 219
Zech. 14:3 92
Zech. 14:3-5 220
Zech. 14:4 220
Zech. 14:4-5 87, 219, 220
Zech. 14:4-11 256
Zech. 14:6-7 219
Zech. 14:8, 10 219
Zech. 14:9 257
Zech. 14.9 219
Zech. 14:9, 11 219
Zech. 14:9-11, 16-19 227
Zech. 14:10-11 256
Zech. 14:11-19 92
Zech. 14:12-15 92
Zech. 14:12-21 219
Zech. 14:17 111
Zeph. 1:7 22
Zeph. 1:14 22
Zeph. 1:14-15 117
Zeph. 1:15-16 86, 92
Zeph. 1:17 86
Zeph. 2:1-2 70
Zeph. 3:13 251

ABOUT THE AUTHOR

Brock D. Hollett is a board-certified physician and psychiatrist. Hollett earned a Bachelor of Science in middle school education from the University of Central Missouri in 2000 and a Master of Divinity from Midwestern Baptist Theological Seminary in 2003. He worked toward a Ph.D. in religious studies at the University of Missouri—Kansas City from 2003 to 2004. He earned his medical degree from Kansas City University in 2014 and completed his psychiatry residency at Centerstone of Florida in Bradenton, Florida, in 2018. From 2015 to 2020 he served as an adjunct professor of science and biblical studies at Southeastern University in Bradenton, Florida. He received his board certification from the American Board of Psychiatry and Neurology in 2020, and he currently practices psychiatry in Bradenton, Florida.

Dr. Hollett's theological interests include the holy Church fathers, eschatology, soteriology, and sacramental theology. After spending several years studying the talmud under an Orthodox Chabad rabbi, he authored *Moshiach Now* (2020), an evangelistic tool intended for rabbinic Jews. His newest book, *Jesus, the Jews, and the End of the Age* (2023), is a four-hundred page exploration of biblical eschatology. He and his wife Staci have four daughters, and they attend an Orthodox Christian parish in southern Florida.

www.ingramcontent.com/pod-product-compliance
Lightning Source LLC
Chambersburg PA
CBHW031409290426
44110CB00011B/320